YOU'RE OKAY
BUT YOU DON'T KNOW IT

E. EDWARD REITMAN, Ph.D.

ISBN: 147748471X

ISBN 13: 9781477484715

Library of Congress Control Number: 2012910145

DEDICATION

I'd like to dedicate this book to Harriet, the woman I married fifty-seven years ago, who still stands by my side, shares my bed, participates in our numerous dinner parties, and has walked with me through jungles, mountains, wetlands, ice, and snow in our quest to experience, first-hand, the world we live in; but even more so, because she has tolerated my ups and downs, fears and frustrations, insecurities and emotionality, all the while believing that I was okay, even when I didn't know it.

TABLE OF CONTENTS

PART TWO   145

ACKNOWLEDGMENTS

The list of individuals who contributed to this book is extremely long. It consists of my secretary, Amber, who typed and retyped the manuscript several times over; the countless number of patients I've seen in therapy, from whom I've frequently learned as much as I feel I've shared; my numerous valued friends, who have always been there to support and encourage me; my wife, Harriet, daughter, Shelly, her husband, Mark, my daughter-in-law, Natalie, and, of course, my five grandchildren, Melissa, Jessica, Lauren, Reese, and Miles. All of you have provided me with love, understanding, and care. Your belief in me has always been far greater than my own self-perceived sense of worth, probably because the little child in me has never fully accepted that I am truly okay.

I sincerely believe that my feelings are similar to those of almost everyone else in the world. That's the reason I wrote *You're Okay, But You Don't Know It.* It's my hope that this book will help each of you to discover your worth and to eventually come to value yourself in spite of the wounded child in you.

—*E. Edward Reitman*

PREFACE

You're Okay, But You Don't Know It is far more than a title designed to sell a book. It's a statement of my basic belief that every one of us is truly okay. Unfortunately, most of us don't know it.

As a result of this dichotomy, we walk through life striving to fit the mold, seeking the approval of our parents, peers, and community. To reach this goal, we fall in step, try to achieve, get an education, and obtain a high-paying job, a fast car, a big house, clothing, jewelry, and fame, all designed to gain acknowledgment, acceptance, and love. If our body weight is an index of our worth, we keep it in check. If the criteria for fitting in demand wealth, success, attractiveness, accumulating possessions, being tough, or being an acquiescent "good guy or gal," we mold ourselves and our actions to fit that image. The problems stemming from this behavior frequently don't come to light until *after* we've lived up to these expectations. It's then that we look around, shake our heads in disbelief, and wonder, "Is this all there is?" You've done everything the world suggested to achieve happiness, self-satisfaction, acceptance, fame, and peace of mind. But, now that you've done it, chances are you might still feel an old familiar emptiness in the pit of your stomach. It's as though the whole ordeal was for nothing. Are you still, for some reason, sad, disappointed, angry, and confused? Where do you go from here? And what is it that you now have to do that will make you truly okay?

For the most part, the answer is always the same and always erroneous. If one million dollars wasn't enough, get two million. If the new house wasn't sufficiently ostentatious, or the diamond ring wasn't big enough, work harder to afford a bigger house or a larger diamond. When that doesn't work, deny, avoid, and refuse to come in contact with the fact that you're in turmoil, depressed, and disillusioned. Hide or run from your disappointment. Drink, take drugs, eat, worry, blame, complain, sleep more, or not at all. But all of these are only temporary fixes. They don't work.

Take the following question as an example: "How many carbohydrates do you have to consume in one day to meet your daily requirement of protein?" If you've heard this question before, you know the answer right away. Zero. No matter how many carbohydrates you consume, they won't satisfy your need for protein.

Think how that applies to your life. How much money do you need to make you feel okay, to experience inner worth and peace of mind? You already know the answer. Nevertheless, time and time again, I see people in therapy who have "made it" on the outside, but not on the inside. The problem is that all of the directions you were given as a youngster were goals that you had to achieve *externally*. You were rarely told that, in order to really be able to recognize and appreciate how okay you are, you have to go *inside* before you can go out.

So, what does that mean, exactly? It means that I am totally in favor of you directing energy toward goals that give you pleasure, such as having status, fame, and fortune. However, I do not believe these behaviors will make you okay. Accomplishments are only the icing. You have to have a cake. That cake is you. You aren't perfect, but inside you is a person who is, without a doubt, okay. Unfortunately, most of us don't know that. Consequently, when we perceive any flaws or bumps, we either cover them up with icing or go so far as to throw the cake away; i.e., give up on ourselves by no longer trying, because we don't live up to our recognized standards. Still others of us make too much icing and, when we're done, we have nothing to spread it on. *You're Okay, But You Don't Know It* is intended to help you recognize that icing can't and won't make you acceptable, long term, to everyone in the world, or to yourself. This book will also help you to first recognize the ways you've attempted, in the past to feel okay, and then provide you with a new recipe for success: a series of steps that will allow you to see yourself as a person of substance—a gourmet creation that's palatable to you, and more than sufficient for anyone whose love you desire.

In the first part of *You're Okay, But You Don't Know It*, I describe *why* you haven't known that you're okay, provide some explanation for why you feel the way you do, and assure you that you're not alone. I firmly believe that the vast majority of human beings go through life similarly to you and me, feeling less than, desperately wanting to be more, drastically driven to improve, to be better and to achieve sufficiently so they can consider themselves okay.

If you're old enough to read and understand this book, then the notion that you're not okay is already firmly entrenched in you. The sad fact is, that notion will never change. It may be mitigated or lie dormant for long periods of time. But whenever you are faced with excessive conflict, stress, or overwhelming situational problems, it will rear its ugly head. At that point in time, you will feel no different than you did when you first began to perceive that you were lacking, or not enough. However, by that time, you will hopefully have acquired some notion of how those feelings came about and gained some recognition of the factors that came into play to create them. This is not to provide you with ammunition to punish parents, to blame others, or to excuse them based on situations or factors beyond their control, but, rather, to understand how you came to be and feel the way you do. Through that understanding, you will also have gained knowledge, which will have given you the power to better cope with your feelings and any problems that come your way.

Even though you may not fully understand it at this moment, the second half of *You're Okay, But You Don't Know It* will provide you with a path, a series of steps you can follow, in order to learn that you truly are okay. They will also help you to see a light at the end of your tunnel that will encourage you to run toward life with greater zest and joy. Eventually, those steps will lead you to a place where you will realize that what, in the past, you considered weak, insufficient, or unattractive may really have been your strengths, and that what you feel now, despite the fact that it may be hurtful, is really growing pains.

These steps are also a paradigm for escaping from the highly habituated, entrenched behavior patterns and coping techniques that helped you to attain what was initially described to you as a means of achieving success in life. The paradox is that, in many cases, it worked. However, emotionally, it led you to feeling disappointed and betrayed. It is rather like a song sung by Peggy Lee many years ago which said, "You built your house and when you thought it was complete, you watched it burn to the ground and you asked, 'Is that all there is?' " Were that question asked by only one individual, I might not be so concerned. But I hear it asked repeatedly, by people of every age, social status, and level of so-called success.

I think that for centuries, man has asked himself, "What is it all for? What will make my life meaningful or give me the sense that I accomplished something during my stay on this earth?" The series of steps in part 2 of this book can help you find an answer to those questions. Following them can help you come to peace with yourself. They will aid you to experience contentment with what you've achieved, to value the individuals you live with and love, or even give you permission to search out someone who can love you better. The only disclaimer is, if you do it the same way you did it the first time, the results will be the same.

To find true success inside, make sure to read *You're Okay, But You Don't Know It* with an open mind. Be receptive to, or at least consider, the notions presented. Once you're able to follow the recipe provided, you can modify it according to your own liking in order to create a "you" that you can relish, feel, and perceive as okay…in fact, *more* than okay.

INTRODUCTION

Some time ago, I heard a minister on television tell a story designed to demonstrate how little self-worth people have. He said, "If I were to offer you a new, crisp, clean $100 bill, free of charge, with no hidden agendas, and all you needed to do was reach out, grab the bill, and it was yours, would you take it?" All the people in the congregation nodded in the affirmative. He went on, "What if I were to take that $100 bill, put it in the street, let cars run over it, and let it collect dirt, mud, and filth from the street? Would you want it?" Again, the parishioners nodded yes. He continued, "Then, what if I were to take that $100 bill which had been run over, soiled from the accumulation of dirt, germs, and mud in the street, and crumple it up into a little ball so it was creased and wrinkled? Would you want it then?" Once again, the congregation nodded in an approving fashion. "Why is it," the minister went on, "that when it comes to a $100 bill, no matter how soiled, crumpled, wrinkled, and dirty it gets, you'd take it? In fact, you'd want it. You'd reach out for it. But when a human being has the misfortune to be crumpled, creased, soiled, defaced, you turn away? Why is it that the $100 bill has an inherent worth that, no matter how soiled or stained it may be, holds its value, but when a human being slips and falls, makes mistakes, takes the wrong path in life, we turn our backs on him/her? We reject him and he loses whatever value he may have had before."

Let me expand that question to ask, why is it that when you make a mistake, behave in an inappropriate manner, fail, fall short of your goals, aren't loved or are rejected by someone whose love you desire, or feel inadequate and insufficient, you lose whatever value you may have previously felt? Why is it that when or if a spouse divorces his/her partner, she/he feels totally destroyed, betrayed, depressed, inadequate, and worthless? Similarly, if a child fails in school, strikes out in a playoff game, has little or no athletic ability, or isn't outstanding academically or socially, he/she loses his/her worth in the eyes of others and himself/herself. Are we only of worth if we produce, succeed, or perform?

Perhaps the real question is, what constitutes worth? Is it based solely on how successful you've been, how many "toys" you own, or how you look? You know the politically correct answer, but is it true in regard to how you go about living your life? Think about it. How many parents feel or express that their children have worth or are of value just because of who they are? How many of them state that their child's out-of-the-box behavior, ideas, and feelings are worthy of being listened to and deserving of consideration, versus how many parents expend tremendous effort helping their kids to conform, fit in the box, color inside the lines, insist that leaves be colored green and that boys play baseball while girls play with dolls?

From my vantage point, it appears that the majority of parents and their children alike expend most of their effort trying to be someone who will be loved, accepted, and approved of by others, rather than by themselves. They live their lives from the outside in, determining their behaviors, thoughts, and sense of value through the eyes of others. Sadly, this behavior appears to be the rule rather than the exception. Years ago, on a live TV program, I asked the hostess to close her eyes and open her mouth. She did so, apprehensively. Then I inserted a thermometer into her mouth and said, "Gently close your mouth and open your eyes and tell me what I'm doing."

She said, "Taking my temperature."

"No, I'm taking my temperature."

"That's crazy," she responded. "You've got the thermometer in my mouth."

"I know, and it does appear crazy. But, the truth be known, most people take their emotional temperature by figuratively putting a thermometer in someone else's mouth. If you introspectively observe yourself, you'll see how sensitive you are to the tone of others' voices, the expressions on their faces—whether approving or disapproving, if they laugh at your jokes or are impressed by your exploits, appreciative of the food you cooked, the way you dress, or how you present yourself. All of which later contributes to your perception of what you're worth." Few, if any, of you are sufficiently courageous to expose yourselves openly, vulnerably, with your pimples, flaws, and shortcomings, because you're too frightened to risk rejection for being who you are.

The truth is, *you are okay, but you don't know it*. What you need to do, the rest of your life, is resolve to be who you are, behave on the basis of what you feel, and risk rejection. You must come to believe that you are a human being who deserves love, whether you're in step with everyone else and march to the same drummer or are trapped in the same emotional box. Ironically, having the courage to share who you are and to act in compliance with what you feel and desire is truly what makes you okay—first in your own eyes and then in the eyes of others, who will envy that you're at peace with being the unique individual you were born to be: someone who has regard and respect for others, but who maintains a rational self-interest, doesn't sell himself short, and doesn't act in a politically correct manner. *You're Okay, But You Don't Know It* is my attempt to help you to become that person. Someone who, despite the doubts he may occasionally have, truly knows he's okay.

PART ONE

The problem with most of us is not that we're broken or insufficient. It's that our fears and lack of confidence disallow us to embrace, live up to, or actualize the capabilities we already possess. The truth is, we don't have to be better or different, but we do have to be who we are. Therein lies the problem. How do we get to be us? It would seem that the first step might be to recognize who we are. Sadly, very few of us have the courage to do that.

—Ed Reitman

CHAPTER ONE

THE FACE IN THE MIRROR

Before reading this book, I'd like to request that you look in the mirror and honestly tell yourself what you see. Is it a positive picture? Do you see someone of value who deserves to be loved, noticed, and listened to by others? Or does the face staring back at you belong to a sad, pitiful person that you wish wasn't you? Are you embarrassed or ashamed of the individual you see? Are you staring at someone who, in your mind, needs to be radically altered or drastically enhanced before you'd be willing to risk openly exposing him or her to the public?

In many more instances than you might imagine, the negative image, in varying degrees, is what most people perceive in that mirror. So it might be safe to say that many of us lack a true sense of inner worth, have minimal confidence, fear failure, and are reluctant to bet on ourselves. It may not be true in every aspect of our lives, but, in relationships particularly, we're frightened to display who we really are

1

and to expose our true feelings or emotions. Consequently, on any given day, we're apt to think, "I would never say that in public," "I don't dare leave the house without makeup and heels on," or "It doesn't matter what I do; nothing will help this face or body. I can't stand my hair. I hate being who I am," or "I'm dumb. I could never be proficient on a computer, learn math, or write a book." How do most of you deal with these feelings? For some individuals, a little fix does it. You lose five pounds, get a new hairdo, a different shade of lipstick, and no one, not even you, would guess how bad you still feel on the inside. In other cases, because your self-concept is so depreciatory, even plastic surgery, liposuction, hair transplants, and veneers wouldn't help, because the person you perceive yourself to be on the inside stays the same.

The truth is, if you start off feeling badly about yourself, no matter how strong you seem on the outside, you remain weak in substance. The reason is apparent. If the foundation you build on isn't sufficiently strong, it can't adequately support the structure you build on it. It doesn't matter how wonderful that structure may be, or how positively others perceive you. When your sense of self-worth is diminished to start with, you wind up filled with self-loathing, which makes itself evident in one of three ways.

One, you exert constant effort to avoid coming in contact with the real you. You do your best to believe your own façade and then feel surprised when something seems missing in your life. Your highs are never quite high enough. But, then again, your lows never hurt as much. That's the compromise you settle for in the end. As a result, your life is contrived and, at best, tolerable. At worst, it's depressing.

Two, you see yourself for the fraud you are, recognize your achievements as only icing covering a cardboard cake, and live your life as a lie. You attempt to be busy enough, sedated enough, angry enough, chaotic enough, drunk or drugged enough to avoid coming in contact with who you perceive you really are. For the most part, your life holds little joy, and you are always fearful of being exposed.

Three, you consciously or unconsciously feel incapable of changing or escaping who you perceive yourself to be. You feel overwhelmed and depressed, retreat from life, risk noth-ing, gain nothing, enjoy nothing, and abhor the person you are. In both instances, your problem stems from the fact that, beneath your outer facade, you harbor doubts about whether or not you're okay. These doubts originated early in child-hood and will endure throughout your life.

I suspect that the initial reaction many of you have will be to take strong issue with everything I've said, because you honestly don't agree. I understand, because feelings of insufficiency and inadequacy are, more often than not, invis-ible to the eye. They're hidden beneath the surface. In most instances, these types of feelings only make themselves appar-ent in vague, subtle ways. However, on occasion, they can be evidenced by inordinate fears of failing, or a perfectionistic need to succeed. No matter which, it explains why so many people take pills to improve their memory, increase their strength and energy, help them to lose or gain weight, grow hair, remove wrinkles, or increase sexual performance—all of which reflect an attempt to fix, rather than to accept the person you really are.

This is why, as a child, you were reluctant to admit that it was you who took the cookies from the jar, misplaced the note sent home to your parents about your poor school performance, or tried to change the grade on your report card before your mother or father saw it. Later in life, you lived with "something in your eye" rather than admit you were crying; wore dark clothes and loose-fitting overshirts and blouses so people wouldn't see how much weight you'd gained; lied about graduating from a university when you had only taken two or three courses at a community college; or fabricated how you had spoken up to the police officer who gave you a ticket, in order to feature yourself as fearless and strong. All of these actions are testimonies to the fact that you are dissatisfied or disappointed with who you are. You very likely fear being vulnerable or perceived as weak, because you don't get loved for being shy, imperfect, a coward, or too sensitive, right?

But, no matter how you attempt to cope with these feelings, you need to be aware that your underlying doubts regarding whether or not you're okay motivate, direct, and control far more of what you do, say, and even think than you can begin to imagine. As a result, you constantly strive to achieve, accomplish, perform, appear, and behave in ways that will cause others, as well as yourself, to think that you're acceptable and worthy of love. The sad fact is that because of those feelings, you tend to question love, even when love is forthcoming, and you have difficulty accepting it. You fear that if this person really knew you, the *real* you, his/her love wouldn't be forthcoming. And, of course, you're not about to reveal what you really feel or who you actually perceive yourself to be. Ultimately, you believe you have no choice but to constantly strive to be better or perfect. Of course, you know, intellectually, that it's impossible to be perfect. Therefore, it's an exercise in futility.

Nowhere else do your feelings of insufficiency manifest themselves more than in your intimate relationships. Over the years, I have heard countless numbers of people just like you, both men and women, say that what they want in a spouse is a sensitive, feeling, caring human being. A man wants a woman who will make him feel that he's okay just the way he is. He wants someone who will understand him, support him when he stumbles, and nurture and love him simply for the person he is. In effect, men are seeking a woman similar to the mother they wished for or imagined they'd grown up with. Years later, that man might complain that his wife is too controlling, critical, and nonresponsive sexually. It's no wonder—he can't have wild sex with a mother figure. It's the same for women. Many women claim to want a feeling, sensitive man, but, in actuality, these same women can be quick to criticize, find fault, and harbor resentment toward spouses and boyfriends who overtly demonstrate feelings. They deem their men as weak, indecisive, fearful, or too sentimental. What a woman unconsciously wants, no matter how successful or independent she might be, is a strong father figure, whether she had one or not, who will always accept her and will provide security— support her emotionally and protect her, financially and physically. It isn't that women don't value a sensitive man; it's that they don't see him as an adequate spouse. It's all right, if not wonderful, to have someone like that for a friend, but not a husband. Interestingly, years later, a woman will complain that her husband isn't emotionally considerate, sensitive, romantic, or empathetic. Therefore, it's no surprise that she's no longer sexually aroused by him.

It's essentially the same for both men and women. The person you say you want and the one you choose are often radically different. That difference occurs because, in most instances, the person you want is determined intellectually by your thoughts, but the person you choose is determined emotionally, by what you feel. That being the case, it follows that the person you get is someone you are attracted to on the basis of your neurotic feelings of insecurity, lack of confidence, and poor self-esteem. All of which causes you to search out someone you believe you can depend on, but what you fail to consider is the price you'll eventually have to pay for satisfying your dependency needs.

A patient of mine, Alex, is a quintessential example of this phenomenon. He's really okay, but he definitely didn't know it. At his first appointment, the first words he said were, "I hate myself. I cried all last night, on the way here, and now I'm crying again. I don't know why I cry at the drop of a hat. When I was a kid, I would go to a movie and be mortified when I'd start crying. If anyone asked if I was crying, I'd just say something was in my eye. I've always been way too sensitive and caught up in my feelings. It's tough, because I want to be seen as a strong man." The paradox is, if you were to ask most of the people who knew Alex, they wouldn't describe him as weak. His ex-wife would say he was emotionally distant, uninvolved with his family, a man who never initiated anything and was consumed by his job. His coworkers would tell you he was a go-getter who didn't jump into things, but thought them out instead. They looked up to and respected him for his commitment and conscientiousness. Do you know why? Because the people in Alex's life didn't know what he really felt. He just put on an act, and it was a good one. The problem was that he was frightened to let anyone get close enough to discover who he felt he really was. In his mind, he was an excessively sensitive, feeling, caring individual who he perceived as weak. The truth is, he was really okay, but he didn't know it.

Now, allow me to let his own words speak for him. "I just returned from a wonderful trip with my girlfriend, Cindy. I was apprehensive about visiting her friends, but by the second day, I warmed up and was pretty comfortable. Cindy is quite a lady. I love her strength, her vivaciousness, and her personality. She doesn't have trouble with people. She's decisive, knows what she wants, and goes after it. I, on the other hand, spend half my life feeling ambivalent and considering all the negative alternatives that might occur if I say or do something wrong. So, more often than not, I wait to see what others think or want to do and follow along. People seem to like me for it, but I feel like an obedient little child. What's going to happen if she really gets to know me? That's why I came to you. I want your help, before she sees me, to become the person she thinks I am. I don't want to live with the dependent, inadequate, frightened guy I am, the chameleon who is constantly trying to fit in."

Unfortunately, Alex isn't alone. On one hand, most of you go through life trying to be the kind of person you think someone will accept and love. On the other hand, you search for a person you believe will make you that way. The problem is that everyone talks about the value of authenticity, transparency, sincerity, and emotionality, but behaviorally, that isn't how you act. Despite your verbalizations to the contrary, as I noted earlier, you ladies still want that handsome knight in shining armor who will whisk you off and protect you for the rest of your life. And men, even more than you realize, feel the need to fulfill those expectations. Consequently, they create an image that portrays them, externally, as strong and fearless. In effect, they hide behind a lie designed to mask or deny their vulnerability, emotionality, and feelings of insufficiency. I wonder how much better men and women might feel if they expended the same effort toward discovering and accepting who they really are?

If you can relate to the multitude of individuals in our society who, like Alex, go through life fearful, constantly trying to prove themselves, then this book is for you. It's intended to help you see that your behavior shouldn't consist of performing a series of endless challenges that will fix you or please someone else. Instead, your energies should be directed toward discovering who you are and learning to accept that person because he or she truly is okay. It is the only way to get off the treadmill you've been on most of your life and to focus on accepting, rather than fixing, the person facing you in the mirror.

CHAPTER TWO

GIVE YOURSELF "THE GIFT OF "ME"

I recently discovered something I never knew about the woman I've slept with, eaten with, and loved for fifty-seven years. On every one of her birthdays, she buys herself a present. This fact blew my mind. I thought, "In a million years, I would never think of doing that," partly because I doubt I'm that deserving. By now you know that's a feeling I've carried with me since early childhood. However, after mulling it over, I decided there's a lot of merit to her behavior. It says, "I matter and I deserve it." Then I wondered what gift would I give myself? A new photo printer? Another zoom lens? A deluxe gas barbecue? They all sounded great, but none really rang a bell.

I didn't come up with an answer that did ring a bell until last New Year rolled around—a time when most individuals introspectively ask, "What would I like to change or augment in myself in the coming year?" You know the typical answers: lose weight, drink less, stop smoking, establish a budget, spend more time with the family, go to synagogue or church more often, learn a foreign language, be kinder to others. Those are only the tip of the iceberg, but you get the idea. Nevertheless, thinking of them made me realize what gift I would like to give myself. It's one I believe is invaluable to everyone. Best of all, financially it costs nothing, although emotionally, it can be very expensive. It's the gift of "me."

I suspect my answer does little more than confuse you. In fact, I would expect you to ask, "What does that mean? Don't I already have me?" My answer is, probably not. You might reply, "All right, tell me how I can tell if I have me." I'll let you determine that by virtue of your answers to the following questions.

How many times have you:

1. Avoided answering a question because you were too fearful to be honest, lest the other person would get angry or reject you?
2. Capitulated and gone along with things that you really didn't want to do, rationalizing that it really didn't matter that much to you, but it seemed to be such a big deal to the other person that it wasn't worth arguing over?
3. Thought about saying something to someone you love—a spouse, a child, a parent, a good friend—and bitten your tongue because you didn't have the courage to speak out, justifying your behavior because you didn't want to hurt him/her?

4. Not responded to a hurtful or rude statement by someone else, rationalizing that it would only put you on his/her level?

5. Overindulged someone, emotionally or financially, because you wanted him/her to love you and were afraid that if you didn't "buy his/her love," he/she would reject or be angry with you?

6. Been reluctant to make a unilateral decision for fear of making a mistake or taking the risk that your spouse, partner, or boss would object?

7. Not extended a spur-of-the-moment invitation to dinner to someone you really wanted to have over because you were afraid of your spouse's reaction?

8. Not spoken your mind or said what you really believed because you knew it was an unpopular or deviant opinion?

9. Not expressed your religious, political, or philosophical beliefs because you believed they weren't acceptable or would be criticized by others?

10. Been in the company of a friend or acquaintance whose behavior or verbalizations were unacceptable, but you let them go by, acting as though you didn't hear them, even though you were appalled by them?

11. Been embarrassed publicly by someone dear to you, but kept a stiff upper lip, acted as though it didn't bother you, but felt destroyed inside?

12. Been so intimidated by your spouse that you were too frightened to let him/her know when he/she has acted inappropriately or hurt you, because

he/she might hurt you even more, all the while justifying your behavior by saying, "I don't like confrontations"?

13. Hidden these things you consider negative or don't like about yourself from your spouse; not told him/her about the hurts you feel, then resented him/her for not coming to your aid and not knowing what you need after all these years?

I'd have you further ask, emotionally, if you:

1. Feel weak, helpless and controlled by others.
2. Hate yourself because of your lack of backbone, feelings of subservience, and inability or reluctance to stand up for yourself and your convictions.
3. Ever experience feelings of hatred toward your spouse or parents, whom you perceive as oblivious to the hurt and/or rejection they impose on you. (Note, this hatred may not manifest itself by overt anger, but, instead, can make itself evident by an absence of feelings altogether, i.e., flat emotions.)
4. Have daydreams of running off, leaving everything behind, and starting a new life.
5. Have the feeling you've settled in life, but don't know what to do to change your situation.
6. Feel trapped by circumstances, such as your age, finances, family obligations, or the expectations of others.
7. Desperately want to change your life, but feel yourself almost paralyzed, physically and emotionally,

by your fear of the unknown and/or a lack of confidence in yourself.

I could go on endlessly, but I think you've gotten the general idea. The degree to which you can answer yes to these questions is the degree to which you haven't given yourself the gift of "me." What you do have is a weak, inadequate-feeling individual who placates others and goes through life justifying behaviors that aren't palatable to you. It's not that you're bad, it's just that you lack the courage to be you. Instead, you are an individual who takes the easy road, capitulates, acquiesces and later resents and estranges yourself from the very people you love and whose love you desire. You do this not because you hate your spouse, children, parents, or friends. Instead, when you interact with them, you hate *yourself* because you lack the backbone or integrity to be honest, to share your thoughts Discover Your LUCAP, and to state your mind. Your excuse? "When I'm around them, I can't be me." But whose fault is that?

At the same time, I suspect you may also relate with or know many individuals who have the same feelings as you, but whose behavior is the total opposite.

1. They bully, intimidate, put down, and argue with those they love to prove they're not weak or lacking in courage. But their exaggerated negative behaviors reveal their true inner feelings.
2. Intellectually and/or physically, they abuse their loved ones. Although they later regret and are often embarrassed by their actions, their false sense of pride disallows them to apologize. To compensate,

they later buy a gift or treat their loved ones in a way they know will ingratiate them to others, as a surreptitious form of apology.

3. These individuals have extremely fragile egos, which they fiercely guard, often to the point of hurting and subjugating people they care for because they are unable to admit, let alone accept, their own shortcomings.

4. They are driven individuals who, by virtue of their neurotic need to prove their adequacy, often achieve great success in the world. But no matter how much money or esteem they garner, in their own mind's eye, they're always lacking. For the most part, their successes stem from their need to prove their adequacy. But it's to no avail. No matter the level of their achievements, they still feel insufficient. Thus, they are quick to be defensive and aggressive in their dealings with others.

Let me stress that the more you can relate to any of these characteristics, the more imperative it

is that you give yourself the gift of "me." The difficulty is that most of you think you have you. You base this notion primarily on what you do on the outside. The problem is that, in the long run, your outward achievements don't count. You can readily see that by asking yourself, "Is my inner worth based upon what I wear, how I dress, the car I drive, the home I live in, the vacations I've taken, the salary I earn, how well my children perform, my acts of charity, the way my husband behaves, or how religious I am?"

Nothing is basically wrong with any of those, except none of them really suffice. You can clearly see that by asking yourself several additional questions.

1. How beautiful do I have to be to feel worthwhile?
2. If my child fails at school, gets drunk, is depressed, or is divorced, am I of no worth?
3. Conversely, if he/she is a doctor, lawyer, or successful businessperson, does that give me worth?
4. How many times a week do I have to go to church, how much do I have to give to charity, and how successful do I have to be for me to feel worthwhile?

The answer is, there is no answer. The only way for any of you to truly feel worthwhile is for you to accept who you are, i.e., the cowardly, fearful child inside you that you frequently run from and often deny, hide, or camouflage; a guy or gal you don't always reveal, stand up for, or protect because you have little respect for him or her.

How do you go about giving that self to yourself? The answer is, one step at a time. Initially, you have to be willing and able to honestly see yourself for who you are. Second, you need to recognize that you can't change who you are on the inside. The hard drive is there to stay. If you're a wuss, lack courage, feel insufficient, are emotionally needy and/or dependent, you have to admit and accept it, because there's no crime attached to it. The third step requires that you stop trying to prove yourself to everyone else in the world, because no matter how much you convince others you're worthy and deserving of love and respect, their opinions are short lived and have to be garnered over and over again. It's a case of only feeling as good as your last magic trick.

In the end, the only opinion that's of lasting value is your own. Therefore, the only person you need to prove yourself to is you. You begin by taking one risk at a time. Thus, you must dare to honestly speak your mind, in spite of your fear of being put down, disagreed with, rejected, or discounted. This, however, in no way gives you license to hurt or abuse others. Instead, it obligates you to share your thoughts and feelings, particularly with those others who are of greatest importance to you. Nor does it imply that you need to be strong, keep a stiff upper lip, or be impervious to hurt. Quite the contrary. When you feel bad, frightened, or sad, you need to nurture yourself, but you must also learn to ask for help. What you can't do is condemn, look down on, or criticize yourself for feeling weak or needing help. Instead, you say, "This is who I am. This is what I feel. I'm not Superman or Superwoman. I'm a human being, with feelings and emotions and a big, soft heart. I care, I cry, and I make mistakes, but I'm beginning to be proud of me, because I'm learning to chance being wrong, to be open and vulnerable to others, and to risk their rejecting me. Most of all, I'm starting to realize that, despite my scars and weaknesses, I'm okay." The bonus is that, by sharing your needs with a loved one, you give him/her a gift; the opportunity to help you and to feel needed, to be of service and, consequently, to feel more positively about himself/herself.

The entire process is best described by the following statement: *Your acceptance of your inadequacies, insufficiencies, and insecurities is the only real actualization of you.* You see, that acceptance is you giving yourself to you. It's trusting that, despite all of your humanness, i.e., your perceived weaknesses and shortcomings, you're okay. The beauty of it is that once you have trust in yourself, you have no trouble trusting everyone else in your world. You can let them in and take the risk of them hurting, rejecting, or not loving you, because you know (with only a little doubt) that you're okay.

Try it. It's the best gift you'll ever give yourself this year or any year in your life, because, as the author George Eliot once said, "It's never too late to be who you might have been." I hope this message resonates within you sufficiently to cause you to want to immediately start the process of giving yourself "the gift of me." If so, all you have to do is to begin is turn this page to discover "how you got that way."

CHAPTER THREE

HOW DID YOU GET THAT WAY?

My patient Eric isn't a truly depressed person, but he is a very sad one. He is preoccupied with all types of crises, which serves to obscure his feelings of inadequacy and despair. The one question that he most ponders is, "How did I get this way? My family wasn't particularly dysfunctional or different from most of my friends' parents. We did all the normal things. We vacationed together. Dad worked, Mom took care of the kids. We went to church. I don't recall being abused or demeaned any more than any other kid. Anyway, that's the way parents punished kids back then. So, why am I this way? Dad always told me I could do anything I wanted. Mom encouraged me. And yet, I feel as though I've been sad and running from that sadness all my life. I always had a project or an activity that I had to participate in or work at. That way, I never had to come in touch with my sadness. But I do remember times when I wanted to cry for no reason at all. At least, I never knew the reason. I just can't recall anybody actually *doing* something to me to cause me to feel the way I do.

The other day a patient came in to see me. He's sixty-five years old, a little out of shape, but generally physically healthy. However, that day, his movements seemed more hesitant. As we walked down the hallway to my office, he almost veered into the wall once or twice. I asked him if he had seen a doctor, or if he was sick. He said, "It's been coming on for about a week or two. I've been getting dizzy and occasionally losing my balance. I just figured it was all these things we were talking about in therapy, but I'm going to see my doctor this afternoon and I'll let you know." That afternoon, he called me and said, "My doctor thinks it might be something neurological or audiological. I'm going to see an ear-nose-throat doctor who can get me in right away and a neurologist next week."

The following week, he was a different man. He looked like the guy who first came to see me. "You wouldn't believe it," he said. "I went to the ear doctor and he said that I was having a hearing problem. I've been wondering about that for the past months. I have this old TV and I thought I'd better get a flat screen or something with a better speaker system, because I kept turning it up and it was never loud enough. I figured it was just an old set and the speakers were gone. But the doctor dug around in my ears and took out a lot of wax. Finally, he took out what looked like a small piece of coal the size of the end of my fingertip. I couldn't believe it. I could hear again! My other ear was clogged up, too, but only slightly so. Today, I feel like my old self. You know, it was such a slow process, I never realized what was happening until I was dizzy and couldn't hear at all. Now that old TV sounds pretty good.'"

It's the same for Eric and so many of us. Our feelings and beliefs develop gradually until they become a part of us without us even realizing what, why, or how it took place. The process of determining who you are emotionally occurs in a similar fashion, slowly, from gestation to four or five years old. You might ask, "Why do you say 'four or five' when you talk about the level at which your child can be considered fully mature, developed, or as old as he's ever going to be?" You might also ask why I state that the adult in you only then begins to make itself present. Let me explain.

Recent neurological studies have shown that the development of the gray matter that covers the brain doesn't begin until age four or five. It doesn't end until age eighteen or twenty-one. The interesting aspect of this is two-fold. One, the gray matter is the area that provides the connecting wires between the lobes of the brain. These connections allow the lobes to communicate and interface with each other. Without that ability, you can learn, but you can't integrate or synthesize information. The second factor is that this gray matter starts and ends its developmental process earlier in girls. By eighteen, the gray matter is pretty much completely formed and the connections between the various parts of the brain are finalized. That's not the case with boys. The project of building these interconnections doesn't end in males until age twenty-one. That explains why, for years, professionals observed that little girls are far more mature than little boys. Girls demonstrate more behavioral restraint, better decision-making abilities, and better ability to curtail impulsive behaviors. There are exceptions to the rule, but, generally speaking, that's the case.

As a result, most of the learning that takes place in children before age four is of a habitualized, kinesthetic, or emotional nature. They do learn, as evidenced by a two-year-old child who crawls across the floor, puts his finger in a light socket, and, lo and behold, for the rest of his or her life, he never does it again. In no way is he or she capable of understanding that by inserting your finger, you create a ground and the electricity that's in the socket goes through your finger and throughout your body. That concept can only be understood intellectually. Nevertheless, the child associates electric sockets with pain and he "learns" no to do it again.

That being the case, you must consider the fact that early learning, though effective in determining behavior, isn't the result of a child understanding the big picture. That only comes later. The differentiating factor is that one type of learning is primarily emotional in nature. The other is intellectual. They are worlds apart. One, emotional learning, is covert, unconscious, and invisible to the eye. The other, intellectual learning, is overt, conscious, and readily apparent.

At best, emotional learning is a covert process that evolves without you really knowing that it's taking place. You gain information from every event, circumstance, and interpersonal relationship with your family and friends. You paste things together, sometimes rightly and sometimes erroneously, and then go about interpreting them based on your DNA, situational factors, such as a divorce or the death of a parent, or parental rearing which may have exposed you to emotional or physical abuse of an overt or covert nature and/or dysfunctional role models. All of these factors serve as major contributors to the development of who you are and how you behave later in life. Early in life, a child's world is very small. He or she can only see a very limited distance. For the most part, an infant only spends time sleeping in a small bassinet or crib—very limited, indeed. Later, as a baby begins to crawl and walk, his world expands to several rooms. But even then, he is restricted from touching or going places that might prove dangerous to him. That being the case, every incident that occurs within his slowly expanding environment is, for him, a major event that can rock his world. As an adult looking back, you might only view it as a minor incident, of little or no significance. But, for the child, it can be an event that stays with him, ingrained deep inside—one that isn't accessible consciously, but significantly affects him throughout the remainder of his life.

Generally speaking, I believe fathers influence who you are on the outside, how you deal with rules, regulations, society and work situations, etc. Mothers, conversely, affect you on the inside, primarily with regard to how you feel about yourself, the way you interact with others in meaningful, long-term, intimate relationships, how you go about reaching out in loving interactions, and what you feel you have to be or do to gain the love you seek.

These influences, however, aren't restricted to parents alone. As your world expands, siblings, relatives, peers, and teachers can all play a significant part with regard to the self-perception you later assume and even the subsequent behavioral patterns you demonstrate later in life. As far as I'm concerned, however, your emotional being is as totally mature or developed as it will ever be by age four or five. Later, you go about selectively recalling and/or reacting to those incidents and events that reinforce your early self-image.

After all these years, I still find it startling to believe how significant a part early experiences can play in the development of someone's adult behavior. To illustrate, let me tell you about Karla, a very attractive, bright, accomplished young physician who repeatedly became involved in long-term, intimate relationships with men she felt she had to appease, chase, and cajole to gain their attention. When I asked her about her favorite game or activity as a child, she said, "I loved to play outside with my two older sisters. But before they would play with me, they'd force me to clean up the mess they made in their bedrooms or in the kitchen. I didn't mind, though, because some of the time, they actually did come out and play." Then she stopped short, her eyes and mouth opened wide, and she said, "It's the same thing I do with men. I'm always chasing them to get them to play with me."

You see, we learn early and we learn well, but, in most instances, we learn without conscious awareness. The process is much like the affect of water dripping long term over rock formations. Similar to the rock, your perceptions of self and your personality take shape and solidify inside you emotionally and psychologically.

I further believe that, from the start, most of you grew up incorporating the same basic insights that I did. For example, when I was a small child, I learned that the world was divided into two categories: One was greeted with applause, smiles, and hugs. It was called "YES." The other was, at least from my perspective, a much larger number of behaviors that were loudly proclaimed "NO."

Later, in my youth, I discovered that YESes were politically acceptable, considered positive, and suggested that I was okay. NOs, however, were associated with rejection, reprimands, and even punishment. They indicated that I was not okay.

As I grew still older, the categories expanded to include not only behaviors and actions, but verbalizations and thoughts as well. I was exposed to the concepts of moral and immoral, good and bad, appropriate and inappropriate. At the same time, I learned that there were advantages that came with being good and following the paths prescribed by my parents, family, and teachers. Those individuals were far older, had lived longer, were supposedly much wiser and willing, if not eager, to share the thoughts and experiences which helped them to achieve the position they had acquired. I learned that if I followed in their footsteps, I would experience few or no problems and be rewarded for my compliance. When or if those rewards weren't forthcoming, I was assured that I would be rewarded in the hereafter and that I should, therefore, not despair.

If, however, I was deemed lacking in ability, accomplishment, or appearance, those rewards would be absent. In retrospect, I now realize that because I perceived myself as insufficient, I unconsciously thought that I had to choose between one of four alternatives: One, resign myself to my lot in life and reap my just reward after death. Two, accept the fact that I wasn't okay and, therefore, didn't have to try. I could just give up, suffer the hand life dealt me, and forever play the role of a victim. Three, rebel against society and its dictates and become a bully and a victimizer. In that way, I could ensure that others would experience the same pain as I did. Four, explain to the powers-that-be how wrong they were by showing them other paths, new beliefs, and alternative ways of thinking. Unfortunately, a goodly number of brilliant, even genius-level minds, such as Socrates and Galileo, etc., were chastised, excommunicated, or even executed because of their innovative ideas and principles or the fact that they chose to think outside the box. But, despite the torment they were forced to suffer, none of them accepted the fact that they weren't okay.

As a child, I lacked their resolve and courage, but, years later, their lives provided an example that left me with a fifth alternative, one we all need to learn. It gave me the wherewithal to begin, at least in part, to live my life with more self-acceptance and freedom. I discovered that I could openly express my personal and professional thoughts, whether they were politically correct or not, and God didn't smite me. Doing so gave me more self-satisfaction than I had ever known before. I began to feel that I was okay, despite the fact that I wasn't the best, the smartest, the strongest, or that I didn't fit the mold or subscribe to all the beliefs of others. Intellectually, I now totally accept and believe that. Emotionally, however, there are still occasions when my feelings of being trapped, insufficient, controlled, and unfulfilled still rise to the surface. The difference is that I am now far better able to live with both myself and those feelings. It is a state of mind that I would love to share with each of you.

You're Okay, But You Don't Know It is my attempt to do that. It is intended as a guide for those of you who feel controlled by or are still fighting childhood feelings of insufficiency and helplessness, but want to learn that you're okay. It doesn't advocate civil disobedience or anarchy. It doesn't encourage rebellion, or even suggest that you can't learn from history or from elders. Instead, it will show you how to value you—your thoughts, beliefs, and feelings. It will give you permission to express them and share them with others. It will encourage you to create your own YESes and NOs. It will aid you to choose your wars, to not be upset by little things or inconsequential issues, and to stand pat when doing otherwise would harm you. It will also teach you that it takes more internal courage to stand up *for* yourself than to stand up *to* others—that, as the axiom states, it is only when you can stand up for yourself that others will fully see and appreciate your strengths and be able to look up to, love, and lean on you.

Dag Hammarskjold said it best. Let me paraphrase his words: the man fell from the narrow ledge he was trying to traverse when, too frightened to stand upright, he dropped to his knees and attempted to crawl.

For a moment, I'd have you close your eyes and ask yourself, "How do I go through life—standing upright, or crawling?"

How do you know if you crawl? Let me tell you. Every child comes into the world with two built-in ways of coping. One, testing the limits, and defy by breaking the rules. Two, *flight*— run, hide, retreat, escape, shut down emotionally, and/or deny. To my way of thinking, despite the fact that they appear to be 180-degree opposites, they're both forms of crawling, ways of avoiding the real issues facing you. They're knee-jerk reactions to the demands of your parents and society, who want you to comply, capitulate, or compromise. As a child, you had few alternatives. As an adult, you have more, but, sadly, despite your chronological age, all too many of you are still children emotionally.

As a result, you crawl. The only question is, how much and how badly does this crawling make you feel?

What your parents needed to tell you was this:

1. Value your person, your thoughts, feelings, and opinions, and express them without anger, blame, or fear.

2. Live proactively. You won't always get what you want, but you'll know you tried.

3. Risk being vulnerable. Stop trying to control others. Instead, take control of you and responsibility for your actions.

4. Feel free to fail and to feel insecure, sad, and anxious. It will help you to learn humility and, in most instances, teach you that you have more inner resources than you realize.

5. *Have passion.* Dare to dream and to love out of strength, not dependence. Know that caring isn't a sin, and expressing your desire for someone to love you takes courage. It is not a sign of weakness, but pathologically needing that love may be, because it stems from your fear that you can't stand on your own.

In sum total, recognize that you're okay, in spite of your fears and feelings of weakness. But, most importantly, know that your primary goal in life shouldn't be to improve or fix who you are. Instead, it should be learning to accept who you are and altering how you react as a result of it.

CHAPTER FOUR

NO ONE ESCAPES CHILDHOOD UNSCATHED

Please hear me. **No one escapes childhood without hurts, scars, mixed messages, confusion, doubts, or worries about who and what he or she is.** Every one of you has, in varying degrees, an emotional hole that's never been filled, but needs to be. But, for that to happen, you have to be able to reach out to people in your world, open up, trust, and allow someone to fill that hole. The problem is that if you have this hole, you've already been hurt. Therefore, reaching out and trusting isn't an easy task. It's a behavior you'll need to work at. In fact, I practice it every day. The difference is that I hope that you start learning it a lot earlier than I did. I want you to know that, one day, you will be able to let your defenses down and feel emotionally safe, because you discovered that there are others in the world who will care and be there for you. You need to know that you're not alone, sick emotionally, or undeserving of love. Instead, you're okay, you just never knew it. You may have negative feelings and perceptions about yourself, doubts about your worth, and fears of rejection, but you would be surprised how many others share those feelings. Those feelings can contribute to your being emotionally needy, willing to pay too much for the love you get or staying in relationships where you don't get it at all. It all stems from the child you were in the first five years of your life. You may find that hard to believe, but once you can get in touch with, own, accept, and love your little child, you'll discover that the adult, the part of you that started to develop after the gray matter grew in your brain, can care for and nurture the wounded little boy or girl inside you. When that occurs, you will begin to feel more in touch with and at peace with yourself than ever before.

The problem is that most people don't want to get close to their child, because it's too painful. Sad to say, this rationale is the norm for all too many people. But I don't want you to be normal. Remember that normal behavior consists of defending yourself in one of two ways: **fight**, i.e., get angry, get mad, push people away so you don't have to feel, or get in touch with painful thoughts or realities; or **flight**, i.e., run away, deny, forget, or obscure the hurts. Drink, drug, eat, smoke to excess. Do anything so as not to feel or get near your hurts. That's normal, and it's the reason so many people eventually come to therapy. They typically say they came to get healthy, and I tell them, "To do so, you've got to be abnormal. You've got to learn to float, not fight or take flight." That means you eventually have to learn to lie on your back while going down the stream of life, look up at the clouds, recognize that some are black and others are white and that you have to be prepared to effectively cope with both because they're bound to be part of your world. When you can do that, your world changes. It sounds crazy, or too simple a solution. But it isn't.

Think about it this way: How much energy does it take when you're feeling bad to try to keep yourself afloat and stay alive? Too much. How much energy does it take when you're feeling good to block out reality, not talk about it or look at it? Too much. Conversely, what if you were able to float, look up at the sky, see the black clouds, and not have to run from or fight them? The energy that it previously took to defend against the hurts in life would then be available to aid you to overcome any challenges you face. Even more, with all your newly acquired energy, you'll find it amazing how much easier it is to confront ordeals that you previously perceived as overwhelming.

But, before that can take place, you need to honestly discern who you are on the inside. To help, let me tell you about myself. If I were to conduct an emotional audit of my childhood, I'm positive that it would wind up in the red. The truth be known, I have only a vague memory of my youth, and none of the thoughts that come to mind are blatantly negative. But I know that at some point in time, I began to have the feeling that I wasn't okay. Throughout the rest of my life, that notion served as a handicap that I continually carried with me, but frequently tried to overcome or hide from. Those feelings grew inside me, to the point that I knew deep down that something was lacking in me, but I was unable to articulate what it was. The interesting thing is, neither of my parents ever said, "You're not okay."

In fact, the times my mother said anything, it was how great I was, which was even worse. You might think it would have been encouraging, but all it did was make me feel that if she was saying it, I had to be it. And the more she told me how wonderful I was, the less I felt okay. The reason: in my mind, there was no way I could live up to it. I wasn't an athlete and my ADHD, which wasn't a diagnosis anyone knew about back then, didn't allow me to be the intellect, the scholar, or the achiever in the classroom. To make matters worse, I felt an emotional emptiness inside. As a result, everything I did was my attempt to feel, even if only for a short time, that I belonged, fit in, and was okay.

In comparison with my peers, I didn't stand out or look peculiar. I didn't have any outstanding physical character-istics that would have singled me out or said, "There's that kid with the humpback, or the big glasses." I didn't speak peculiarly; in fact, I was fairly articulate and verbal. I tried to capitalize on that, but, as is generally the case for people who feel inadequate, I overdid it. I talked too much. I couldn't stand any lapse in conversation and felt I had to fill in the empty spaces. So, if anything, I was a motor mouth who was always trying to be funny. It was my attempt to prove that I was someone of value.

At the same time, I didn't have the confidence to jump in conversationally or to feel like one of the group. Instead, I always saw myself on the fringe of a group, never in the middle. I recall that, on all too many occasions, if some-one was driving and said, "Let's all go to the deli," I never knew for sure if "all" included me. So I'd awkwardly wait to see if somebody said, "Hey, Eli, are you coming?" If they did, I was quick to respond. If they didn't, I often stood there and watched them drive away, validating my fear that I wasn't wanted. I should add that my name is Eli Edward Reitman and, at that time, everybody knew me as Eli. I genuinely like the name now, but, as a kid, I was teased about Eli Whitney and the cotton gin, so, somewhere along the line, I switched my name to Ed. Interestingly enough, the excuse I gave was that another guy came into class whose name was Eli and I said I didn't want people to confuse us, so I'd be Ed. Let me note that there were a half dozen other Eds, which made it even more confusing, but it served as my escape.

The point I'm trying to make is that when I honestly look at my youth, I realize that I never felt okay. I learned that very early on, and I'm sure my ADHD had something to do with it, particularly at school, where I often thought, "I'm as smart as him or her." Then, when it came time to do the work, I couldn't concentrate or focus. My mind wandered off in a myriad of directions. I'd sit in the classroom and hear the teacher tell another student, "Please close the door," and it took everything in the world for me to sit in my seat and not run over and close it first. Similarly, if she asked somebody a question, it took everything for me not to answer.

But I felt equally lacking at home. My father was the most wonderful guy in the world. He was funny, he was compassionate, he was caring, but he was hardly home, because he was working. When he wasn't, he had a project. I now realize it was his escape. I also recall that the few times I tried to work with Dad, I could never do anything well enough. He wasn't critical. He would just say, "Let me do it, this is too hard." So

I never learned to make mistakes, or realized it was okay or normal to struggle and then to learn how to do things better. As a result, I spent a good portion of my life trying to do things perfectly, or not doing them at all and beating myself up for my imperfections. Interestingly, Dad would always tell me, "Don't put your hands in your pockets." I don't remember exactly how he worded it; it was something like, "Idle hands are the devil's workshop." (Back then, I didn't understand what he meant, but I knew it wasn't good.) It was frequently followed by, "How can you help with your hands in your pockets?" Would you believe that, years later, when I lived in Alaska, I'd go out in weather that was twenty degrees below zero and I wouldn't be able to put my hands in my pockets? I'd start to, but a voice from somewhere inside said, "No." So, you see, the messages you get early on, even if you don't realize it, stick with you throughout your life.

But that wasn't the only message I got. In retrospect, it's apparent to me that my mother was so engrossed in her own depression and feelings of disappointment that she only went through the motions of being a mother, not the emotions. No one would have called her a bad person. She didn't beat me. She said the right words. But, many years later, I realized that she was totally emotionally involved with her family of origin. She was consumed with anger over the surrogate mother role that she perceived she was forced to play as a child, and she still felt unappreciated, rejected, and unloved. She lived with those feelings all her life. Even worse, she had no awareness that she was "mothered out" as a youth and probably resented having to care for her own children. She literally didn't know how to hug, hold, comfort, or nurture. The one emotion she excelled at was anger. Without any warning, she would explode, and I wondered where it came from, or why. If I heard her footsteps coming down the hall, my first inclination was to say, "I didn't do anything," because I knew an emotional tirade was about to be unleashed. The worse she felt, the more exaggerated her behavior became, to the point that she frequently had one-hundred-dollar reactions to five-dollar problems. I don't recall her ever being involved with what was going on with or in me, or at all understanding what my feelings were. Then again, I must admit that I never told her. But my feelings then and my thoughts now are that if I had, she wouldn't have had any idea what I was talking about anyway.

The primary emotions I experienced were aloneness and sadness. Dad was gone, Mom was a potential threat, and my younger sister was too timid and scared to provide support. In retrospect, I always had a feeling of estrangement. What I wasn't aware of was my desperate need and desire for someone to be there, to understand, and to care. However, even if I had been aware, I didn't know how to ask for those things and probably didn't feel I deserved them. Deep down inside, those feelings are still alive, and, on occasion, they're quick to come to the surface. Fortunately, I now realize that although the feelings are valid, they belong to the little child inside me, not the adult. They have, nevertheless, stayed with me and, in too many instances, have caused me to overreact in ways I later regretted.

I'm sharing this with you because I want to impress upon you that whatever you truly felt about yourself as a child, on the inside, from the bottom of your chin to the tips of your toes, inside your stomach, your chest, or in your heart, is what you will feel and carry with you for the rest of your life. It doesn't go away. Let me explain. Those feelings are learned early in life. They become, figuratively speaking, part of your hard drive. It's a type of learning that takes place at an emotional level. For example, let's go back to my initial example of emotional learning. If you're a year old, crawling on the floor, and you look up at the wall and there's a plate there with some holes in it, what do you do? You stick your finger in it. And guess what? You get shocked. You have no intellectual awareness, but I promise you will remember it emotionally, so much so that you never again shove your finger into an electric plug. It's no different from a child who, on numerous occasions, has been told by his mother that the stove is "hot, hot." He knows only the words. But the day he puts his finger on the stove and gets burned, he understands the words for the rest of his life and never again purposely puts his hand on a hot stove.

It's a form of emotional or kinesthetic learning that takes place before the gray matter develops in your brain. The various lobes of your brain may develop earlier, but they're not connected. Thus, there's no way the various regions of the brain can communicate or interact with one another. For that to happen, you have to wait until the wiring grows and allows for a connection between them. The problem is that the gray matter, in which the wiring is encased, doesn't really start growing until age three, four, or five. That, by the way, is one of the reasons that I have difficulty with parents who go to extremes to childproof their homes. They're the same parents whose children aren't permitted to get dirty, venture out in the rain, jump in puddles, or attend school if they feel the least bit out of sorts. They're the ones who eliminate all breakable or valuable items from their homes rather than teaching their children "No" or "Don't touch." They're also the ones who fill the electrical sockets with little plastic inserts so their child can't get electrocuted. I've never heard of a child dying from putting his finger in a socket, but I've seen lots of children deprived of learning experiences because of the excessive protection and overindulgence provided by their well-meaning but overprotective parents.

These examples of emotional learning are also the reason that today, some seventy years later, I can, on occasion, still feel sad, alone, unloved, and unimportant. It has nothing to do with my intellectual awareness and everything to do with early learning.

Let me provide you with another example that will even better exemplify this process. I was a successful Ph.D. psychologist in practice for about five years when an attorney, who was my best referral source, called me up one day and said, "Ed, I'd like to ask you for a favor." I said, "Sure, anything I can do for you," because 50 to 60 percent of my referrals came from him. He said, "I've never asked you for anything, and I've sent you every referral I can. I need you to do something for me. I want you to see a young lady in my office."

My first thought was, "Oh, my God, he's probably involved with her and I'm going to wind up in the middle of a messy relationship and lose all my referrals." That was my fears and insecurities talking, because I later heard him say, "She's a young lady whose husband divorced her, left her with a child, and ran off with his secretary. I offered to give her a job, just to give her a chance, and she's very good at work. I really like her. But, Ed, she only comes in two or three days a week, at most. The rest of the week, she arrives on time, but then she's called by the day-care center to pick up her son because he's crying, he doesn't want to be there, he needs his mommy, or he's sick. If she has a sick child, I'm really sorry, but what can I do? I can't keep somebody in the office like that. Would you please see her two or three times, for no charge? If you can't, I'll understand and I'll pay her bill."

I said, "Of course I'll see her." I had no choice, anyway, at least in my mind.

Several days later, the young lady came in, looking totally distraught, as though she were carrying the world on her shoulders. She repeated the story about her work situation and talked about how frustrated and depressed she was. I asked her to describe her typical day and she said, "I wake up in the morning, get my son up, dress him, make him breakfast, and drop him off at day care. I go to the office and, two or three times a week, I have to leave because the day-care center calls. On good days, I take him home after work, take his clothes off, and wash them, because he's gotten them dirty. Then I try to give him a bath. He hates the bath, and there's water all over the bathroom. All the while, he's screaming and yelling. I feel guilty saying this, but at times I wish I didn't have him. I'd almost like to just shove him under the water until he stops, but I could never do that. I get him out of the bathtub, dry him off, put his PJs on, feed him dinner, and put him to bed. Then I clean the bathroom up, make lunches for the next day, and, if I have the strength, take a shower and get in bed to get ready for the next day."

My heart went out to her. Her life sounded so bleak. Her elderly parents lived in another town and there was nobody she could lean on. After hearing her story, I asked her, "What's the worst time of your day?" You probably already know what she said. The bath.

I said, "Okay. No more baths."

She looked at me with astonishment. "That's crazy. What do you mean, no baths?"

I said, "Well, it's the worst time of your day. You've got to do something to lighten your load. Drip-dry him."

She said, "What's that?"

"Wipe him up with a wash rag and dry him off," I answered. "On Friday or Saturday or Sunday, you can fight with him about a bath. There is one more thing. You have to spend half the time you save from fighting about the bath, and cleaning the bathroom afterward, doing something with him. I don't care what it is, but something he'll enjoy."

She came in the next week and said, "Things seem to be a little bit better."

I said, "Okay. I want to see you again, next week."

The following week, she arrived looking like a different woman. She had makeup on, her eyes were bright. She seemed alive and far more attractive than the first time I saw her. "Things are so much better," she said. "I only had to pick him up early once last week. Even then, I think I could have left him and it would have worked out. I know my boss is happier and things are going well."

"What do you attribute this change to?"

"I did what you said."

"What was that?"

"Drip-dry him."

"And what do you do with the extra time?"

She said, "I only have this tiny, one-bedroom apartment now, but I did salvage a few bits of furniture from our house. One of them is a rocker that's now in the living room. So I turn the lights low, put on soft music, and wrap him, after the drip-dry, in a huge terry-cloth towel. Then we sit down in the rocker and I hold and cuddle him in the half-lit room and sing to him softly."

After I heard that, and even now when I tell the story, I almost always get a lump in my throat and, deep down, I want to cry. Mind you, I've told that story a lot of times. But that day, when she first told it to me, it took everything in the world not to openly bawl. My eyes teared up, my throat got thick, and I thought, "I had a lot of baths as I grew up, although I don't remember any one of them specifically. But I was never, ever wrapped in a Turkish towel, lovingly held in a quiet place, cuddled, and allowed to feel the closeness, warmth, and security that I imagined her son experienced during those occasions." From the intensity of my reaction, I realized it was something I had desperately needed as a child, but had never experienced and still desired.

That need is still there in me and always will be. It will never go away. But accepting that fact mitigates the pain, makes it easier to live with the sad kid inside me, and helps me to accept that it's what I still need in my life today. Now, on bad days, I'm able to ask for the emotional nurturing I need without perceiving myself as a weak child lacking masculinity.

I learned something else from that experience. It's that I have a right to feel sad about my emotional hole, to mourn the fact that the love and nurturing I needed as a child weren't there, and to know that I deserved it then and do today. That wasn't always the case. For much of my life, I'm sure I felt that something must have been wrong with me if my mother didn't "love me." I now understand why it wasn't there. Sadly, my mother was dead by the time I understood it fully, but it did help me to forgive her, at least in my mind. That hole is still there. The difference is that I no longer see it as a negative or weak characteristic I have to hide. Instead, I accept that my little kid is a needy, ADD human being. A person who requires lots of reassurance, who doesn't fully appreciate himself, and is always searching for new mountains to climb to prove he deserves that love. I can now recognize and accept that. I no longer feel ashamed or embarrassed by it. It's just another part of me that affects the way I cope and feel.

Of even greater importance, I hope you can come to feel the same way. What I don't want you to do is wait ten or twenty years before you come to the same conclusion. Nor do I want you to think that your only other alternatives are to suffer or commit suicide in order to escape from your little kid. There were several times in my life when I thought about it, but thinking about it isn't crazy. Doing it is. Sometimes, however, feeling that low can bring about an epiphany, which can open up your eyes to the fact that where you're coming from and the way you felt was terribly hurtful, but it needn't be permanent. That realization can bring about an opening in the black clouds over your head, which will allow light to penetrate the dark world you've seen up until now.

I don't expect you to immediately accept this notion. But I hope that I'm sowing seeds, some of which will take root and begin to grow. It's even possible that two or three days or weeks from now, something will happen and you'll say, "That fits exactly what I read. I'm not alone, unique, or crazy, so maybe I can start to deal with myself differently." It may also open your eyes to the fact that you can't change the little boy or girl you are from the bottom of your chin to the tip of your toes, but you can help the adult man or woman you are from your chin to the top of your head to direct you toward any goal you desire. It is also possible that one day, your adult will be able to take over and become your own parent or therapist. Then, when painful thoughts or events occur, the adult in you can emerge and say, "It isn't the end of the world. You don't have to run or hide, even though you may occasionally feel like it. You have the strength to overcome those urges and to stand up, face life, and deal with your own reality." Initially, it'll feel difficult to do, but over time, when you no longer see yourself as sick, insufficient, or not fitting in, you'll realize that despite the hurts you experienced in childhood, you were able to escape, to cut your emotional umbilical cord, and to realize you're okay.

CHAPTER FIVE

THE DYSFUNCTIONAL FAMILY

E ach of us has a family portrait. It may be invisible to the eye or to the conscious mind, but it is nevertheless indelibly engraved in our psyche and is responsible in many ways for the self-perception we live with, the attitude we present, and the manner in which we behave.

For a moment, I would like to ask you to close your eyes and try to visualize the family portrait that you carry within you. The one that includes all of the primary members of your family from when you were age zero to six or seven. Look closely, taking pains to note who is standing next to whom, checking to see the expression on each individual's face, the feelings that you see in their hearts, and the labels that might be affixed to each one. This portrait wasn't necessarily posed consciously or with malice aforethought. Quite the contrary, it is the conglomeration of any number of snapshots that were taken over and over again during your early childhood. The photos share a motif that persists over time and identifies each individual. On the surface, it may appear to be a picture of a perfect family—father, mother, sister, brother, all involved in presenting an image that is acceptable to the camera and to the world. But if you look deeply, you will see the captions describing each individual. There is the "good" kid, the "bad" kid, the "athlete", the "comedian" and the "dunce." There is the "pretty" one, the "mean" one, the "powerful" one, the "weak" one, and the "victim." You may also recognize the "weak father," the "strong mother" (or vice versa), and the "alcoholic" or "sick" parent. They are all there. You need just to press your memory and look deeply into the recesses of your mind's eye to see the nuances of the portrait you carry with you. In some instances, unfortunately, the portrait you harbor can include a blank space where you feel you should be.

A portrait photographer once related to me a very meaningful example of the impact this portrait can have. She was asked to update a family's picture because every time their three-year-old went by their old portrait, taken before his birth, he asked, "Where am I in this picture?" She was able, with the aid of modern technology, to insert the youngster into the picture. I don't know that this was necessarily positive psychologically, but I do know that, unlike that photograph, the emotional portrait we each carry with us is almost etched in stone. It will never change, regardless of your intellectual level, how much you grow, or how much therapy you experience.

Although not necessarily comfortable, the contents of the portrait are familiar to each of the family members and, to some extent, it is comfortable because it is familiar. Moreover, anyone attempting to change this picture stands the risk of upsetting this comfort level. Thus, any attempt to modify or change the photo is perceived as a threat to every person involved, because if one person alters his role, it affects the emotional state of everyone in the portrait. Consequently, many of you choose to live with the familiar, no matter how uncomfortable or unpalatable it may be, because you dare not risk the possibility of rejection. Furthermore, should you attempt to change your position within the family, the other individuals will inevitably attempt to bring you back into the fold. They might say, "This isn't the good little boy that I raised. He wouldn't say the things you're saying," or "I can't trust what she's telling me. She's lied before. She's always fabricated stories, and I need to believe that she's still behaving in the same way. I need to believe it because anything new is scary and frightening and may disturb the status quo." Even when the status quo is not palatable, too many of you view it as preferable. In truth, however, most of you live double lives: one at the office, or with "the guys" (or girls), another at home, or with your family. I can't begin to count the number of successful, bright individuals I've seen who are viewed as proactive, hard-driving professionals at work, but return home on holidays and play the role of the obedient, subservient, acquiescent little boy or girl at the Thanksgiving, Christmas, or Easter dinner table.

In my book *Hungry for Love,* there is a chapter titled *"Lessons from a Lobster."* It states that in order for a one-pound lobster to become a five pounder, it needs to shed its shell. You see, the lobster grows, but its shell doesn't. Thus, in the first year of a lobster's life, it leaves the safety of its shell seven or eight times. It sheds the shell which provides it the ability to mobilize, defend, and feed itself. In the course of this process, it is forced to enter a very frightening world in which it is prey to the fish it normally feeds on and is helpless in the water currents that carry it to and fro, or could crush it against coral formations. But in seventy-two hours, a new, hard shell develops, one which will enable the lobster to swim, to protect and feed itself, and, most importantly, is large enough to give the lobster room to grow.

In essence, that's what life is all about. Growing, changing, learning. That's what therapy is—a process of learning to grow, to risk change, and to better oneself. But in order to do so, you have to brace yourself against the currents of life, the pressures of others, and your own need to conform to the images and preset pictures or expectations of others. To live effectively requires that you swim against the tide, that you not maintain status quos, and that you initiate change or growth.

However, if you don't know where you came from, you will never know where to swim. One way to determine where you came from as opposed to where you might want to go, is to close your eyes and try to visualize another portrait—one that portrays you at work, with friends, or in any group of people with whom you feel the most comfortable and adequate. For some of you, the two pictures may be identical. For most of you, the two portraits will be vastly different, with the picture of you at work or with good friends being far more palatable than the one of you with more intimate relations. Your ability to see this disparity is the first step in the very difficult process of altering your image for yourself and others in your world.

It is very important to be aware of the portrait you have carried with you throughout your life—the one that predetermined whether you are a winner or loser, the pretty, scatterbrained kid or the egghead, etc. You need this accurate picture of your past in order to create a new portrait for your future. For both lobsters and people, growth, whether it is measured by physical size or by the achievement of a successful, happy life, requires you to risk being vulnerable. In other words, be the lobster. Break free of the hard, impenetrable shell you've hidden inside since childhood. You must live by the axiom *you have to let go to grow.*

CHAPTER SIX

WHOSE SHOES DO YOU FILL?

A s a child, I recall, similar to every young man, trying on my father's shoes, which, as you can imagine, were five to ten times larger than my feet. I then wrapped myself in his jacket, which trailed on the floor, my hands only reaching down to where his elbows would have been. In full regalia, I shuffled into the living room and proclaimed, "I'm Daddy." But I wasn't Daddy at all. I was a poor imitation in ill-fitting clothing.

I'm sure that many women recall putting on their mother's dress, stepping into her high-heeled shoes, and clunking across the floor, thinking they were Mother. But their costumes on the outside in no way gave credence to the notion that they were adult women.

Sadly, years later, many of us, whether we're male or female, are still trying to walk in our parents' footsteps. But it didn't work then and doesn't work now. In effect, we're trying to be grown up by assuming the image of our primary role models. Unfortunately, the price for that transformation is giving up our freedom to be who we potentially were then and who we could be now. As a result, far too many of us go through life stronger in form than we are in substance.

Our behavior is obvious when we don someone else's clothes. It's far more difficult to recognize when we assume his or her beliefs, self-perceptions, fears, and neurotic attitudes. Yet that's what most human beings do. We either become carbon copies of our parents and emulate the behaviors and roles we were exposed to in childhood, or we behave the opposite of them. In either case, our behavior isn't our own. Many of us attempt to deceive ourselves by thinking that our oppositional behavior is a sign of self-sufficiency or independence, but it isn't. It's still predictable, based on our role model's actions or verbalizations. In actuality, few of us ever fully cut our umbilical cords, even if we move thousands of miles away and openly criticize our parents' behaviors or find fault with their orientations and values or the way they raised us. All of these are attempts to liberate ourselves by living our lives differently, but, more often than not, they only result in compensatory behavior that is diametrically the opposite of theirs. However, our behavior doesn't reflect who and what we are or want to be in the future. The sad thing is that when you come to this realization, you'll look back and discover that the role you've played, the relationships you've created, and the feelings you've experienced were all learned in early childhood. It makes me think of a saying that I've frequently seen embroidered on pillows: "Mirror, mirror on the wall,

I am my mother, after all." I've never seen this one, but I believe it's equally true: "Mirror, mirror on the wall, I am my father, after all."

Some of you might say, "What's wrong with that? He or she was a good person." Yes, but he/she isn't you. Therefore, you aren't able to live your life in an emotionally honest and healthy manner. To do so, you have to be able to find yourself, accept yourself, and open yourself to whomever you want to share your life with.

I cannot begin to tell you how much this hits home for me personally. As a youngster, I saw my father as the most wonderful, loving, caring human being you could ever imagine. He always had an infectious smile on his face, a wonderful sense of humor, and an inexhaustible reservoir of energy. He was constantly busy. He worked more than most people, but was never really successful. To the extent that he was, he never gave himself credit for it. Although he wasn't rich in dollars, he appeared to be wealthy in terms of friends. Everybody loved David Reitman. He was a friend to all and would give you the shirt off his back, even if he didn't have another one. He was a giver who never asked for anything in return. As a child, I viewed his behavior as meritorious. Today, I see it as a sign of his overwhelming weakness.

If I were to describe my mother, it would be quite the contrary. She was downright mean, miserable, and a horrible person to be around. She found it difficult to allow herself to smile, even when she wanted to. She had few friends and was basically a very unhappy, controlling individual whose behavior (I realized only many years later) stemmed from her fear of other people running over her, rejecting her, or ignoring her. As a result, her habituated response to any question, even before you finished asking it, was *"No."* I now realize that "no" was a form of self-protection, which disallowed her to take risks, i.e., to give you permission to do anything that might result in negative consequences. Why? Because she couldn't accept responsibility for anything that might go wrong. Today, I fully understand why. She was the eldest of eight children. Her parents owned a small store and both of them worked there, twenty-four hours a day. As the oldest child, as I mentioned previously, her job was to be a surrogate parent for her siblings. As a result, she saw them given privileges and opportunities which were never afforded her. I doubt she ever realized that it was the source of her lifelong depression and anger. She certainly never spoke of it. But throughout my life, her anger and depression were omnipresent. I should add that she was incapable of showing physical or emotional love to anyone she was intimately involved with, probably because she was so egocentrically involved in her own misery.

As I describe her, I find myself experiencing more compassion for her at this moment than I ever did during her lifetime. Nevertheless, without that understanding, you can readily see why, as a youngster, I gravitated toward my father. For years following his early death, I recall having a smile on my face whenever I thought of him. Factually, however, he was gone most of the time. Despite his jovial, good-natured, confident appearance, I now see that he lived his life fearfully and blamed most of his lack of success on my mother, whose response to him was the same "No" she gave her children. She served as a wonderful excuse for his never having to look at his own fears and shortcomings. In describing him, most individuals, at one time or another, uttered the words, "Poor Dave, having to live controlled by his angry, depressed wife." I now realize that it was far from the truth, but that was another insight I was late to recognize.

The one memory that most vividly stands out in my mind regarding my parents occurred on a Sunday when I was nine or ten. Dad had taken me to visit someone he described as his best friend. Actually, he was only one of the many acquaintances who certainly liked Dad, but took advantage of him, used him, and, I suspect, viewed him as weak. During the course of our visit, his friend, who owed him a considerable amount of money for purchases he had made on credit at Dad's small army and navy store, pressured Dad to buy several chickens and a dozen eggs. I need to mention that he required Dad to pay cash immediately. Sadly, my father lacked the backbone to say, "Why don't we put this against your account?" It seems ironic to me, but I still recall that the chickens were twenty-seven cents a pound. When we left the man's house, two things occurred. First, we drove past an A&P store with a huge sign in the window saying, "Fresh chickens, eighteen cents a pound"—another fact that stayed with me for years. But what impacted me the most was walking up the stairs to our home, with Mom formidably standing there and accusingly asking, "What did you get now?"

"Two chickens and a dozen eggs," my father said.

"Where are you going to put them and what did they cost?"

My father looked up at her and, without hesitation, said, "Nothing. He gave them to me." There was a pregnant pause. My mother turned and walked into the house, and my father shrugged his shoulders and followed her.

It's no wonder that, years later, I frequently found myself responding excessively whenever I perceived my wife as accusing, questioning, or attempting to control me. It also explains why, throughout my life, I attempted to take over, be responsible, and direct my efforts toward feeling independent and self-sufficient. I didn't allow myself to lean on or to need anyone, but encouraged others to lean on me. I worked to ensure that my outward behavior was completely the opposite of my father's. But would it surprise you that I still carry with me the work ethic he displayed; that I find it difficult to say no to anyone; that, for too much of my life, I said yes on many occasions when I wanted to say no; that I hated the weak little kid inside me that I constantly tried to hide? The truth be known, I walked in my father's shoes all too often, and they fit all too well.

More telltale than anything else is the fact that, during a good deal of my life, despite the love, care, and involvement I received from others, I always carried in me an unconscious, amorphous feeling of dislike for who and what I was. Those feelings didn't abate until many years later, after I finally came to see my father's weakness, feelings of insufficiency, and lack of a backbone. When I was finally able to accurately see him, accept him, and love him in spite of these factors, I found it easier to accept myself. Even more, I was able to admit that, in many ways, "I am my father after all."

I relate this story for still another reason. I want to share with you that recognizing my father for who he really was, realizing that I have attempted to behave and act absolutely differently (i.e., I'm forever living on the edge, taking chances, and thrusting myself into activities that others, and sometimes even I, feel are rather precarious), allowed me to see, own, forgive, accept, and share myself more openly and honestly with others. I'm now able to clearly recognize the similarities between him and me. But, most importantly, I don't have to run from either of us anymore. Moreover, the energy I previously used to run can now be directed toward more productive goals. I can even smile at myself when I find that underneath my bravado is a level of fear and that my humor, similar to his, covers up my insecurities. I'm aware that my willingness to become involved and help others is genuine and stems from other positive attributes within me, despite the fact that, to a great extent, that involvement comes about because it elevates my sense of worthwhileness. I could go on at length, but the purpose is to say that I no longer have to be different from my father, or the same as him. I can be both. In effect, I can recognize that the baggage I carry in life consists of the collective assets and weaknesses of both my parents. I feel proud of some of them, disturbed by many of them, but, in a wonderfully peaceful way, I accept all of them, although not 100 percent of the time. This now allows me, for the most part, to be able to walk in my own shoes, rather than act as a chameleon who wears whatever shoes fit the situation. The end result is that I no longer hate me. I accept me, can laugh at me, and, most of all, honestly share myself with others.

Unfortunately, my story isn't unique. To some extent, I'm sure many of you can relate, even though the outward facts may differ. To give you an example, let me tell you about Jerry, a patient of mine, who was anything but a chameleon. His father was a very prominent physician who was acclaimed worldwide for his achievements in medical research. As a child, wherever Jerry went, he was asked, "Are you Dr. So-and-So's son?" After years of these repeated encounters, Jerry began to say, "No." Still, it seemed, at least in his eyes, there was no way to escape his father's fame and accomplishments. As a result, without conscious awareness, he came to view himself as a failure who could never achieve enough to successfully compete with his dad.

As a result, Jerry compensated by reaching for negative attention. As a youngster, he was a royal pain in the butt, forever getting in trouble, defying authority, messing up, failing academically, and becoming an embarrassment to his family. As he grew older, the problems he created increased, starting with drugs, gambling, petty theft, and driving-while-impaired charges, and, finally, ending up with his incarceration for possession of drugs with the intent to sell.

When I first met Jerry, he was thirty-eight years old and unemployed. He had two failed marriages, a child out of wedlock, and no means of support. His only income came from a trust fund set up by his father and grandparents. By some standards, the subsidy he received was sufficient to live on and possibly even to invest with. Jerry, however, saw it as a huge neon sign that repeatedly displayed the same message: "Jerry, you're a failure. Jerry, you can't make it on your own. Jerry, if it weren't for your parents and grandparents, you couldn't eat, live, or take care of yourself." As a result, Jerry viewed the monthly allowance as a reinforcement of his own feelings of inadequacy and developed a disdain for the support it provided. In no way could he invest it, use it positively, or allow it to be the basis for any success he achieved, because any success that stemmed from it wasn't his, it was theirs. But he couldn't live without it. So, each month, he cashed the check, felt increasingly depressed and inadequate, and spent most of it on drugs or alcohol. He was in a double bind. He couldn't win for losing. It's apparent, from this brief description, that Jerry's behavior was designed to be the exact opposite of his father's.

It was only after leaving prison that Jerry finally was able to cut his umbilical cord. It took his parents' total rejection of him for Jerry to feel that he had finally paid his debt to the world for the air he breathed and the space he occupied. As a result, he no longer had to sabotage himself or be the opposite of his father. Figuratively speaking, he was finally able to take some fledgling steps in his own shoes. He, very slowly and awkwardly, adopted a new orientation, one that included feelings of hope and the notion that the world might hold something positive for him.

When you look at Jerry's and my histories, you realize that until you can recognize and accept your past, you will never be able to fully accept you in the present. You have the choice to continue to strive to be someone society will pay attention to, positively or negatively, or to learn to walk in your own shoes. Choosing the first option will only ensure failure, because you will never be able to achieve enough success, money, possessions, love, fame, or notoriety to make you okay. Therefore, the only healthy choice you have is to be yourself.

My former patients Louise and Jim are another example of the same theme, one that made itself evident in their marital relationship. They were well-meaning people who never shared themselves with each other, probably because neither had sufficient introspective awareness about himself/herself. They were bright, educated, articulate individuals who outwardly appeared to have a wonderful family, a beautiful home, fancy cars and even a second residence in Colorado. Emotionally, however, they had very little. Jim made work his priority. He directed his time and attention solely to that endeavor. Doing so enabled him to amass a small fortune. However, when he finally reached a point where he was able to say, "I have all the money I'll ever need," he began to realize how emotionally empty and sad he felt.

Louise devoted herself to their children. She satisfied most of her emotional needs from her relationships with them and claimed that made up for her disappointing marital arrangement. At the same time, it was evident that she was extremely angry and resentful toward Jim. She saw him as cold, rejecting, and only interested in her for one thing, sex. Consequently, his advances failed to turn her on, which resulted in a sexual relationship that ended eight years prior to entering therapy.

At Jim's insistence, they finally came for counseling. After three or four therapy sessions, they planned a romantic weekend together that wound up extremely disappointing, emotionally and sexually. The following Monday morning, Jim arrived at my office in tears, demonstrating more emotion than I had seen previously. He said, "I'm through. I've had it. It's the end. I want a divorce. It's not that I don't love her, but I have no intention of spending the rest of my life this way. I refuse to live like a monk anymore. I arranged for a suite overlooking the water, had wine, hors d'oeuvres, and flowers in the room, and all she did was complain that if there was a fire, the ladders wouldn't reach up to our floor. How romantic would you say that was?" He was, to say the least, furious. I felt, however, that his heightened emotionality was a significant improvement over the flat line personality he typically exhibited.

When I told him so, he angrily snarled, "Is that some kind of psychobabble observation?"

"No", I answered, "but tell me, what's the opposite of love?"

"Hate," he responded.

"No. Although most people would agree with you, that's wrong. The correct answer is indifference. You see, love and hate are similar. You don't love someone unless you're really involved. Similarly, you don't hate someone unless you're equally involved. Both of them reflect involvement and emotionality."

He stopped almost dead in his tracks, and I could see the wheels in his head turning. Some time later, he left my office with one resolve—to tell his wife where he was coming from: that he loved her, wanted her, and would fight to get her, but he refused to do so unless she was equally committed to working on herself and their relationship. He added that without her cooperation, he couldn't stay because he felt too empty to work on it by himself. She agreed, and, over time, each of them realized where he/she was coming from and what he/she wanted. Though fearful of being vulnerable, they began to risk being honest regarding their feelings and needs. For example, Louise was able to share some of her traumatic childhood sexual experiences. Jim is now aware of her fear of only being loved for sex. His understanding enables him to see her sexual behavior as her problem, as opposed to her rejection of him. Consequently, he can be himself, instead of feeling he has to submit to being controlled by her and having to meet her every need. They are now in a far healthier place emotionally. Consequently, their marriage has a very good chance to succeed. The reason is threefold:

1. They are no longer blaming each other for their problems. They recognize that they are their own problems and that they can't fix anyone but themselves.

2. They're learning that they have self-worth and are entitled to be loved, but that their partner isn't a mind reader. Therefore, they have to be sufficiently vulnerable to ask for what they desire but, at the same time, accept the fact that they might not get it.

3. Most of all, they're no longer trying to get what they want by filling someone else's shoes or expectations. Instead, they've gained insight regarding themselves and expect to be respected and nurtured for who they really are, instead of who they've tried to be.

The basic fact is this: if any of us ever wants to walk in our own shoes, we have to come to the same three realizations. To do so, we need to first ask ourselves, "What do I really want?" The answer won't immediately make things better. Instead, it's likely to contribute to thoughts of having previously lived your life as a lie. It will demand that you give up old defense mechanisms which once served as your way to cope. It will contribute to fear over a future that will involve anxiety and change, which can cause you to be apprehensive. But it will also enable you to feel a simultaneous sense of excitement and challenge. It's similar to going from riding a tricycle to a two-wheeler. You're bound to be scared. As a child, your thoughts were things such as, "Can I do it? Can I pedal and balance myself at the same time?" As an adult, they'll be, "I don't know if I can be me, because I really don't know who I am. I've lived so long filling everyone else's shoes, I'm afraid to walk in my own, because so many of the things I might feel or say won't be popular, politically correct, or acceptable, and then I won't be loved." Granted, in the past, you may have elicited love through acquiescent behavior, but you certainly didn't get it for being yourself. If you had, you would never have settled for the bad marriages you made or stayed in the destructive relationships you helped to create. This applies to almost all of us. Therefore, despite our fears, it's time for each of us to go shopping for a pair of shoes that fits us. The fact is that when you're authentic, you feel comfortable from the start, and, surprising as it may seem, the people who stay with you are the ones who truly love you. Those who leave are the ones who needed you to meet their needs. You can't call that love.

What I'm about to say might seem overly repetitive and passionate, but I try to remind myself, and every human being I come in contact with, of the following: "You must learn that you're okay the way you are, even though you doubt it." I'm fully aware of how tough a challenge I'm presenting to each of you. I know how terrifying it was to me when I first discovered that I had options. It was far easier to feel trapped, helpless, and hopeless. Instead, I'm saying to you, "Here is a blank sheet of paper. Write on it what and who you want to be. But then you have to take responsibility for being who you are, fat or thin, happy or sad, loving or mad, forgiving or punishing, etc." That's frightening, especially when you've lived all your life similar to everybody else in the world, explaining and blaming who and what you do, feel, and say on others, while only rarely looking at yourself. I suspect that what I'm asking you to see and do is a far greater challenge than almost anything you've ever undertaken before. Whether you eventually get a divorce, lose a job, or have problems with a child, these are secondary to you finding yourself. In the end, that's the best gift you can give to those you care for in your life.

I know that being you is much harder to do when you're with a person who has unconsciously supported and reinforced the roles you've played throughout your life. What you need to know is that they didn't, in most instances, do it with malice aforethought. Their actions came about because they unconsciously needed you to be that way. Think of it in this manner: a giver always needs a taker, a helpless person always needs somebody who is constantly helpful or controlling. Weak people always need someone strong. Subordinated individuals need subordinators. Abusive people need persons willing to be abused, etc. Thus, you search out your neurotic or symbiotic match and then live out your life complaining about him/her. As I noted earlier, it's far easier to blame someone who dominates you than to see yourself as too terrified to stand up on your own and behave independently. That is, unless you one day decide to clean up your own act, be who you are, and walk in your own shoes. But beware, shoes wear out, and if you don't resole them or buy new ones, you'll gravitate back to the old ones. Why? Because for the rest of your life, the little kid inside you (age zero to four or five) will be there, attempting to control, direct, and guide you along the only path he knows: your old status quo. Thus, the adult in you needs to constantly be on guard, asking, "Is this really who I want to be? Is this the right way for me to act? Are these the shoes I want to fill?" These questions are intellectually easy to answer but difficult to actualize. First, you'll wonder, "Who am I?" because you've probably never fully discovered you. You've just blindly lived your life, similar to every other sheep in the flock.

If it gives you any comfort, let me assure you, you're not atypical. You're just another member of the human herd. It's not a pleasant thought. Therefore, it's no wonder you might have turned to drink, drugs, gambling, anger, and depression to hide from what really pains you: the fact that you've been too frightened to be you. Not that you didn't try. I believe that you first attempted to actualize yourself during the "terrible twos," then later as a teenager. But, after going too far in the direction of destructive teenage rebellion, society's so-called voice of reason prevailed and you capitulated because you didn't want to be a black sheep or be ostracized by family and friends. Then, twenty, thirty, forty years later, you turned around and thought, "I did what everyone said was right, and I'm sad, angry, and feel empty. Life holds no meaning, and I don't know who I am or what I want." That's when you were described by others as going through a midlife crisis. It's also when you might have listened to Frank Sinatra sing "I Did It My Way," and the lights came on. You realized that your song was "I Did It Their Way." Now you decided you could change things.

So, what do many people do? They decide to change their lives, their spouses, and/or their jobs, when all they really had to alter was themselves. Their resolution was wonderful. They're right that life is too short to waste. But, if you want to deal with your life constructively, you have to direct your energy and efforts to first fixing what's broken that you're able to fix. That's you. *You're Okay, But You Don't Know It* will aid you to do just that: to do it your way—to buy a new pair of shoes that not only fit, but are comfortable. I also want you to have a rational self-interest and to learn to live with yourself in a healthy manner. That means integrating your little kid with the adult that's already there inside you but 80 percent of the time lies dormant.

In essence, I'm saying that we live lies and marry people who will live our lies with us. As a result, we wind up creating marriages and relationships that are based on lies and then try to make them work, without directing any energy or effort toward making ourselves work. Why? Because to make ourselves work, we have to face our truths. That's difficult to do, because most of us can't differentiate between what we feel and what's real. The sad thing is that it's only when we reach that point that we can begin to successfully and honestly live with someone who is equally in touch with himself/herself. Someone who has the courage to give you the best gift that anybody can ever give you, your own reality. That's someone who can tell you what he/she really believes, because he/she is not afraid of your reaction, because he/she is okay with himself/herself and can emotionally survive without your approval or love. Because of that, he/she can aid you to see who you are or when you're regressing back to being your little kid. The result is a relationship and a life that are honest and real—one in which each of you can walk in your own shoes without fear of rejection, abandonment, or loss of love.

CHAPTER SEVEN

WHO ARE YOU?

"Who are you?" may seem like a foolish question, one that you might be asked during a psychological party game at a gathering of friends. But it isn't. It says, "Who are you, really? What are you? What's your identity? Is it one you've chosen, or just fallen into? Is it one you've created or chosen, because, after taking an honest appraisal of the person you are, warts, scars, fears, and all, you found yourself lacking?"

In part, I discussed the development of identity in a previous chapter titled "The Dysfunctional Family." At that time, I strongly suggested that a sense of self is unconsciously formed by a myriad of often barely perceptible interactions, verbalizations, and experiences, all of which occur even before you have the ability to intellectually conceptualize. It's the type of learning that occurs when the toddler crawls up to the wall and puts his inquiring fingers into a wall socket. He/she has no understanding of electricity, but he/she never does that again. The process can be observed very early in life, when, for example, a little girl is brought home from the hospital. The room she is brought to is usually decorated in pink lace and ruffles. It is doubtful that a "tomboy" will emerge from that room. Nor is there any doubt what her parent or parents desire her to be. Similarly, a father who places a football, basketball, or baseball glove in a child's bassinet makes a strong statement with regard to his expectations of his son, or even his daughter. Whether or not the child fulfills these expectations will eventually determine whether he or she perceives himself or herself as a winner or loser, or a loved or unloved individual. Either way, it will strongly affect a child's sense of who and what he or she is.

For example, consider the mother who says "I'd like you to meet my son or daughter, the Little League player/president of his class/the pianist/ the gymnast." Years later, she or her husband may well introduce their children in the following manner: "This is my son. He's in Johns Hopkins Medical School," or "This is my daughter. She's getting an MBA at Harvard." What they're saying is, "Our identity stems from the fact that we are the parents of a future doctor/ business executive." It is no different from the woman I see in therapy who always introduces herself as "the wife of Dr. Smith." Well, you certainly know who she's married to, don't you? You also know what she feels gives her a sense of worth or an identity. Unfortunately, you have no idea who *she* is or what her real identity may be. The sad fact is that in many cases, she doesn't either.

What you can certainly see, however, is that people search for their identities in a thousand and one ways.

Most of the time, it involves defining themselves by their accomplishments or professions, which is readily obvious in the previously described examples where identity is almost synonymous with achievement or failure. There is a second way: you determine who you are by looking for yourself in the eyes of others. Anita, one of my patients, is a wonderful example. She is an exceptionally attractive thirty-one-year-old woman who models for a living. She is intellectually bright, extremely verbal, and has a wonderful sense of humor. In most men's eyes, she would be considered a very desirable individual. While still in therapy, she met a man at a party who swept her off her feet. In her words, he was "perfect," the man of her dreams. Coincidentally, he was also a patient of mine. They dated for about six weeks and then agreed to take a trip together for an extended holiday weekend. On the second evening, they felt it was desirable, appropriate, and timely for them to become sexually intimate. Despite their heightened state of arousal, or perhaps because of their intense attraction to one another, he was unable to perform. In spite of all their efforts, no means of stimulation could resolve the problem. They finally went to sleep after numerous apologies from him, reassurances from her, and disappointment for both of them.

The next morning, I received a frantic call from this "outstanding woman," who was overcome by her fear that he wasn't attracted to her and that she was lacking in sexuality. Her total sense of identity was being determined by his behavior, or lack thereof. I might add that the following week he came to see me and told me about going on a trip with this extraordinary woman and being unable to perform because he was "intimidated by her beauty and fearful he would not satisfy her." At that point I, of course, realized who each of their partners was and encouraged him to speak to her about his concerns and our conversation in therapy. Needless to say, they immediately recognized that I was their mutual therapist, and made a joint appointment. By the way, they are still dating and are seriously considering marriage.

A variation of this theme involves blaming who you are on others. I cannot count how many of my patients have said in one fashion or another, "No wonder I feel so inadequate. He always criticizes me," or "I feel I'm a failure because she never gives me any credit." I would accept that statement more readily if it came from the mouth of a youngster of seven or eight years old, but not from individuals some twenty or thirty years older. By then it's far too late to attribute or blame who you are on a friend, colleague, boss, or spouse. Your sense of worth or lovability is something that was established long before you met any of them. Later in life, believe it or not, you unconsciously search out individuals who can and do help to perpetuate and reinforce the identity you earned in childhood, either positively or negatively. But you cannot attribute who you feel you are today to an individual with whom you're presently involved. At some point in your life, you have to recognize that how you feel about yourself was determined early in your youth. From there on, only you can determine whether you're going to behave in accordance with your feelings, or in spite of them. You decide whether you want to blame others for what you do not like in yourself; deceive others and possibly even yourself regarding who you feel you are; choose to impress others with your accomplishments, possessions, or financial success; attempt to use your early perception of self as a victim to elicit attention and sympathy from others; or consciously muster up the courage to honestly see the true you and then reveal what you've discovered to others. It's a risk that makes you very vulnerable, in that you and/or they may not like who you see. But when you and they do, you'll know both of you care for the person you really are.

With the exception of the last alternative, all of the previous choices, when practiced long enough, become ingrained behavioral patterns which serve to obscure who you really are. Your identity, however, whether you're a doctor, lawyer, golfer, tennis pro, scholar, model, mother, dictatorial father, consummate caretaker, alcoholic, depressed individual, criminal, or gambler, does not reveal who you are. These identities only attest to your behaviors and accomplishments, or lack thereof.

Think for a moment: What is a doctor after he retires? Or a professional golfer after he's over the hill? A model who ages? A dedicated mother whose children finally cut the umbilical cord? Or an alcoholic who no longer drinks? Maybe that's the reason some doctors never retire, some mothers refuse to let their children out of their emotional grasp, some alcoholics and drug users never stop drinking or using, or become as addicted to AA as they were to their drug of choice. It's their way of hiding from who they fear they might truly be if they were no longer what they portrayed themselves to be.

What I'm suggesting is that a majority of people never discover their true selves. Instead, they cling to false identities consisting of stacks of testimonials to their accomplishments and worth, which they have no place to hang because they have no "self" on which to hang them. It stands to reason that if all you are able to recognize about yourself is what is on the outside, you can't be very content with what you believe is on the inside. That being the case, your only choice is to compensate by adding to your outside trappings. This attempt, however, always results in failure. No matter how much you add to your stack of credentials, it doesn't alter who you really are. It only causes the stack to grow higher, heavier, and more burdensome to maintain—the notion being that if you start with one lie, it only leads to more lies. If you're caught in this trap, you need only to ask yourself, "How many cars, how much money, jewelry, trouble, lies, intimidation, control, sex, academic degrees, fame, and acceptance does it take to achieve a state of mental health?" As I mentioned previously, one of the questions I always ask my patients is, "How many carbohydrates do you have to consume in one day to fulfill your daily requirement of protein?" The answer, of course, is zero. No matter how many carbs you eat, it won't satisfy your need for protein. It's the same with your mental health. Mental health consists of the integration of all your emotions, feelings, and desires inside—whether you perceive them as lacking or unacceptable—with that part of you that intellectually knows right from wrong, good from bad, and constructive from destructive. The problem, however, is that you need to be able to recognize, accept, and forgive what you previously deemed unacceptable, i.e., not okay, within you. In most instances, those feelings, emotions, and desires weren't that bad at the outset. They were only human characteristics shared by everyone, but you don't know that, because no one told you so. Quite the contrary, it was probably implied that feelings of anger, inadequacy, fear, insecurity, neediness, etc., were signs of weakness. It's no wonder that you hid them, felt guilty about them, and tried to conceal them with a bevy of socially acceptable achievements, excuses, or even problems and negative behaviors.

The irony is that even when you are admired and loved for your achievements, it doesn't last very long. Why? Because the admiration stems from how you present yourself, not how you truly feel about you. One additional thought I would have you consider is this: the larger the stack of accomplishments or problems that you feel you need to make you "okay," the worse you must believe, at some level of awareness, that you are. Figuratively speaking, it only takes a small wall to conceal a forty-gallon garbage can. It takes a much larger one to hide a dumpster.

It is much like building a house out of cards. When it collapses, there's nothing there. Everyone knows that to build a house, you need to first construct a solid foundation. It is no different when you want to rear a solid human being. You must first construct an emotionally healthy child so the adult has something on which to hang his awards, diplomas, and certificates of achievement. It is extremely important, however, to realize that "health" does not imply perfection. As I indicated earlier, it involves the ability to be sufficiently introspective and to recognize your imperfections. The purpose is to be able to emotionally own, forgive, and accept your weaknesses in order to later capitalize on your strengths. It should be an essential part of the process of raising healthy children. Unfortunately, most of your parents weren't able to provide you with the nurturing parental figure needed to help you develop a positive view of yourselves. In most cases, they themselves were cheated in the same way. No one taught them that, early in life, you have to recognize, forgive, and accept your shortcomings, fears, and insecurities and then adopt appropriate limits, boundaries, and consequences in order to govern your behaviors, but not depreciate or undermine your strengths and assets. The reason is that the energy and effort you might have otherwise used to hide, disguise, or run from who you actually are can now be directed toward enhancing you.

If you weren't taught that, don't waste time or energy blaming your parents. It doesn't accomplish anything. Instead, direct your attention to learning to parent yourself, because without the acceptance and realization that your inner child is okay, you will never emotionally appreciate all the achievements and love you later receive or earn, even though you recognize them intellectually. As a result, these achievements will hold little meaning and won't be beneficial long term. It can be likened to making spectacular improvements on a rented house. You may appreciate the improvements, but in the long run, you do not benefit from the effort or expenditure; the owner of the house does. Psychologically speaking, it would then seem that before you can fully benefit from your accomplishments, you have to embrace your inner child. One who has imperfections you accept, as well as strengths you value.

Perhaps the best example I can give to you about accepting and owning the child inside you is a movie entitled *The Kid*. Three or four of my patients individually expressed the opinion that I had to see the film. Coincidentally, after my wife took our grandchildren to the movie, she called from the car and said "I told the kids that Papa had to see this picture." They were right. I went to see the movie and, for the first fifteen minutes, I questioned why in the world everyone recommended it. It was contrived and more in keeping with what a child might enjoy. But when it finally hooked me, I decided it was a picture all of you need to see.

The following week, I asked some of my patients if they had seen the movie. Several had. Three or four of the men, particularly, but one woman as well, described it to me. They knew the facts, but I felt they'd missed the message. I had seen so much more. Perhaps I read into it what I wanted to see, but I believe that if you're reluctant to fully see yourself, you need to blind yourself to those parts of the world that might force you to become more introspectively aware. In *The Kid*, Bruce Willis played the role of a Dapper Dan, arrogant, insensitive, self-confident, goal-oriented, no-nonsense image consultant. In his own words, he didn't listen to people; he told them what to do. His problem, however, was that he was beginning to become depressed. He couldn't sleep at night. Something was bothering him. He tried a crash course in therapy, which consisted of one visit to a psychiatrist, during which he requested medication that would just allow him to sleep and get those thoughts out of his head. In the interim, before his second appointment, he discovered a rather unkempt, chubby youngster breaking into his house.

When he finally caught the youngster, he found him to be a whiny, clumsy, awkward, overweight, careless kid, lacking in confidence and dependent on others—the antithesis of his the man's outward image. His disdain for the youngster was immediately apparent. Willis's character attempted to get the boy to stop his whining, avoided feeding him because he was too fat already, and tried to rid himself completely of the kid. Eventually, he discovered that this child wasn't just any eight-year-old, it was him when he was eight years old. He was everything he couldn't accept in himself and had tried to obscure or disguise throughout his entire adult life. The problem, however, was twofold. One, the kid was still there, lurking in the background, and, two, his new image brought him no long-term satisfaction. Quite the contrary, it left him emotionally empty and estranged from others, as well as himself.

What he needed, similar to many of my patients, was to reconcile with himself. Most of them think they come to therapy because of conflicts with spouses, friends, lovers, bosses, coworkers, or the world in general. They perceive their problems as stemming from outside them, but that isn't the case. Their real problem is within them. Unfortunately, like them, you've probably never reconciled with who and what you were growing up—with what you felt as well as the emotions you experienced as a result of the hurts, fears, threats, and punitive or abusive interactions. Instead, you might have spent a lifetime running, avoiding, obscuring, and, similar to Bruce Willis, disguising the youngster within you—cloaking yourself with academic degrees, designer clothing, affected attitudes, and poor treatment, or excessively nice treatment, of others. As a result of your attempts to hide from who you really are, you exert a horrendous amount of energy and effort, which often depletes you of the energy and effort you might more effectively use to enhance your position in the world. Consequently, you become strong in form, but weak in substance, i.e., you have little foundation to support you.

There is an alternative solution: reconcile with your little kid. You need to accept him or her with all of his or her limitations, shortcomings, and fears. You must forgive his or her trespasses, mistakes, and poor judgment. Most of all, you need to champion and assimilate him or her into a whole human being with a solid foundation.

Perhaps that's what psychologists and theologians mean when they talk about discovering a "centeredness" within you and creating a oneness with yourself. Once a person achieves that state of wholeness, he or she can then devote his or her efforts to moving forth in the world without wasting the time, energy, and effort to avoid, hide, disguise, or deny his or her four- to six-year-old child. It is the championing of your kid that allows you to live peacefully with your heretofore unacceptable child. No matter what circumstances you were brought up in, how malicious, inadequate, or insufficient your parents were, you must learn to parent yourself on your own, in a healthy manner. To do so, you need to discover a new parent—yourself. Once you realize that you can care for yourself, support, and love yourself, you will no longer need to change or blame others. If your parents weren't the parents you wish you could have had, you must become the parent you wished for all your life. Essentially, you must learn to parent and nurture yourself. You need to realize that if you can take control of you, you can climb to whatever heights your capabilities will allow you to reach. You will come to know it isn't how high you climb that counts, it's the reason for the climb—the underlying motivation behind it—and the attitude you demonstrate while trying to climb that determines the eventual satisfaction you will experience from your climb.

All of this can occur when you realize that you are of value, that even your perceived weaknesses can serve as strengths if you learn from them and behave in spite of them, not because of them. It is then that the energies you previously used to hide or obscure yourself can be directed to more positive endeavors. It is also then that you can define your identity and, when asked "Who are you?" can truthfully answer, "I am a person of worth, whose feelings, emotions, desires, fears, insecurities, and insufficiencies add up to a unique individual whom I love and appreciate, and who is worthy of being loved by others because I'm okay." *You're Okay, But You Don't Know It* will show you the steps you need to take to reach that end.

CHAPTER EIGHT

THE STRUGGLE INSIDE YOU

There is a truth that you need to know: if you never come to realize you are free, you inevitably wind up hating yourself, the people you perceive as controlling you, and the situations you feel have trapped you. Over time, you even experience difficulty recognizing whether what you do is what you want to do or what you feel obligated to do. The confusion thwarts your wherewithal to enjoy or relish any situation, because you constantly question, "Am I drinking this milk because I want to, or because my mother told me to? If I'm drinking it because she told me to, then, somehow, the taste is contaminated. If I'm drinking it because I want to, I can enjoy the frothy, creamy, cool liquid. I can relish dipping a chocolate cookie or graham cracker into it, or mixing it with ice cream to make a milkshake. The possibilities are endless." Of course, so are the potential pleasures, because you are no longer governed by rules you learned in childhood. Nor are you restricted by an emotional umbilical cord that mandates that you "follow the leader" rather than choose the path you want to explore. As a result, your fears and resentment subside, because your rational adult has taken over. You now realize you're going to college because you want to, not because your parents told you to do so. Or you're taking out the garbage because it's trash day, rather than because your wife "ordered you to do it."

Your DNA, your parents' child-rearing practices, role models, peers, and the situational factors that you were exposed to as a child all contributed to your present behavior, reactions, and attitudes. Understanding derived from each of these areas can help to put your emotional jigsaw puzzle together so that it supplies you with a fairly accurate picture of why you are who you are. However, no matter how much insight you acquire, you can't change your past. What was, is. What happened has already taken place. The scars, the hurts, and the emotions associated with them are there to stay, for the rest of your life.

How you deal with them, how they affect the way you react and relate to people in the future, is another story. With knowledge and awareness regarding why you are who you are, you can then proceed to make a decision regarding how you want to behave, who you want to be, and what goals you want to direct yourself toward in the future. Those decisions are entirely yours to define. Unfortunately, they are too often predetermined by habituated knee-jerk reflexes that cause you to act without thinking, or without giving any consideration to questions such as, "Will this get me to where I want to be? Will it contribute to a positive self-image? Will it allow me to be at peace with myself?"

Your initial thought may be, "If my behavior is contrary to my thoughts and desires, something must be wrong with me." That's not necessarily the case. This duality exists in all of us. It may vary in degree or intensity, but it's there. You may be consciously aware of it or blind to it entirely. It really doesn't matter, because, in both cases, it has an extremely important impact on the way you behave, the orientation you choose to take, and the degree of satisfaction you will experience in your relationships with others and with yourself. Let me provide several examples.

It wasn't the first time that Philip had worked his posterior off, only to be told that he was lacking in managerial skills and wasn't sufficiently motivated. He almost anticipated the criticism. In fact, he had heard it so often throughout his life that he partially believed it. Overtly, he shrugged off the comments. Inside, however, another piece of his ego slipped away. He felt demeaned, depressed, and hopeless. His only saving grace was that no one would ever know. He would never utter a word in defense or let them see his emotional hurts and pains.

Ramon was just the opposite. When his "redneck" boss inferred that, possibly, the company needed to establish a longer lunch break to accommodate those individuals accustomed to taking a "siesta," his boss found himself lying on the floor before he knew who or what hit him. His boss later received a written reprimand for his inference. Ramon, on the other hand, was fired for having a five-hundred-dollar reaction to a fifty-dollar problem.

Another patient, Helen, was sexually abused as a child. As a result, she thought she knew what every man wanted, and she thoroughly resented it. This resentment contributed to her thinking and verbalizing a desire for a close, meaningful relationship, but experiencing a great deal of trouble with the "close" part. Her defense was to view every guy who showed any interest in her as a sexual predator, although, intellectually, she knew better. Essentially, she went through life with an invisible sign hanging from her neck that said "Beware of vicious animal." At the same time, she couldn't understand why men showed little romantic interest in her, and why those who did went away saying "she has larger testicles than I do."

Carol abhorred conflict. She experienced her fill of it while growing up. Thus, despite the fact that her husband was an alcoholic who ran around on her, she rarely complained or found fault with him. She lived in her own world, reluctant to cause upset or controversy. She was willing to pay any price to keep her life, at least on the surface, free of dissension. To do so required that she restrict any display of emotion and preoccupy herself with her children and her work. Consequently, over the years, she and her husband grew farther and farther apart, emotionally, but they stayed together "for the kids." It was a compromise she was consciously willing to make. At least that was the case for twenty-eight years, until her husband "fell in love" with one of his paramours. It was then that she sought out therapy, questioning how this could have happened when her husband had always described her as a "perfect wife," one who never caused problems and was always accommodating. That, of course, was the reason he described her as "perfect."

Philip, Ramon, Helen, and Carol are four examples of the countless number of people I have seen in therapy who, figuratively speaking, live unhappy lives and resolve their problems by either killing canaries with a cannon or battling grizzly bears with a penknife. In either case, the results are disastrous for them, for the individuals with whom they interact, for their children, and for their relationships. Ironically, these behavioral patterns have little to do with a person's level of intelligence, social class, or ethnic background. They are, instead, emotional in nature and were learned early in childhood.

Although these individuals would readily state that you should not hang up a picture hook with a sledgehammer or pry open a fifty-gallon steel drum with a nail file, they threaten divorce because a spouse arrives home late for a dinner party, or fly into a rage because their child accidentally drops a glass of milk. Some of them, similar to Ramon, behave with knee-jerk reactions, while others knowingly live for years with spouses who abuse or cheat on them, saying, doing, and seeing nothing. At the same time, these over- or underreacting individuals know better. If a friend arrives late for their dinner party, or the next-door neighbor's child drops a glass of milk, their reaction is radically different from the way they react to their spouse or their own children. It's the same duplicitous behavior you see when an abused wife or husband is asked what advice he or she would give to someone living in his or her situation. The majority of them are quick to give advice that is psychologically right on target. Thus, they might say, "You should never accept abusive behavior." But their words don't comply with their actions.

It's apparent to me that most individuals possess an emotional tool chest that, figuratively, contains every implement from a crowbar to a screwdriver small enough to repair a fine watch. The problem is that they fail to use them in accordance with their intelligence. Instead, they behave out of their emotions. Although they know not to pound a watch with a large hammer, or to attempt to cut through a metal chain with plastic scissors, their feelings and emotions cause them to try it anyway. In order for any of them, or you, to deal effectively with conflicts, problems, and relationships, you have to approach life with sufficient thought and awareness to choose the appropriate tool for the job at hand. None of you can afford to impulsively reach for the first available implement. You must take the time to think what tool, what approach, will

1. Best help you to achieve the goals you set
2. Solve the problems you face, or
3. Enhance the relationship you claim to desire.

Then, you must dig deep in your toolbox to find the appropriate tool (behavior). In almost every instance, you know what it is and you're capable of it. Let me say it more concretely. To reach your goals, to be successful in your endeavors, and to better your interpersonal relationships, you need to search within yourself for the right words, the right actions, the right behaviors that will help you to proceed in the direction you desire. Think about it. If you can treat the next-door neighbor's child more appropriately than your own, if you are more compassionate and forgiving of others than yourself, and if you treat your clients, customers, and business associates better than your spouse, it isn't a question of whether or not you have the knowledge or where-withal to deal with your problems. It's more a matter of not choosing the proper tools, or your emotions interfering with your behavior.

You don't need a Ph.D. in psychology to recognize that the major hindrance to healthy behavior is that most of us act out of our emotional selves rather than our intellectual selves. The result is that our behavior is impulsive, frequently occurs without forethought or malice and is, primarily, designed to protect us from hurt, rather than to help us grow. One way you can understand and deal with this conundrum is to view yourself as two people—an emotional one and an intellectual one. In most cases, you will discover that in those areas where you function primarily on the basis of the good common sense you possess, the innate intelligence you have, and the training you experienced from living in the world, you are most suc-cessful and most content with yourself. But, when the emo-tional you controls or takes over your behavior, your actions include hidden agendas. They are defensive, rigid, unbend-ing, closed minded, and resistant to any influences from other individuals or the facts. By virtue of that, they rarely contrib-ute to solutions or positive interactions with others.

Let me add, however, that I am in no way suggesting that you should be entirely governed by your intellect, common sense, and experience. I would never negate your emotional self. Instead, I am stating that the two need to be integrated, to function together, to be resilient, open to new ideas, to be creative and think and act, on occasion, outside of the box. All of which will allow you to appreciate and value your own feelings, emotions, and desires without self-criticism or self-hatred. The integration of the two individuals inside you will make for a unified whole that is greater than the sum of its parts and will permit you to behave and achieve in ways that far supersede how you have behaved up until now. It will leave you with a sense of independence, self-sufficiency, and freedom from being entirely controlled by other individuals, society, mores, or conventional thinking. To be able to reach this emotional state, you first need to have some understanding and awareness of the two people residing inside you. You must then learn how to access their strengths and benefit from their unification.

There are several factors, however, that make it difficult to achieve integration. One, most of us will periodically forget that there are two of us residing in our body. Two, there is a constant power struggle going on between which one will control us. For example, how many times when you were a student did you feel conflicted about "Should I go out or should I study?"; "Who should I please—my girlfriend or my male friend?"; "What do I want, versus what do my parents say?" All of these quandaries can result in extreme internal conflict, anxiety, and stress, and the degree to which these emotions occur is an indication of how much of a struggle you experience when trying to cope in the world. Why? Because too much of your energy and effort goes into satisfying others, toward fitting in, staying in the box, and forfeiting your own desires and identity. To change this, you have to fully accept the fact that there are two separate individuals living in your body, who are almost constantly engaged in a power struggle to determine which one will control how you act and react. By embracing these two individuals, you will come to peace inside with both.

CHAPTER NINE

YOU LIVE LIES

You don't start out by lying about who you are. At first, it's more a case of emulating what you've learned is acceptable and appropriate. If you're a girl, you don't necessarily fit in if you're rough and tumble, assertive and pushy, or loud and overly aggressive. If you're a boy, you don't play with dolls, dress frilly, act too sensitive, cry, or show weakness. If you're confused, you don't tell anyone.

I'm not exactly sure where or how I learned those rules, but somehow parents, peers, teachers, and society collectively united to say, "Don't be a sissy boy." It was a dictate I had no choice but to follow. As a result, I knew I should show no fear, insecurity, or weakness. I needed to be sure, confident, brave, and courageous. There was, however, one very large problem. Inside, I felt the opposite. I was often frightened, intimidated, sensitive, and conflicted. All of which contributed to my feeling that no one would want me if he or she knew who I was or what I really felt.

This thought was further aggravated by the fact that no one ever told me that I was "okay" because of who I was, or that most young men and women were faced with the same dilemma. Nor did they say that I wasn't the exception, the oddball, or atypical. As a result, I began living a lie. I tried to hide any trace of fear or insecurity, softness or sensitivity. It was the way I, and probably many of you, attempted to fit in, to be accepted, and to feel that I was "normal and acceptable." Inside, however, I secretly wondered and feared that I might be gay, less of a man, or, at best, weird. It never occurred to me that many other young men and women, so-called tomboys, felt equally confused and worried.

Still later, as a young teenager, the fears multiplied. I was consumed by the thought that if any girl was going to be interested in me, I had to be cool, a stud, a smooth talker, confident, and assertive. Inside, I didn't feel that way. Thus, I felt forced to act the part. Needless to say, I wasn't good at it. But that was the real start of my living lies. The curious paradox is that society advocates this behavior, and some professionals even tout it as a means of achieving success. Simply put, I've heard it said that if you act the way you want to be, you'll become it.

Similarly, while wandering through a book store recently, I came across a self-help book by Jo-Ellan Dimitrius, Ph.D., and Mark Mazzarella, entitled *Put Your Best Foot Forward (Make a Great Impression by Taking Control of How Others See You)*. It essentially advocated being who you want to be to gain the approval and acceptance of others. It may well be that this behavior works well in the world of business, but I suspect it's the reason so many professionals and businesspeople do poorly in their intimate personal relationships.

It was years before I came to realize that I wasn't alone. Most people live lies. That's because most people don't believe that they are okay just as they are. Of course, some people do lie better than others, i.e., they are better at. People live lies to different degrees, depending on the extent to which their DNA, primary family, and other situations contributed to their inner feelings of inadequacy. The formula is that the more deficient you feel, the more lies you live.

Let me tell you about Scott, a prominent attorney, whom I have never seen when he wasn't irritated, angry, or upset over something or someone. To a great extent, that served him well in his litigation practice. But, on occasion, he went too far, lost control, dug himself into a rut, and then found that he had lost his advantage because of his "overenthusiastic" orientation. His wife filed for divorce. His partners warned him about his abusive tone of voice when dealing with secretaries.

In one of our meetings, I said to him, "Scott, you always appear angry. Your teeth are clenched; your voice is elevated. Your very appearance is intimidating and pushes people away. It may work well in a courtroom, but look at the difficulty you're experiencing with almost all of your colleagues, staff at the firm, and your wife."

"I'm not angry!" he shouted. "I don't feel angry."

I'd like to ask you to consider the facts and then decide; is he lying? Do you believe what he says? I do, but I also believe he's lying to himself.

Let me tell you about Janice. She is a forty-two-year-old, once unbelievably beautiful woman. I had first seen her in therapy almost eighteen years earlier. At that time, there was no way she could enter a room or walk down the street without turning heads. Her beauty was more than just physical. There was a radiance about her. She seemed to exude sensuality, yet she had class. Her voice was deep and throaty, her figure was perfect, and there was a kindness about her that invited you to feel comfortable around her and think all her attention was directed only to you. In addition, she was a bright, tremendously insightful young woman. The package was totally complete. But her behaviors and achievements were completely the opposite of her outward appearance and qualifications. She completed nothing she started. That went for jobs, education, careers, and relationships with men and women alike. Her sense of adequacy, in my opinion, was far different from her own words when she described her feelings about herself. She saw the world as her oyster, envisioned no end to the possibilities available to her, and made highly plausible excuses for every failure and/or endeavor she refused to complete. Inside, this wonderful individual was an extremely needy young child who desperately desired love and assurance beyond anyone's greatest imagination. Her mother, who had been married three or four times, was a physically and emotionally abusive woman who had never wanted children and resented the very fact that she had one. Her father was a highly successful, extremely verbal, accomplished man who had pulled her out of so many financial, emotional, and physical difficulties that he finally reached a point where he only shoved money at his daughter. It was his way of protecting himself emotionally whenever he dealt with her.

I could go on at length about what occurred during the fourteen- to fifteen-year interval following my first seeing her in therapy, but suffice it to say Janice continued to sabotage every opportunity and to create havoc and pain for anyone who cared for her. When she arrived at my office the second time, the outer shell was tarnished. Many of the qualities were still there—the throaty voice, the ability to intellectualize, the capacity to draw you in with her charm. But time, emotional stress, and, I believe, excessive periodic use of alcohol and prescription drugs had taken their toll.

The impetus for returning to therapy was an auto accident. She was miraculously uninjured, but she had nearly killed two other people and had totally destroyed her vehicle. It wasn't the first time. Therefore, the court ordered her to therapy.

On our first visit, I said to her, "I don't know if I want to see you. I could be there for you, support you, and help you to look at where you're coming from, but I doubt if you're ready to accept therapy, whether it's from me or in a rehabilitation center. You see, you're an alcoholic. You're a druggie. And until you can see that you're using these things to avoid your internal emotional pain, you can never start to examine who and what you are, let alone who you want to be."

She looked at me, almost incredulously, and said, "How can you say that? I may drink on occasion, but you don't understand. My problems stem from physical difficulties. I can't sleep. I have migraine headaches and bodily pain that I need the meds for. It's all prescription medication. The doctors wouldn't give it to me unless they thought I needed it."

I ask you, is she lying?

In the case of both Janice and Scott, the attorney, I believe that you, as an independent, objective, individual would say, "Both of them have difficulty with the truth." I agree with you. At the same time, after forty-eight years as a therapist and seeing countless other individuals of the same ilk, I've come to a different conclusion. It's that most people, not just these individuals, live a lie. Most of us protect ourselves from ourselves. We don't want to see who we really are, what we really are, or take responsibility for who we really are. As a result, we lie to others and ourselves. I understand that, if you listen to Scott and Janice, you feel as though they're lying to you. But they can ill afford to see the person that you or I see before us.

I contend that most people live their lives similarly, by avoiding their truths. You believe what you project to the world. You do it when you apply for a job, when you put yourself on Facebook or eHarmony, when you go out on an initial date, when you speak to strangers. It all consists of initially putting your best foot forward. But when you deal with people over a long period of time, particularly the ones you love the most, you become complacent and drag in the other foot. Oftentimes, it's not very pretty. It can be abusive, distance making, nonconstructive, even destructive to relationships and to yourself. You tell yourself what you'd like to believe. You see yourself as a victim who in no way contributed to your problems, and you defend your positions. Later, you may voice responsibility for what took place, but you fail to genuinely believe it. It's politically acceptable and easy to say, "We were both to blame" for the misunderstanding, accident or divorce. But often, it's too gut wrenching and guilt provoking to actually believe it.

Are you lying? Yes, to yourself and to others, and it always proves disastrous to your life, marriage, and interpersonal relations. But the lie is not, in most instances, fabricated to deceive. Its primary purpose is to protect, to deny, and to allow you to avoid looking at the truth about you. Why? Because that truth can be painful, even devastating to your already fragile sense of worth and lovability. Not only insofar as what others think of you, but what you think of yourself. Even more, that truth might push you to realize that you need to change; a very difficult task to achieve. But if you want to be emotionally healthy, you cannot continue living lies. You have to risk being vulnerable. That's the reason you will hear me say, time and time again, that you always need to look at *you* first. All the things that happen around you are the facts. The problem, in most instances, isn't the facts; it's you, the reactor, the interpreter, and, on too many occasions, the falsifier who first attempts to aggrandize self and then comes to believe your own lies.

All of which brings us to Keith, a sixty-year-old patient of mine who was a financially successful individual who looked forty-five. His outward appearance, however, was deceptive, particularly when it came to his emotional health. Emotionally, he was an extremely needy individual. He desperately required and solicited love in all the wrong places, from all the wrong people, and repeated the process over and over again. When he came to see me, he was working on his third divorce. The emotional turmoil, the devastating feelings of rejection, and the complete sense of unworthiness he was experiencing were no different from the reaction he'd had during his two previous divorces. It was evident he'd never read AA's *Big Book,* which, clearly states, "The definition of insanity is doing the same thing over and over again and expecting different results." Well, if that's the case, Keith could be considered insane.

He could also be seen as a quintessential example of the type of "liar" that I have been discussing in this chapter. In every new relationship, he presented himself as the confident, successful individual he physically appeared to be. His checkbook was quick to open and his credit cards were freely used. It was all designed to portray himself as the generous, caring person he wanted others to believe he was. But, his underlying purpose was to create dependence in his partner. His payoff was that their weakness made him feel stronger. Ironically, he didn't have to do a great deal, because he consistently selected women who, no matter what their outward appearance, were tremendously manipulative, streetwise females who were basically angry toward men, seductive in their dealings with their partners, and dependent in their intimate relationships, a fact which, to a great extent, accounted for their anger toward men. Generally speaking, these women were initially attracted to and emotionally responded to men who appeared strong and successful. But, once they took the bait, once they were hooked, they discovered that the fisherman was an emotionally fragile, dependent human being himself. Men like Keith harbor inner feelings of self-worth that are so poor they can't believe that anyone would love or care for them if they knew who they really are. Thus, they feel the need to buy their partners and attempt to solidify their love by giving gifts. These types of men and women don't accept that they're okay, that they don't need to impress, lie, or spend ridiculous amounts of money to get someone to love them. In Keith's case, the gifts consisted of buying women new houses, trips around the world, or supporting them, ever hopeful that they'd respond to him appreciatively and love him for the benevolent role he played. But that never occurred. Instead, he inevitably wound up feeling and becoming the victim, the unloved, rejected suitor, the "generous guy" who cared tremendously, but was unappreciated and taken advantage of in his relationships.

Keith's own words denoted his disdain for himself and his lack of regard for who he really was: "I'm coming to therapy to change who I am. To become strong." Sadly, that goal was out of the reach of therapy. As disappointing as it may sound to you, no therapist, no amount of therapeutic hours, can help you to change who you are. That person is written into your hard drive. It's been there since you were five, six, or seven years old. The emotional child you are will never change. Therefore, you have no alternative but to learn to live with yourself, to accept him or her, and to learn to forgive, to be amused by, and to love that person. To be okay with who you are, to accept that you're okay. That's something that therapy can help you with. It can point the way and help you to live with yourself. It can also help you to recognize that feeling weak, having fear, and not being the strongest, fastest, smartest, best-looking, most successful person in the world isn't a tragedy. In fact, when you reach that point, I would perceive you as the strong person you want to be, because accepting you involves having the courage to see you. Conversely, fixing you implies you have shortcomings you can't accept.

Once you can grasp this concept, you and the myriad of other individuals similar to you and Keith no longer need to live lies. You can begin to cope differently, to act positively, and to present yourself honestly.

One of the best examples I can share with you is Chuck, another patient of mine, who was divorcing for the second time. It wasn't a decision he relished. Quite the contrary. He was facing his future with more dread than joy, all of which was in sharp contrast to his first divorce, one he described, in retrospect, as an almost knee-jerk reaction to a bad situation which he felt incapable of changing and which he perceived to be the primary problem in his life. He had come to realize that the divorce he was presently embarking on wasn't going to solve all his problems. It was only going to provide him with a new playing field, on which he had strongly resolved not to reproduce the mistakes he'd made in his previous two marriages.

In his own words, "My first wife, Joyce, wasn't very smart. I'm embarrassed to say, she wasn't the sharpest knife in the drawer. She was pretty, passive, compliant, and dependent. Six years and two children later, I realized I had no idea what she was thinking, where she was coming from, what she truly desired, and certainly not what she thought. But it was easy to be married to her. She created few bumps in the road, posed no challenge, offered no resistance, and contributed little or nothing to our relationship, in sharp contrast to the intimate, adventurous relationship I desired and fantasized about."

Marcy, his second wife, could hardly be described that way. If there was any bump in the road, she'd find it. If she had a thought, it was never censored. She was quick to criticize, depreciate, and aggravate. There was a haughty arrogance about her that was founded on hot air. Although she was far more intelligent than his first wife, her accomplishments were equally few and far between. She rarely finished anything she started, yet she constantly bragged about her accomplishments. Her arrogance served as a compensatory behavior to hide the fact that she probably felt as frightened, inadequate, and insufficient as wife number one.

Unconsciously, Chuck had reproduced his first marriage with a woman who was 180 degrees different on the surface, but whose emotional dynamics were exactly the same. It's no surprise, because he hadn't changed and he was the common denominator in both relationships. He was the same person that grew up in a home which contributed to his feeling just as inadequate as his two wives. The only difference was that he was able, by virtue of his job, to build financial success and to garner the good will of others because of his outward role of "Mr. Good Guy." Few people ever got to see the real Chuck. His periodic, volatile outbursts were reserved for his wife's ears only and occurred primarily as a consequence of coping with life by hiding his real feelings, not expressing his genuine desires, and trying to accommodate in order to gain approval and love. At least until, similar to a volcano, his internal pressure caused him to emotionally erupt.

The second time around, however, his eyes were wide open and he was better able to see his own reality (i.e., his little kid) than ever before. Consequently, his focus was directed primarily toward how he (the adult) could alter his behavior and what he needed to do to handle, deal with, and cope with situations and people in a healthier manner. He had, at least partially, learned that mental health can best be determined by the degree to which you deal with yourself as well as the degree to which you don't distort, deny, run from, or hide from your truths. The rule is, if you start with a premise that's based on falsehood, your behavior, decisions, actions, and reactions will all be based on lies.

That being the case, a mentally healthy Chuck or Keith might say to any individual with whom they want to become involved, "Hi, I'm Keith/Chuck. I'm a very emotionally needy person. I have fears, self-doubts, and feelings of inadequacy, but I also have dreams, wishes, and goals, and I work hard to try to achieve them. I desperately want to love and be loved by someone. Because of that, I'm a potentially good partner. I give, I care, and I'm sensitive and empathetic. I try not to be too possessive or controlling, and I'm not a stalker, because I understand that it's difficult to catch a butterfly on the wing. It's easier to stand still in a bright-colored shirt and wait for it to light on you. If you can love a person like me, I promise you, you'll be loved back two- or threefold. But no more, because I don't want to be run over or taken advantage of by my partner. I am, nevertheless, willing to give more than I get and show you who I am from the get-go. I try not to live a lie. The foot you see is the foot that is, and the other foot I'll drag in will be no different. Hopefully, you can care back.

But if you can't, tell me quickly; be honest, and I'll be on my way, because I know that somewhere out there, there's someone who will love me in spite of my flaws and weaknesses."

It's the antithesis to living a lie. It may sound fairly simple, or easy to achieve, but it's not. It's a process very different from the one most people follow. It is truly, in renowned author and psychologist Morgan Scott Peck's words, "the road less traveled." It is, however, a road that leads to a new world, one filled with hope, truth, and loving relationships that you can honestly savor and trust, because the person who is loving and being loved is who you honestly are.

CHAPTER TEN

YOU LEARNED TO BE HELPLESS

If it's true that you're okay but you don't know it, then you might be thinking, "How can he say I'm okay when my life is a mess, when so many things have gone wrong, when I'm looking out and my world is bleak, black, and breaking apart?" My answer is, "I understand where you're coming from. I recognize how much stress you may be experiencing, and I believe that you feel inadequate, insufficient, helpless, hopeless, or even trapped in the situation or relationship you're in. But, in spite of those feelings, I still feel you're okay. The problem you face is that inside of you is a person who failed to learn that he/she is of worth. Because of that, you've built the trap you're in right now. You limited the opportunities available to you and probably blamed others for the problems you face. That's a rationale many people follow. But, if you can truly accept that you are the one who put yourself in that position, whatever it may consist of, you can also come to realize that you can get yourself out of it."

It's the same for everyone. You get into situations with far more ease than you later experience trying to extricate yourself from them. Nevertheless, it is possible. It requires, however, that you first realize that whatever is causing you stress, upset, sadness, or anger may indeed be real, but it's not your problem; it's a fact. You may be in a job with an abusive bully for a boss. You may be married to someone who is emotionally detached, hostile, or unfaithful. You may have flunked out of school, become addicted to drugs or alcohol, or been faced with a countless number of other problems. But they're the facts, not the problem. The problem is you. That doesn't mean you're bad, a failure, or a loser. Quite the contrary. It only means that you are the problem, and now you have to determine how you are going to deal with it. For the most part, you can't do very much about the hand life deals you. But how you cope with it and how you react to it can affect whether your world is bleak and black or if there's a light at the end of your tunnel.

Sadly, many of you learned early in life that there is no light, that you're trapped; that you are a helpless human being who is destined to be controlled, influenced, and governed by others. Even more, that standing up would only cause you to lose the affection, acceptance, love, or approval you desperately desire. So, similar to a hungry dog, you settle for a bare bone with no meat on it. As a child, you had no choice. But as an adult, you do. The problem is, you don't know it because the feeling that you are trapped or helpless in life still resides deep down inside you. It affects your outlook, sense of worth, and actions throughout most of your life.

But you are not alone. You cannot begin to imagine how many human beings there are who also feel trapped, helpless, or discouraged by their situations, but do little or nothing to alter their status. It isn't that they don't want to; it's that they feel incapable and overwhelmed. They're blind to the positive alternatives available to them and are paralyzed, emotionally and physically, by a negative self-perception inside them. So much so that they become resigned to their fate and accepting of what they feel is inevitable. For them, there is no light at the end of the tunnel.

In many instances, the negative orientation they harbor isn't apparent, even to them. They, and probably you, would say, "That's not me. I'm a positive person. I believe I can do anything I want. I don't think I'm trapped, hopeless, or helpless." In some instances, you might even support your statements by adding, "Look at what I've accomplished socially, educationally, or financially." The problem is, you're speaking about surface factors. The issues I'm talking about are subtle, emotional, and, for the most part, internal and unconscious. They have little to do with what you think and far more to do with what you feel. It's the reason that, despite knowing right from wrong, good from bad, healthy from unhealthy, and constructive from nonconstructive, you choose to behave in nonconstructive ways or are too frightened to take risks, to be vulnerable, or to act at all.

Despite the fact that, from the outside, your opportunities for change are readily apparent to others, they are invisible to you. On those few occasions when the clouds part and you can see them, you can become excited by the possibilities available to you, but only for a brief period of time. Then the clouds close and you feel as though they never parted. It's odd that, to others, they appear easily within your reach, and yet you are oblivious to them. It's difficult for them to understand and almost impossible for them to believe that you don't take advantage of your potential or that you stay in situations and relationships that cause you emotional hurt and are destructive to you. Let me share several stories of patients I've seen over the years that exemplify this issue.

Helen hates George and has almost from the start of their forty-seven-year marriage. But she stays with him, fantasizes about leaving him, and laments her life.

Grant has been unhappy for as long as he can remember. The night before his wedding, he recalls wanting to call it off, but he lacked the courage to disappoint Nancy or to face his friends and family if he did. So he has had numerous affairs and constant conflict with his wife, but divorce has never been an option.

Bucky hates his job. Every morning he wakes, dreading going to work and complaining about his boss and his co-workers, but he stays because he's too frightened of losing the security it provides.

Helen, Grant, and Bucky are only the tip of the iceberg. I suspect there are millions of other individuals who feel equally trapped by their situations. They complain but never leave or do anything about them. Why? To answer that questions, ask yourself, "Have I ever wanted to do something, but didn't, and then hated myself for not having the courage to risk 'being me'? As a child, did I see myself restricted by my parents? As a student, did I blame my teachers for my grades? Later in life, was the culprit my boss at a job I disliked but was afraid to leave? Still later, did I carry that behavior over to my marriage or other relationships, where I stifled my thoughts and refrained from saying what I felt because I didn't want to hurt my spouse, risk his or her wrath, or make waves?" The rationale being that it's not an important enough issue to fight about.

If so, in every instance, you stayed, mitigated your resentments, and hid your true emotions. You lived a lie and justified your actions on the basis of political correctness, religious teachings, or the welfare of others. There may have been times you let your feelings out, but, for the most part, it was probably only after you'd built up sufficient anger to provide a sense of false courage, which often led to you overreacting. The rest of the time, you probably grinned and tolerated it, thinking, "This is the way life is."

I can't count how many people I've seen in therapy who fit that description. They complain about their employers, parents, the spouses they chose, or the errors they made by marrying them, and they lament the price they now pay for that mistake. They are insensitive to the fact that their spouse probably pays a similar price, that having a partner who resents them because he or she doesn't have the courage to break off an engagement doesn't make for a happy marriage. Some of them eventually divorce, but, sadly, several years later they're back in therapy with a new spouse, singing the same song, second verse.

It makes me think of the nineteen-year-old prisoner who is sent to jail for twenty years. Every day, he rattles the bars of his cell and shouts, "Let me out." Upon his release, he goes out into a world that has changed from iceboxes to refrigerators, typewriters to computers, and Victrolas to iPods. In desperation, he runs to a familiar spot—the corner drugstore where he and his buddies used to hang out. But when he gets there, he finds a high-rise. The environment, the people, and the technology have totally changed. He feels so detached and frightened, he robs a 7-11 across from the police station and is immediately caught, placed in his old cell, and, within an hour, begins rattling the same bars, shouting, "Let me out!" Again, it's the same song, second verse.

As a child, you learned to live your life as a helpless individual, trapped by forces beyond your control. That wasn't your imagination; it was reality. But, by eighteen or so, you were free to make decisions, exercise your own judgment, and express your viewpoints, i.e., to be your own person. But you don't realize it because you haven't outgrown your learned feelings of helplessness. As a result, you continue to live your life as an emotional child, still governed by the thoughts, beliefs, and controls of parents, who were formidable in your eyes as a four-year-old, but shouldn't be now that you are an adult.

Why didn't you grow up? Because there are many payoffs for remaining a child. You don't have to take risks. You can blame everything on someone else, feel anger toward those who control you, and view yourself as a victim. Consequently, you continue to live your life influenced by early childhood messages, such as, "Be a good little boy or girl," "You're the little man in the family now," "People don't like you when you cry or get angry," "If you want to be loved, you've got to earn it," or, "You'll never amount to anything." In essence, you let the intimidated, wounded child inside you determine the actions, feelings, and expectations of you, the adult.

Years ago, a group of psychologists began a study they entitled "Learned Helplessness" that best illustrates how and why this phenomenon occurs. They constructed a box four feet wide by ten feet long, with solid sides five feet high. In the center, they placed a partition three feet high, thus creating two four-by-five compartments. In one compartment, they placed an iron grid attached to an electrical charge. They randomly selected a large group of adolescent dogs and began their study. They would take a dog, put him into the side with the grid, and sound a bell. Several moments later, they would send an electric charge to the grid. Without deviation, when the electrical charge hit the grid, the dog yelped and jumped over the partition to the other compartment. It was almost one-shot learning. It showed that an animal automatically avoids pain and hurt. It's a natural aversion behavior. Then, one by one, they again placed the dogs into the compartment with the grid. This time, however, the compartment was covered by a thick piece of Lucite so that the dogs couldn't escape. The psychologists then rang the bell, which was followed several moments later by an electrical charge. The dogs yelped, barked, bit, defecated, urinated, or curled up in the corner compliantly, awaiting the charge that they learned would follow the bell. After approximately thirty trials with each dog, they removed the Lucite cover. Once again, they placed the dogs into the grid side of the box and rang the bell. It was a signal the dogs had previously learned indicated they would soon be shocked. Despite the fact that there was no cover above them and the dogs had the means to escape, each of the dogs repeated its previous behavior. It barked, bit, urinated, defecated, or crawled off in the corner and yelped, resigned to the inevitable, that it was going to be shocked. Although all were free to leave the noxious, hurtful situation they were in, not one of the dogs jumped over the partition. They had learned to be helpless. The smartest dog, only with the help of the experimenters, took over two hundred trials before it learned to avoid the shock.

This study isn't particularly palatable, and I'm sure PETA was on the case, but the implications with regard to human behavior are startling. They suggest that once you're exposed to enough repetitions of hurtful behavior, you can become so accustomed to your helplessness that you go through the remainder of your life trapped by invisible "lids" that are no longer there. Thus, you may fear making simple decisions, standing on your own two feet, or expressing your opinion. In part, it explains why battered spouses stay in abusive marriages, why husbands and wives who feel controlled or depreciated never speak up, and why people capitulate to demands and behaviors that are unacceptable. As a child, you had no choice. As an adult, you do. But if you are unable to recognize that you're free to be you, you still behave as though you're trapped. As a result, your world becomes a cell with a door you rattle but never open, even though it's not locked, all because you are restricted by invisible fears from your past. Recognizing this will enable you to see that the only limits you have are those you carry with you from childhood. But, most importantly, this study shows that when you are free of your past, you needn't go through life feeling like a victim and wasting precious years, resenting your world and the people in it. You have the power within you to make a change in your life for the better. The only problem is that until now, you didn't know it.

CHAPTER ELEVEN

THE ORDEAL OF CHANGE

Based on the results of the learned helplessness study, it's readily apparent why, of all the ordeals you will face in a lifetime, there is probably none more difficult than attempting to alter or change your own behavior. You would think that simply wanting to change would be sufficient to motivate a person. But, after forty years of watching people in therapy, it's apparent that knowing right from wrong, good from bad, appropriate from inappropriate, or constructive from destructive isn't enough. Think about it. How many people do you know who are overweight, despise their body image, and repeatedly make resolutions to go on a diet, but never do? They know their weight will result in hypertension, a heart attack, kidney problems, circulatory problems, and their premature death, but it doesn't seem to matter. Similarly, how many individuals do you know who smoke, even though the package informs them that it is injurious to their health? Every day, the literature reinforces the notion that smoking not only causes cancer, but is associated with a myriad of other diseases. Nevertheless, they persist in buying cigarettes. They may even verbalize, "I have to stop smoking," but it doesn't translate into behavior. The same can be said for persons who drink excessively, take drugs, gamble, are addicted to pornography, or engage in physical and/or emotional abuse of their spouse or children. Most of them know their behavior is unacceptable. After every episode, they are remorseful, repentant, and apologetic. Still, their behavior continues. Saying it's an addiction is only a definition. It is not an excuse, a justification, or a solution.

More often than not, human beings just like you need to be hit over the head with a baseball bat to wake them up; to motivate them to initiate changes they've always wanted to make but were too fearful or lacked the confidence and resolution to actualize. It often takes a heart attack to put you on a diet or to start you exercising. It might take cancer to cause you to stop smoking, or a divorce to finally make you recognize that your own behavior contributed to the situation you're in and that you desperately need to look at yourself and your behaviors. It's then that you come to realize that it is useless to make excuses, blame others, or plead ignorance. There is only one way for change to occur: you must resolve to take responsibility to become the person you truly want to be. In the long run, change needs to come about not because others are pushing or motivating you, but because, deep down inside, you want to be thin, stop smoking, stop drinking, stop gambling, stop taking drugs, stop mistreating others, or stop staying in unacceptable jobs or relationships with people who mistreat you. You must want to be able to think, act, and feel what is inside you, not what others dictate you should do, feel, or think.

Otto, a man whose children I saw in therapy, was a prime example of someone who needed a catastrophe to initiate change. He was a basically well-intentioned individual who loved his family, but dealt with them in a highly self-righteous, authoritarian manner. He pontificated, restricted, demeaned, and subordinated his spouse and children, all of whom were frightened and intimated by him. In spite of that, each of them strongly desired his love, approval, and attention, but he didn't know how to give it. For him, demonstrative feelings only reflected weakness. He learned that early in life, from his father, a stern, dictatorial individual who had experienced considerable persecution during World War II as a German immigrant living in the United States.

Throughout the time I saw his children, Otto periodically visited me. His manner was always abrupt. His words lacked emotionality and were always critical of others. It was difficult for me to listen to him without becoming irritated. Despite my numerous attempts to help him see the negative impact his interactions provoked in others, his self-righteous defenses disallowed him to face his reality. As a result, he cancelled his appointments, but called every other week to discuss his children's behavior. To be truthful, it came as a welcome surprise when the calls ceased for a period of almost six weeks. During that time, his children were at summer camp and I went on vacation. Thus, I had little information about what was happening at their home. Then, one weekend, he called again, but something was different. He asked how I was, whether I had enjoyed my vacation, and seemed far more animated and responsive than I had ever perceived him to be. He was far more emotional, and the negativity that usually accompanied his conversations was noticeably absent.

He said, "I thought it appropriate to call and let you know what's happening with me. I guess you noticed I haven't called for about six weeks, because I've had a bout of surgery. My doctor discovered a tumor during a routine examination and, to make a long story short, I have melanoma. I have no idea what's going to happen. But, no matter what the future holds, I want to live the present differently. I'm trying to be positive about things, and I want to tell you a funny story involving an associate of mine. He called and told me about a friend of his whose father was diagnosed with cancer and was informed that he only had a short period of time to live. As a result, he decided to fulfill his fondest dream, to go to Africa, along with everyone in his family and several select friends. He spent a tremendous amount of money on one of the most wonderful trips that any of them had ever been on in their lives. That was twenty-six years ago, and he's still griping about all the money he spent! But this associate called me and said, 'Otto, in case you are of the same mind-set, I wanted to say that I'm available to go on a trip with you.' "

Then Otto broke out into laughter. I was talking to a different man. I thought how sad it was that he and many, if not most, people need a catastrophic event to cause them to grow emotionally and to alter their behavior and attitudes. On one hand, I felt sorry for him. On the other hand, I was glad. It was, nevertheless, sad that it required getting diagnosed with cancer to motivate him, to get him off dead center.

Unfortunately, sometimes even a heart attack, cancer, divorce, or repeated involvement in dead-end relationships isn't always sufficient to motivate change. For example, another patient of mine, Melissa, a thirty-four-year-old, very attractive, bright, professional individual, found it almost impossible to behave according to what she wanted. Instead, she was controlled by covert feelings of insecurity and inadequacy, stemming from being raised in a home where emotions and nurturing were all but absent. As a result, she desperately longed for a meaningful, close relationship with someone who would care for, love, and support her. Her longing, however, was a concept built on fantasy and wishful thinking. In actuality, she never really experienced love. She only knew the dream. Thus, although she knew what it was that she wanted, similar to most people, she behaviorally clung to and searched for what was familiar with. Consequently, she repeatedly became involved with men who, over time, provided the same empty emotional relationship that she'd experienced as a child.

In the end, she always felt used and unappreciated, both very familiar emotions. Still, she was unable to extradite herself from these relations. In her mind, if she lost who she had, there would be nobody to fill the void. Because of this, she stayed in at least two relationships long after she knew they weren't providing her with what she wanted. She tolerated behavior she perceived as unacceptable and stayed angry with herself for her inability to change. In both instances, she stayed despite her pain. She was unable to leave until her hurt, depression, and feelings of unworthiness became so acute that she felt she could no longer survive emotionally. At the same time, it appeared as though she deliberately created her own increasing discomfort to the point that it would give her the courage to leave. It is similar to an individual who first has to gain sufficient weight to reach a point where it is so unacceptable to him or her that it provides the initiative to go on the diet he or she spoke about ten pounds earlier.

From the outside looking in, the picture appears absurd. If you know what you want, feel positive it would be beneficial to you, and hate yourself because of your inaction, it's obvious you need to do something about it. But you don't. Instead, you stay frozen in place, despite the fact that you make repeated promises to yourself to initiate a change. Time and time again, you say, "I'll do it tonight," "I'll start this weekend," "After the holidays," or "When the kids' finals are over." But the deadlines come and go and you're still in the same place you were weeks, months, or years ago. It doesn't seem to make sense, yet thousands of people find themselves facing the same dilemma. The content may differ, but the situation and emotional dynamics are essentially the same. It doesn't matter whether you accept a sales job and are reluctant to cold-call; want to start a diet and exercise but can't stop overeating; desire a divorce, but are afraid of hurting your children and soon-to-be-ex-spouse; are looking for a raise, but are afraid to ask for it; want to escape an abusive relationship, but are afraid to be alone; or have to make any one of a thousand different decisions that someone emotionally important to you might find fault with in the end.

Think of it as though you're a novice trapeze artist, standing on a high platform at one end of a tent. Your goal is to reach a platform on the other side of the tent. Your partner hangs by his feet and swings toward you with his arms outstretched. Your job is to swing out on your trapeze, let go, do a flip in the air, and grasp his hands as you fall. There is one problem: once you let go of your trapeze, you have nothing to hold on to until you reach his outstretched hands. It doesn't seem absurd for you to stand frozen on your platform, or to swing back and forth, gaining momentum for your jump, but never letting go. Think of it as being paralyzed by procrastination. Based on your fears, all of this makes a lot of sense, because fear of failure or the unknown can be a very strong motivator.

That isn't the only motivator that controls us. As noted in the learned helplessness studies, early habituated attitudes or orientations can paralyze us as well. They can almost act as a double-edged sword. On the one side, we punish ourselves for being too weak, dumb, frightened, etc., to initiate change. On the other side, we blame the people we perceive as controlling us and the situations we feel trapped by. Over time, you even experience difficulty recognizing if what you do is what you want, or what you feel obligated to do. The confusion thwarts your wherewithal to enjoy or relish any situation, because you constantly question, "Am I drinking this milk because I want to, or because my mother told me to?" The potential pleasures are endless when you are governed by your own thoughts—when you are no longer restricted by an emotional umbilical cord that mandates that you be controlled by your inner child. As a result, your fears and anger subside, because your rational adult has taken over control of you.

Let me tell you a story that a friend of mine told me years ago. He was a Central Intelligence Agency agent who had been traveling in Russia during the Cold War. At one point, he found himself waiting for a train at a railroad station in central Russia in the middle of winter. The station was freezing. There was a crack in the wall and the cold Russian air was seeping into the waiting room. The men and women waiting in the station with him all sat in their parkas with their hats and gloves on, tolerating the cold. At one point, he got up, moved several nearby suitcases in front of the crack and, after a period of time, the station warmed up to the point that many people took off their parkas, hats, and gloves. One group of men even started playing cards. Some time later, a train arrived, and the man who owned the suitcases my friend had put against the wall picked them up and left to catch his train. The room began to get cold again, and the people put on their parkas, hats, and gloves and stopped their card game. My friend found this totally confusing. It was so obvious that all they had to do was move some other suitcases in front of the opening. He asked me if I could explain this behavior. I told him about the dogs and learned helplessness and suggested that human beings often learn a state of helplessness, as well. They become resigned to disappointment, hurt, failure, even abuse. Though they complain bitterly and resolve time and time again to change their behavior, they remain in the same place, too frightened (and cold!) to try something new, not believing that if they do, they could succeed, or that they deserve any better than life has already dealt them.

There is another group of people who experience no pain, no upset or fear, because their coping techniques function so effectively that, on the one hand, they see no need to change (i.e., "if it ain't broke, don't fix it"). On the other hand, you probably recognize, at some level of unconsciousness, that if you do change, you may have to face or come to grips with issues you've effectively avoided dealing with all your life. For the most part, people who fit that bill are persons who, when asked "Are you happy?" answer, "I'm not unhappy." Any discomfort or conflict you experience occurs primarily when others in your world express discomfort or distaste for the way you are. Thus, you only enter therapy at the request or insistence of someone else. All the while, however, you think, "I don't need this. I'm perfectly content with how things are."

No matter which group you're in, or how you cope—by snarling, biting, yelping, waiting for the inevitable, etc.—change is extremely difficult. Because of that, some of you can live your lives without ever changing. You remain in situations that are noxious and unrewarding and view yourself as a martyr or victim. Despite your wishful thinking and desire for something new or better, nothing in your life will ever change until you convert your wishes into actions. For the most part, that won't take place because you're afraid of the unknown and frightened you won't be able to live your life the way you desire, as a thin, sober, self-controlled, lovable, independent, happily married, or successful human being. So you remain where you are, despite how painful it may be. As I noted earlier, change, when or if it does occur, often comes about only as a result of a catastrophic or life-threatening event, instead of from positive motivation based on the belief that you needn't live your life controlled by childhood fears and that you have the right to act in accordance with your own wishes. This should be the goal for everyone and, in fact, it may well be yours. But, too many times, your fears don't make it possible. To help you to achieve your goals, you need to follow the guidelines below:

Ask yourself two questions, which I suggested earlier were important for you to answer. They are: "What do I want?" and "Where do I want to go?" You may even have to write them down and answer them every day. Your response to these questions can serve as a daily guide to the direction you need to follow.

Be aware that change doesn't take place with one big step. You first have to crawl, then walk, and finally run toward what you desire.

---

1. Act, in spite of your fears, your feelings of insufficiency, and your reluctance to ail. Your success will eventually come about just because you tried and failed enough to succeed.
2. Remember that progress only comes about as a result of forward thinking, and it almost always involves taking three steps forward and two steps back. Although two steps back may be interpreted as a failure, these steps are very necessary, first, because you will learn from your failures and benefit from your mistakes, and second, because success is built on a platform of previous failures.

Don't be disheartened when your first attempts to change result in your going overboard, or to an extreme. For example, the passive, compliant person first acts angry and hostile before he/she levels off. The pattern that change takes is similar to the behavior of a pendulum on a cuckoo clock. You start it by positioning the pendulum at one extreme and letting it go, causing it to swing to the opposite extreme. Then you wait for it to level out. Human beings react in the same manner.

Finally, force yourself to take the first step toward the goals you've chosen. Thereafter, your body will follow. Even more, you will be pleasantly surprised to discover that your fears were groundless and, instead of losing the person you love, you will gain his or her respect and affection.

CHAPTER TWELVE

COMING TO PEACE WITH "ME"

While on a trip on the Red Sea, two fellow travelers and I entered into a discussion about our lives. In the course of our conversation, one asked, "What do you consider the most significant accomplishment you've experienced in life?"

He then began to answer his own question. "Mine is my second marriage. I have a wonderful, meaningful relationship with a woman I truly love. My life is so much fuller with her in it. So I'd say my marriage to her and the relationship we both have with our children is my greatest accomplishment."

The second spoke up and said, "I've had many accomplishments that I'm very proud of, but greatest of all is fact that I left the practice of law and took a teaching position in a small university, which enables me to significantly affect the lives of many students and even some of the faculty. It's the most rewarding accomplishment I can think of."

Then they turned to me and said, "Well?" I hesitated and finally said, "It's not something I can easily answer. I don't know why, but the question is so meaningful to me that I need more time to genuinely consider my thoughts. Several things come to mind, but to answer truthfully, I feel as though I have to look more deeply inside me." After several moments, I blurted out something that surprised even me. I said, "The greatest accomplishment in my life is that I have finally come to accept me, with my warts, scars, shortcomings, fears, and insecurities. I doubt that I'll ever be able to do it 100 percent. It's a work in progress, but, more often than not, I've learned to laugh at my failings and foibles, to minimize my anger and defensiveness, to be who I am, and to say what I genuinely think or feel without overwhelming concern regarding what others will think or say. In a sense, I could say that maybe 75 percent to 80 percent, I've come to peace with me."

I felt guilty later that evening as I lay in bed and thought back to my response. In part, I felt guilty because I hadn't said, "My fifty-four year marriage with my wife; my relationship with my children and grandchildren; the individuals I hope I've touched in a positive way throughout the course of my professional career; the numerous friends I have; the degrees I obtained that I thought were impossible goals for me; the articles I've written, and, most of all, the hearts I've touched." But, at that moment, it became so very clear to me that all of those achievements were really my attempts to somehow prove, I thought, at first to others, but then I realized, far more to myself, that I was okay. It was a testimony to the fact that I must have started out with the notion that I really wasn't okay, good enough, or worth loving to begin with. My thinking must have been that if I could collect enough medals, degrees, or accomplishments to my name, I would be okay, worth loving. But it never worked.

Nor did it work for so many other, much more notable people, such as Marilyn Monroe, Michael Jackson, Elvis Presley, Ernest Hemingway (my hero), and a host of others who, despite all their successes, were emotional failures. On the surface, they seemed to have it all, but they left this world prematurely, often by their own choice, because they also must have felt something was lacking in them. Nothing better illustrates this than Marilyn Monroe's statement, "A wise girl kisses but doesn't love, listens but doesn't believe, and leaves before she is left." Her own words fully describe her inner child, who was obviously frightened to be emotionally vulnerable, reluctant to trust, and terrified of being rejected. It's apparent that the way she and the others were viewed by the public was significantly different from the way they saw themselves. All of which led me to see something I had never before fully realized: that I had spent most of my life at war with myself and experiencing constant conflict between **what I thought and what I said, what I wanted and what I dared ask for, what I believed and what I did, and what I felt and what I couldn't afford to risk sharing with myself, let alone others.**

Having said all this, I'd like to ask you, "What makes you okay?" Or, "What do you consider to be the most significant accomplishment you've experienced in your life?" Please don't answer hurriedly. Give it several moments of genuine thought and consideration. Then, at least for yourself, try to discover the meaning of your life. I'm asking you to think about what you have done, achieved, accomplished, or given that gave you the sense that you genuinely deserved the space you occupy on this earth and the time that you were given to spend here. Did you build a sports car from the ground up? Win a drag race? Earn sufficient money? Help enough people? Own enough houses? Win enough legal battles? Intellectually impress and/or intimidate enough people to prove you're okay? Did you play the role of being the "good guy"? The tough task master? The loving, caring individual? The industrious, hard worker? The helpless, dependent individual who needed all the nurturing and attention he/she could garner from others? What did this do for you? Did you spend your whole life, no matter how prestigious, important, successful, or financially rewarding the activities you engaged in were, feeling as though you were in a rat race, going through the same maze or running on the same path day after day and having no real sense of accomplishment? Did you search for fame, only to discover that fame has a very short shelf life? That, five to ten years after any notable achievement, most people will have forgotten your name, or even the fact that you ever existed?

I now realize that, in the course of living my life, I constantly searched for some way to feel okay. Although my memories of childhood are minimal, I'd like to provide some more examples from my life to which you may be able to relate. (I almost want to start by saying, "Once upon a time, there was a little ADHD child who grew up in a dysfunctional family before anyone had ever heard of ADHD or dysfunction.") One I will always recall is how thankful I was for a young man in our neighborhood by the name of Jerry Cohen. You see, I lived in a low-class area on a street where there must have been thirty or forty kids. When we had a baseball (we called it stickball) game, there were fifteen to twenty guys on a side, depending on how many of us showed up that day. The ritual was that the two most athletic, physically large, or intimidating guys in the group threw a bat up in the air and, after catching it, alternated putting one fist after another around the bat until they reached the top. The purpose was to determine who would choose players first. Well, if it hadn't been for Jerry Cohen, I would always have been the last one chosen, instead of Jerry. But it really didn't matter, because the position I played (not by choice) was the out-out-outfield. So far out that few of the kids could even hit the ball that far. Still, I can't ever recall this ill-coordinated, ADD kid ever playing without returning home with some sort of minor injury. So the vote was in: I was not destined to become an athlete.

In junior high, I recall identifying with a movie star named Donald O'Connor. (Only those of you who are, shall we gently say, up in years, will recall him.) He was a nerdy kind of guy whose claim to fame was co-starring with Gene Kelly in the movie *Singing in the Rain*. However, I best recall him starring in a film where he was depicted as a rather awkward, geeky-looking guy who lacked confidence with regard to girls and whose social acumen was severely impaired. He didn't play sports, wasn't outstanding academically, and was more or less looked down upon by his peers, particularly those members of the "in crowd." It's sad to say, but I related. In one scene, he wandered around the gym looking lost while the cheer-leaders, dressed in their short skirts, bobby socks, and saddle shoes, flirted with the members of the football team. Finally, he sat down at the piano and began to "tickle the ivories." The music that emanated changed the atmosphere of the whole room. The cheerleaders all gravitated to the grand piano in the gym. They sat on top of it and swayed back and forth to the music, while looking at him with adoring eyes filled with newfound affection and respect. The more they responded, the more energetic, vibrant, and exciting the music became. It didn't take me long to decide that that was the way to go.

Six instruments later, it became apparent to me I wasn't going to make it to the top of the music world. I started with the piano, gravitated to the guitar, the clarinet, the saxo-phone, the Hawaiian guitar, and the violin. My innate lack of ability to carry a tune, to keep time, and, most of all, to read the music when the flats and sharps became increasingly present, was a testimony to the obvious—I would never become a musician.

It was about then that I discovered I had a knack for humor. Unlike other kids, whose little black books were filled with names and phone numbers, mine was filled, alphabeti-cally, with punch lines. I figured I could become a comedian. As a result, for a period of time, my interactions with others consisted of "Can you top this?" In my quest to stand out, I assumed the role of the jokester, the funny man, the one who always had something humorous to say which would make me the center of attention. Needless to say, long term, that didn't work, either. Too much of a funny facade can cause you to become a joke, as opposed to a jokester.

To say the least, having ADD didn't aid in the development of my sense of worthwhileness, intellectually or academically. To the contrary, it contributed to a deficit in my wherewithal to develop, sustain, and maintain successful interpersonal relationships. Because of my feeling that I was unable to perform intellectually, I predictably attempted to compensate by excessive behavior, i.e., being too quiet, too loud, too hyper, too needy, or too ready to impress or gain the attention of others. When or if that failed, I strove for negative attention by being a disruptive pain in the posterior. It always worked. I got plenty of negative attention. Sadly, it took me far too many years to realize that, no matter how you attempt to conceal your feeling that you're basically lacking, in almost every instance, your compensatory behavior is never as palatable to others as is the real you. I didn't yet know that I was okay. I should add that I can't help but recall the numerous times I sat in a classroom, hyper to the point that I'd answer a question with the first thing that jumped into my head, and, of course, being laughed at by my classmates. On other occasions, I was too fearful to volunteer an answer that, in more cases than not, was accurate. Sadly, the fear of being wrong and being criticized was too great to allow me to open my mouth. However, moments later, after another student verbalized the very answer I had at the tip of my tongue, my knee-jerk reaction was to shout, "That's what I was going to say." Thank goodness, I was astute enough to understand that reaction would only have made me look even more ridiculous than I already felt.

Without a doubt, life isn't easy for any youngster who feels he's lacking but wants to be noticed, accepted, cared for, and popular, i.e., to feel "okay." Mostly because, for him/her, feeling okay is an emotional state that is impossible to achieve. Yet, if you're that kid, you desperately desire it and question, at least internally, "How do other kids do it? How do they get to be popular, well-liked, looked up to?" But, no matter how many times you ask the question, the answer isn't forthcoming. There's no textbook that tells you how to achieve that state. There are only thousands of suggestions telling you what you should do that you lack the courage to attempt. As a result, you wind up feeling that you are on the outside of every group, somewhere near the perimeter but not really accepted or included. It's as though you're only a spectator looking in from outside, but never feeling like a member. Little did most of us know, the popular kids don't feel okay, either.

That point in my life was the time when my sense of well-being and adequacy hit a new low. I had only two alternatives: fight or flight. I was too cowardly to fight, so I chose flight. First, by flight of thought, daydreaming, and fantasizing, i.e., hoping for a miracle. Finally, my ultimate flight was when I quit high school after only one month of my freshman year. It didn't take very long for my difficulties with English grammar, Spanish, and history to convince me that scholastics were no more the pathway toward "being okay" than were my athletic, musical, or comedic abilities. There was no other choice but to run. Not to any one specific place, but away from a place I thought caused me to feel inadequate. I was far too naive to even remotely realize that you can't run away from yourself, because wherever you go, you're there.

Years later, while in the service, I saw my peers finding girl-friends, being confident, and having fun. I thought, "There's got to be a reason for their success." I erroneously decided my lack of social achievement was due to the fact that I didn't have a car. So, I worked my regular job in the service and found two part-time jobs off base that would provide me with sufficient money to eliminate that problem. Six months later, I had a car and payments, but no girlfriend. This time, however, I immediately realized why. It was because I had a used car. What I needed was a new one.

It was about the same time that I began to experience a modicum of success. The service proved to be a place where I could excel. My willingness to work hard without complaining was consistently rewarded, and my confidence began to grow. Additionally, I met someone who tried to convince me that I was smarter than I believed. She even suggested that I needed to go to college. The thought was as preposterous to me as if she had suggested I could fly. Had she left it to me to provide the initiative, I would probably never have applied. But, she persisted until I found myself standing in a long line of individuals, picking out my classes, but not telling them that I was admitted conditionally, on the basis of a GED from the territory of Alaska and a letter begging for admittance. A letter, by the way, that was written by my "delusional" muse, whose regard for me was far greater than her grasp of reality, at least in my opinion.

Two-and-a-half years later, I had a bachelor's degree. I wore the gown proudly and looked the part of every student in the graduating class. But underneath, I still wasn't okay. This time, I realized why. "Everyone knows you're not okay unless you have a master's degree." It shouldn't surprise you that, two years later, with a master's degree in hand, I felt no better and no more adequate. Fortunately, I had the wisdom to recognize that it's only with a Ph.D. that one can feel sufficient. So I put my nose to the grindstone and, several years later, to my great disappointment, I realized that wasn't the case, either. It was one of the most disheartening emotional experiences I can ever recall.

I was standing in the pavilion at the University of Houston, having just received my Ph.D., when a thought went through my mind that totally devastated me. At that time, there were only twelve thousand Ph.D. psychologists in the whole United States (I knew that because I had read the figure somewhere about a week earlier), and I was one of them. But my thought was, if they had a baseball game, you guessed it, I'd be the next to last one chosen. But it didn't stop there. For years, I engaged in the game of competing in every facet of my life. I had to be more energetic, sleep less, and accomplish more. I was a person who had to work longer and harder than anyone else. I always needed to be doing something; I couldn't ever just be. Just being seemed wasteful, nonproductive, and lazy. Besides which, you didn't accomplish anything, and, in my mind, it meant you were an unambitious, worthless person. Only many years later did I come to realize that, underneath, people of that type have little or no intrinsic sense of self-worth. They and I see ourselves as only having value if we earn it. Even worse, I believed that the harder the task completed, the more I was worth. My orientation was based on the notion that "nothing of value comes easy." I now see that thought as not being entirely true. Hard work and dedication are certainly valuable attributes. Good luck and being in the right place at the right time also help. But, most of all, being confident and free of fear and stress—and, therefore, willing to risk failure—play an even bigger role in determining how much real success you eventually achieve.

It's now also apparent to me that, for too much of my life, I strove to please everyone except myself. "No" was a word I didn't accept. Nor did I know how to say it. Essentially, I directed my energy toward satisfying everyone else's desires in order to gain their acceptance. As a result, I was viewed by others as a good guy, a nice guy, everyone's affable, agreeable friend, except my own. I didn't like the person I felt I needed to be to buy the acceptance I desperately desired. Even more, I discovered that I didn't like the price I paid for acceptance, or even the people who accepted me. Underneath, deep inside this affable, good-natured guy was a fat little kid, adolescent, teenager, and later adult, who was a basically angry person. Someone who couldn't accept himself or fully benefit from the acceptance he received from others. Deep down, I knew that any acceptance I experienced was derived on the basis of the erroneous image I portrayed, not for who I genuinely was. The consequence of all this was to feel severely lacking as a person. In order to prove the opposite, I attempted to conquer every challenge I faced, because I couldn't accept failure and hated myself when it occurred. What I failed to realize back then was that competing with others, or distorting who you are to gain the favor of others, will never lead to making you feel good enough, because, eventually, you're bound to encounter someone who is bigger, stronger, smarter, richer, more capable, or more successful than you. The only person you should ever compete with is yourself, and the only person you should ever be is who you are. Although those words are basic truths, they constitute a challenge that often feels impossible to achieve, but I promise, if you open your eyes to what's going on around you and in you, your world will change.

For me, four events occurred which emotionally steered me in a new direction.

The first was my son going on dialysis because of childhood diabetes. It forced me to face something I couldn't control, change, or fix. I was unable to make it better. The helpless feeling inside me was as difficult for me to swallow as his illness was. Years later, he was the recipient of double transplant surgery, giving him a kidney and a pancreas, which also gave him a new lease on life, literally and figuratively. Still, the awareness of my own impotence to fix everything prevailed. The realizations I later came to were:

1. I couldn't control the world. At best, I only needed to control me.
2. I didn't have to be perfect to be okay. I always verbalized these thoughts intellectually, but I never before fully owned or embraced them emotionally.

The second event was a huge economic downturn in the late 1980s, which resulted in me losing everything that I had accumulated in the previous twenty-eight years. The realization that came with it was that my life wasn't really radically different. I hadn't changed. I was the same person with the same feelings, thoughts, and issues. It became very obvious to me that my possessions never made me any more or less okay. What I felt about myself inside determined what and how I felt and acted on the outside. I always knew that as well, but knowing it emotionally gave me an entirely new outlook on living.

The third was our house burning down. We lost all our possessions, particularly a large art collection we had put together throughout our travels all over the world. I should add that none of it was insured, and even if it had been, most of it was irreplaceable. Still, life went on and, emotionally, I remained the person I always was.

The last and crowning blow was our next home being invaded by kick-burglars. Three of them burst through the door of our townhouse wearing ski masks and waving revolvers. They pistol whipped me and took my wife from our bed to the bathroom to get the diamond ring off her finger. My fear was they were going to cut off her finger to get it and/ or they were going to kill us. Needless to say, I pleaded for our lives and offered them everything of value in the house. In less than fifteen minutes, they left, loaded down with jewelry, leaving the two of us totally nude in a closet, with blood dripping down my face. Meanwhile, any thoughts of me being "Rambo" vanished forever from my brain. I had to be resigned to the fact that the guy inside was not a tiger, he was a pussycat, but today, even that's okay.

I'd be lying to say the losses were easy to accept. But the realization that followed was that I was no different after them than I was preceding them. I still went about my life working hard, needing love, and feeling I wasn't good enough. All of which boils down to the fact that it isn't what you have or do outside of yourself that really counts. That doesn't mean that medals don't matter or that we shouldn't strive to achieve, to do good things, to help our fellow man, to be successful, to get close to others, and to love and care for our families and children. All of those are very worthwhile endeavors. But, in the end, none of them will significantly alter your basic feeling about who you are on the inside.

The truth be known, the scarred, inadequate, or needy-feeling little kid of your youth that most of you harbor inside never changes. He or she is part of the baggage each of you brought with you from childhood. Some of you are more fortunate than others—your suitcases are less damaged, less scarred. Others are fastened together by bits of tape and rope that temporarily hold you together. Still others are locked shut, and the key or combination to that lock was lost years ago. No matter the condition, there's no plastic surgery, no form of psychotherapy, no magic pill that can alter you on the inside. Your inner child is part of your hard drive. The only way you can ever come to feel okay about him or her or you is to come to peace with who your child is and what he feels, i.e., to recognize, forgive, accept, and love him.

That is the mountain you eventually have to climb if you truly want to feel okay. The alternative is to continue to camouflage yourself, to hide in costumes or behind badges, degrees, and bank accounts. Sadly, none of these behaviors succeed. At the risk of being redundant, let me say it once again: nothing on the outside can permanently fix or change what you are on the inside. It is only by learning to recognize and own, accept, forgive, and love the inner child you harbor that you can ever truly feel okay about the person you are inside and the adult you have become on the outside. The obstacle that makes this difficult, if not impossible, for some individuals is that recognition alone can be a very painful experience. Consequently, most people choose to deny their inner child and his or her feelings.

In retrospect, it took me too many years to accept that, as a child, I was very sad inside. In fact, I now remember occasionally crying for what I then thought was no reason at all. Today, I realize I was crying for the pitiful little kid inside me who felt estranged from his peers because he felt so lacking in worth that he didn't dare let anyone see him, not even himself. He was a person I was critical of, found fault with, and even punished. At one time, I buried him under an extra sixty pounds of weight. It was an effective smoke screen that temporarily hid him from me and others. Whenever I got close enough to really see him, I'd redirect my attention to how fat I was. Perhaps you did, or still do, the same thing, using alcohol, drugs, anger, or one of the numerous other self-defeating behaviors available to you, as opposed to my choice, mashed potatoes and macaroni and cheese. It's no wonder I felt others didn't like me. I made it impossible for them to really see or know me. Any rejection I experienced, I saw as coming because of my weight. But, in truth, the person who couldn't accept me was me.

This isn't a new concept. William Wordsworth once wrote, "The child is father of the man." The logic is that the man or woman you create is built on the foundation laid down by the child you were. As a result, no matter how adequate the man or woman you create, the stability of that person will be determined by the strength of the child that supports him. Susan Batson, in *The Drama of the Gifted Child*, went a step further. She said, "The inner child is the center of your weakness, but it is also the center of your strength." I see her words as saying your inner strength consists of your creativity, your capacity for joy, sensitivity, understanding, compassion, and, most of all, your wherewithal to genuinely love yourself and others. All great people get in touch with their inner child. But those who are really healthy are the ones who then learn to accept him or her. You see, confronting and effectively dealing with your little kid eliminates the fears that keep you from access-ing and fully appreciating your strengths. Consequently, until you face and accept your fears and weaknesses, you will never be fully be able to realize, benefit from, or fully access your inner strength.

The best examples of this fact are those individuals who, despite all their successes, never feel satisfied. They need more and more medals, possessions, and money. Nothing is ever enough. All because they never accepted the child within them. As a result, their foundations remain shaky. This isn't surprising because, no matter the degree to which you alter you, the extent of your alterations, or the cost of the changes emotionally, physically, or financially, they're only cosmetic. What really counts isn't that you're feeling happier today, appear more attractive physically, or are enjoying more financial success. Those are all positive changes, but they're not necessarily permanent in nature. The rule is that the structure or person you create is only as stable as the foundation you build him or her on. You need to realize that, as long as you go out in the world trying to improve who you are, you will never feel you're good enough. The reason is that the path to feeling "good enough" can't be reached by fixing, improving, or altering who you are or what you have. Instead, the first step is recognizing your feelings, accepting them the way they were to begin with, and learning to act in spite of them, or because of them, whichever coincides with what you think, feel, and want.

Accepting you is a reward in itself. However, once you learn to accept you, there is a wonderful bonus you can look forward to. You will be far more willing to take risks and to be vulnerable, because you'll recognize that there is no penalty for failing, but there is for not trying. You will also feel more accepting and deserving of the love and approval you receive because you came by them honestly. Even more, you will become more approving, loving, considerate, and forgiving of others who are still engaged in their war to achieve okayness. The axiom that prevails is that "The acceptance by you of the insufficiencies and inadequacies you perceive in you is the only actualization of you." It is the way to find peace within yourself and to feel closer to and more comfortable in your world. Let me stress, once again, that it is certainly no crime to do better. But you need to remember that doing better doesn't necessarily make you better; accepting you does.

One last thought is that your story, at least the specific facts or content, may differ significantly from mine. However, I believe, with some degree of certainty, that the feelings and emotions accompanying your story are the same or very similar to my own and to those of any number of others. I further feel that you must face your feelings, no matter how painful they may be, because recognizing, owning, and accepting them (i.e., your little kid) is the first step toward you being able to find, forgive, and love yourself.

TRANSITION

Haven't you always heard that nothing you do can be considered a failure if you learn from it? That's the way I want you to approach the second half of *You're Okay, But You Don't Know It.* It can help you not only to recognize you're "okay," but enable you to reach the point that you are happy and satisfied with who and what you are, where you are, and what you do. Please read and consider each step carefully. You can question, modify, and improve on the design of the path, but not on its goal. It can help you find peace within you, cooperation between your adult self and your inner child, and the realization that the joy it can provide you for the time you have left on this earth is well worth the energy you will expend and the pain you may temporarily experience before getting there.

PART TWO

'm not a perfect girl. My hair doesn't always stay in place and I spill things a lot. I'm pretty clumsy. Sometimes I even have a broken heart. My friends and I sometimes fight. And some days, nothing seems to go right. But when I think about it and take a step back, I remember how amazing life truly is and that maybe, just maybe, I like being imperfect.

—Anonymous

There is nothing or no one so damaged that it or they can't be put together or mended. If that weren't the case, half the world would be driven to madness.

—Hercule Poirot
Appointment with Death, by Agatha Christie

The easiest thing in the world to be is you. The most difficult thing to be is what other people want you to be. Don't let them put you in that position.

—Leo Buscaglia

CHAPTER THIRTEEN

CREATE A NEW YOU

T he general notion is that only people who are in trouble or have serious problems should go to therapy, read self-help books, or strive to delve into the depths of their emotional beings. That isn't at all the case. As I've repeatedly suggested, everyone can enhance the quality of his or her emotional health by increasing his or her insight, knowledge, and acceptance of self. Certainly, those of you who experience serious problems in coping should, by all means, search for help. However, oftentimes, the most overtly successful-appearing individuals you know, admire, or envy are just as desperately in need of guidance to help them cope with and live their lives more productively, i.e., in a manner that causes them far less stress and provides more enjoyment of living than they've known heretofore. Let me provide some examples:

Shirley has an MBA from a prestigious university. She is in an executive training program for a large company and has twice been singled out for her outstanding performance.

However, at home, she is constantly berated by her husband, who depreciates, criticizes, and keeps her in a subordinated position. She wants to leave, but is frightened no one else will want her.

Garrett is an extremely successful litigator. He has a national reputation for being a "top hired gun." He is also in the midst of his third divorce. He works, gambles, and drinks to excess and is basically depressed. His two children from his first marriage are estranged from him, and he has no close friends.

Lyle is squeaky clean and straight as an arrow. He is the chief financial officer of an international oil supply company. His reputation at the firm is that of a fair but tough individual who knows no gray areas. His world is either black or white. At home, however, he is surrounded by gray. He is passive, unable to make decisions, kowtows to his wife and kids, and capitulates to their wills. His children are totally out of control. They know no limits, and his wife, unbeknownst to him, is having an affair. His world is on the verge of self-destruction, but he is oblivious to all of it.

It is difficult to count how many other truly bright, successful, sensitive people I have seen in therapy whose external lives appear to be the epitome of success. Their social status and professional achievements are models that many of you might envy and strive toward. Yet, at one stage in their lives, everything starts to crumble because their worlds are made up of a fragile, delicately balanced house of cards—one that gives the appearance of stability, harmony, and happiness, but is really an illusion. When that fact finally becomes apparent to them, they sink into depression and despair. At that point in time, supporting them becomes difficult. Pointing out their previous successes and achievements accomplishes very little. It may brighten their lives for a few moments, but it doesn't last. Their lives are emotionally shattered because they were built on the erroneous premise that what they accomplished tangibly and externally would equal what they felt emotionally or internally. But no amount of amassed fortune or fame can achieve that end. Thus, these individuals find themselves on a constant treadmill, having to do more, give more, be more, and make more in order to sustain a delicate balance holding up their house of cards. There are numerous famous names that might also fit this example: Marilyn Monroe, John Kennedy, Bill Clinton, Jimmy Swaggart, Jim Bakker, Michael Milken, and Jeff Skilling.

What all these individuals needed to know was that every human being carries within himself or herself a self-perception that is fully developed early in his or her childhood. It stays with you throughout your lifetime. For many of you, that picture consists of an emotionally wounded or damaged child, someone who doesn't measure up, isn't good enough, lacks worth, and isn't deserving of love. The picture isn't necessarily accurate, but it strongly affects the way you act later in life. Many of you are totally unaware of that wounded little child. In fact, you would staunchly deny him, maintaining "I don't feel lacking. I like myself." At the same time, a review of your life's history might include interpersonal and professional disappointments, numerous traffic tickets, an unhappy marriage, a divorce, or problems with your kids. You might attribute all of that to being young and impulsive, having bad luck, picking the wrong partner, or the actions of others. These events may, however, be the behavioral evidence of a hurting little kid living inside you, one you are unwilling to consciously face. All the while, he is the underlying source of your occasional bouts of anxiety, periodic depressive feelings, or dysfunctional, immoral, or unethical behaviors. Your negative self-perception, though frequently erroneous, because most of us have far more worth than we realize, can become a permanent part of your hard drive, a part that can never be erased. No amount of work, effort, or achievement will alter it. Accomplishments, awards, degrees, and recognition can, for a short period of time, cause you to pay it less attention, but that damaged inner child will always rear its head again when you least expect it. That being the case, it is essential that you accurately recognize your self-perception and then develop a healthy means of coping with it.

To that end, as I have stated throughout this book, numerous people live their lives consciously and unconsciously trying to compensate for or negate their self-image. They work to excess, accumulate money and property beyond their needs, and relentlessly endeavor to prove that they are more adequate, sufficient, and worthwhile than they feel. But, no matter how successful they become, in terms of the way the world views them, their wounded self-perception persists. Other persons attempt to deny, to run, to obscure or obliterate that image. Often, they're successful, at least in terms of their conscious self. But underneath, the damaged little kid survives all attempts to outrun, discredit, or mitigate him. He or she is ever present, much like a dormant disease or virus that lurks in the background, waiting for any sign of weakness in your immune system which will permit it to come to the surface. Thus, denying, running from, or discrediting your inner child is not an effective way of dealing with him or her.

That being the case, you might ask, is there really any hope? When you can't bear to look at your dirty laundry, you can't possibly put it behind you and go on to live life successfully. Nor is it ever possible to wash your laundry so thoroughly that you truly believe "it never was soiled." Going out and buying new garments to cover up doesn't work, either. All of these behaviors—avoiding, expunging, and covering up—are only your futile attempt to escape a you that you can't accept. But that's impossible. You can't eat, drink, take drugs, lie, gamble, or screw your way to mental health. Even if you become obsessively involved in seemingly constructive activities, such as work, children, and charities, if it's to excess, it is still a form of escape. Similarly, you can't hide behind anger or blame your unhappiness and your depression on your parents and your spouse. It's to no avail. They may be wrong. They may be at fault. But, in the end, you still remain in your emotional trap, all because you can't face, accept, forgive, or love yourself.

There is only one other choice. You need to look your self-image in the face, to run toward him/her, rather than away from him/her. Whether he/she is reality based or not, he/she is real to the extent he/she resides within you. Consequently, you have little choice but to accept the child within you for who and what he/she is and forgive him/her for what you cannot abide in him/her. That is the only process that can result in the psychologically healthy actualization of you. At the risk of being repetitive, let me say, **the**

acceptance and forgiveness by you of the insufficiencies, fears, and threats you perceive in you is the first step toward the actualization of you.

The acceptance of the wounded or damaged child in you becomes the foundation on which you can later construct a healthy, positive, successful you, limited only by your individual capabilities, interests, and desires and the energy you are willing to expend. However, without taking the first steps of accepting and forgiving, you will never reach your full potential. Instead, you will direct much of your efforts toward denying, rationalizing, or obscuring who you fear you are. As a result, you are left with little energy to build that solid foundation. Similarly, when you build without establishing a foundation, you wind up forever asking, "Is that all there is?" until eventually, everything collapses because there is nothing to hold it up. Whatever accomplishments you may have realized, no matter how positively they are perceived by others, will have little value in your eyes. They will fail to provide the satisfaction you desire, or the sense of self-worth for which you are searching. The foundation that can provide these healthy feelings only comes about with the acceptance of whoever you learned to think you were during the first four or five years of your life. Using it as your base, whatever you later construct will be long lasting and emotionally constructive because it is supported by honest introspection, instead of lies or illusions.

It is ironic, but three or four of the internally angriest individuals I ever saw in therapy were people whose early memories of life consisted of pictures of perfection, harmony, unconditional love from mother, and a home environment that emulated *Little House on the Prairie.* None of them could accept the truth of their childhoods, I suspect because it was too painful for them to explore. Therefore, reactions of this type aren't always the result of a punitive or emotionally abusive childhood. Some of these individuals experience something insidiously more damaging. They are "chosen children," those whose parents needed to perceive them as perfect. Why? Because they are designated by their parents (usually their mother) as the savior, the person they can turn to, lean on, and expect to care for them in their old age. The result is a reversal of roles where the child, actually, or at least in his mind, assumes responsibility for the parent. In return, he or she is idealized. He can do no wrong and is showered with love. But the price for this status is enormous. The child is treated differently than his siblings, a fact which often contributes to considerable guilt. Moreover, he feels constant pressure to excel because he was selected to parent his own parents, a task at which he is destined to fail, eventually causing him to see himself as inadequate and insufficient. These feelings are further reinforced by his inability to live up to the idealized picture held by his parents. Later in life, he not only carries with him a sense of responsibility for his parents' disappointments, but also feelings of guilt for any wishes he has to estrange himself from his "loving relationship." In either case, whether he deceived himself regarding his past or feels a failure for not fulfilling his parents' needs, these men's and women's lives are filled with conflicting relationships: first, because no partner he finds can ever live up to the fantasy of love he created as a child; second, because he needs to be in total control of any relationship he forms to avoid the possibility of being hurt again; and third, because of the covert anger he feels over his inability to rid himself of his earlier feelings of obligation and responsibility and his continued need to please everyone he loves.

If you are one of these individuals, do not be disheartened. There is a solution. You need to learn to see yourself, accept yourself, and forgive yourself. Therapy can often help, but only if you view it as an activity designed to aid you to live your life differently. It does not cure you. It helps you to cope, not out of habit, not because of childish emotions and perceptions, but based on what you learn and then accept about yourself. Uncovering an accurate picture of yourself will permit you to see who you are, where you came from, and why you feel the way you do. You can then build upon that picture by becoming the person you intellectually want to be, in spite of your fears and feelings of insufficiency, inadequacy, or lack of worth. But even then, throughout life you will continue to be nagged by your inner child's feelings. They will cause you to doubt yourself and to question your decisions. At those times, you must have the courage and resolve to behave on the basis of what you have learned and know, as opposed to what you feel. Many of you will think "This is something I can do for myself." However, more often than not, if you haven't accomplished these steps by your late teens, they won't change by themselves. You will have to force yourself to reach out to someone who can guide you through the emotional maze that leads from your heart to your head. In most instances, that person will need to be a therapist.

However, whether or not you choose to seek, or are even in need of professional help, let me try, throughout the remainder of *You're Okay, But You Don't Know It* to provide an emotional road map of the actions you can take to make the rest of your life emotionally healthy, more rewarding, and far more positive.

CHAPTER FOURTEEN

DECIDE WHO THE PROBLEM IS

Thirty to forty years ago, dentists had the highest rate of suicides among professionals. For over a decade, they topped the list. It wasn't difficult to understand the reasons. For the most part, dentists were viewed as "rejects," particularly in their own eyes. During that period of time, dentists, generally speaking, were individuals whose primary career choice was medicine. Those who, for whatever reason, weren't accepted into a medical school often wound up going to dental school. The result was simple. Their sense of self-worth was severely damaged by the failure they felt they had experienced because they'd "settled." In their eyes, many considered themselves second-rate doctors whose prestige was considerably lower, whose income was far less, and whose sense of accomplishment and professional image were inferior to those of an M.D. Viewing themselves as failures contributed to their feeling trapped in a career they didn't respect or desire. For many of them, the image was intolerable, and the only way they knew to escape the trap they saw themselves destined to live in was to escape life by committing suicide.

During that period, some dentists tended to compete with and judge themselves in comparison with physicians. Consequently, they took no sense of worth from who they were, what they did, or their own accomplishments. Instead, they perceived themselves as inferior because their evaluation of self stemmed from an external comparison with others, as opposed to an internal appreciation for who and what they were.

Today, if you look at what has transpired in the world of dentistry, you will see tremendous change. The role that initially implied "reject" is now frequently sought after as a primary choice. However, the same growth isn't evident in medicine. It has become a business, governed, to a very great extent, by the insurance companies, Medicare, and the government. One doctor after another can be heard saying, "Practicing medicine isn't fun anymore. Our image has been tainted. Our capacity to make money has been diminished, and the freedom to practice medicine as we see fit is something of the past." Not so for dentistry. It has been much less constricted by the changes in the medical system. The practice of dentistry today is far more lucrative than years ago. Dentists not only have the opportunity to earn more, but to work a five-day week, to have few, if any, night calls, and to be booked up, in many instances, for months in advance. By virtue of that, practicing dentistry affords dentists a way of life that enables them to have more time for their spouses and children and that is far more compatible with maintaining a healthy family life.

I should add that dental schools have instituted far more classes in business management, running an office, billing, dealing with employees, and other pragmatic aspects of running a practice than any other professional training programs. Few, if any, of the medical schools, law schools, psychology, or social work programs even remotely consider courses of this nature. As a result, a dentist leaves school ready to start a practice and often feels more competent to run his practice professionally. It's apparent that dentists have found their own identity. They needn't and don't compete with physicians as they did in the past. And, surprise of all surprises, the rate of suicide in dentists has shrunk to normal levels.

The story and facts are interesting in themselves, but you might wonder, what does that have to do with you, with psychology, or with people in general? My answer: a great deal.

Let me explain: Many of you, in your own way, feel trapped by your lives, jobs, income level, and problems with your spouse, children, or marriage. The majority of you stay where you are, feel disgruntled, blame others for what has been dealt you by the fickle finger of fate, and either suffer in silence or constantly complain. In either case, you do nothing to alter your situation. Many of you believe that if you could only trade in what you have for something or someone new, you'd change for the positive, e.g., "If only I were a doctor instead of a dentist, I'd be okay." Others of you feel, "If I had more money, a bigger house, a better job, or a new sports car, I'd feel good about me." But, I strongly doubt it. It didn't work for dentists, and it's unlikely to work for you. What did work for them was altering their image of themselves.

There are many valuable lessons you can learn from the dentists' story. The three most important ones are:

1. *When you compete with anyone else, you never win.* The reason is that if you're competing to begin with, it's probably because you originally started out questioning your own adequacy. Even clearer is the fact that, no matter how much you excel or possess, you will eventually come across someone who is faster, stronger, smarter, or richer than you.

2. *Emulating a doctor, changing your children, or getting rid of your spouse will in no way alter you.* Recall lesson number one: you and your dissatisfaction were probably the problem to begin with, anyway. Therefore, you have only one alternative: you have to alter or take charge of you, because getting rid of you isn't a viable choice.

3. *The way to feel good about yourself doesn't come about as a result of how you stack up with others.* It comes about as a result of how you feel about yourself. Enhancing your self-image, your value of self, and your perception of self is the key to eventually feeling adequate about you. You might say that who you are is the ingredient you were originally given to work with. What you do with it is your responsibility.

So, if you're unhappy with who you are or where you are, before deciding to do anything rash—divorcing your spouse, quitting your job, or ending your life—look to your primary problem, i.e., you. It is only after learning to live comfortably with you that you can adequately judge whether you need to change where you are, who you are with, where you want to go, or if any change is needed at all.

Most of all, do something different. Don't stay in the rut you feel trapped by today or complain about it for the rest of your tomorrows.

This sounds all well and good, but doing it is an entirely different story. Even when you intellectually accept the fact that you have to discover who you are before you can be an emotionally healthy person, taking the steps in that direction isn't easy, primarily because, initially, the process requires that you fully accept responsibility for who, what, and why you are where you are and why you have the problems you're experiencing. Typically, your first inclination is to blame others or your circumstances, or attribute your situation to an emotional problem, DNA, or bad luck. On the surface, that may suffice, but, over time, it does nothing to resolve your problems or contribute to your emotional growth. That's because those things are only an explanation or an excuse, not the problem. Even if they were, you can't change them; you can only fix you by learning new coping techniques to help you deal with your world in a less overwhelming or stressful manner.

I have tried, on countless occasions, to convey two basic rules of thumb to every one of my patients, but most find them too large a pill to swallow. The first is, **you have to take responsibility for yourself.** Few people want the guilt attached to that step, because it implies that, if you got yourself where you are, you have the capability to get yourself out. That notion contributes to a good deal of fear and doubt. Think about it. Being a victim elicits sympathy, care, and support, whereas being responsible places the ball directly in your lap. It forces you to face your insecurities regarding how capable you are and to come to grips with your fears. It makes you face the fact that you aren't perfect or, even worse, might occasionally fail. In this instance, failure doesn't only mean not making the grade, or passing. It also means not living up to your own expectations.

The second rule of thumb is, **you can't change anyone else**. You can hear those words and repeat them, but, more often than not, you don't totally believe or act on them. Instead, you continue to get angry or resentful toward others because they behaved in ways that disappointed you or let you down. Your knee-jerk reaction is to accuse them of being unloving, egocentric, lacking in understanding, or unsympathetic, all because they disappointed you, triggered your insecurities, or couldn't read your mind. For example, your husband walks into the house to hear, "You should have thought, on the way home, that we needed bread and stopped at the store to buy a loaf. Remember last night, I said, 'We're almost out'?" Or, a wife is told, "I don't have a clean shirt to wear. You should have known that. I told you about the meeting I have today." Basically, you're angry because you want so much for that someone to meet and fulfill your emotional needs. It could be a person you're married to, a child whose love you desire, a boss whose acceptance and approval you're trying to get, or even an entire company whose respect you want and feel you deserve. When it isn't forthcoming, you feel cheated, unappreciated, and resentful, even though you know, intellectually, you can't change somebody else.

That's when I repeat, "Look at yourself."

"I know I should," said my patient Paul. "But first, let me tell you how Carole acted last night. Here we are, in the midst of a divorce. Finally, she's crying and emotionally upset. She's gotten past threatening me with lawyers and telling me she's going to take everything. She's seen you in therapy and she says, 'Why don't we try, one last time, not to find fault with each other, but to deal with each other out of the best of who we are? So, for a brief time, as an experiment, instead of you cutting me down or finding fault, try to be kind to me, and I promise to do the same.'

"Two days later, I said to her, 'You know that young lady that works in my office, the one from out of town, whose father just died? Well, she just got back and she has no place to go on Thanksgiving. Why don't we invite her to come over with our family? Also, there's a male intern who's from out of town. I'd like to invite him as well. They're two young people who are going to be alone, and Thanksgiving is a time to have people over.' I couldn't believe it, but she said yes. I began to think, maybe this will work. She seems genuinely different, accepting and willing to go along with a suggestion.

"The next morning, I woke up and, while eating breakfast, she said, 'You know, I thought about it last night. It's going to be uncomfortable. We're having so much stress right now. We really shouldn't interject two other people into our problems. It'll make them feel awkward. So, I've changed my mind.' I became furious. In my mind, I took the check mark off the positive side of my score sheet and put it on the negative side. My first thought was, 'I definitely need a divorce.'

"Then I recalled your words and thought, 'Paul, look at yourself before you explode.' Almost immediately, I heard another voice inside me saying, 'I don't have to look at me. I've got faults, I admit it. But look at her. She's a liar. She makes promises she doesn't keep. She doesn't care what I feel. She has no compassion for other people. She's totally egocentrically concerned with whether she's comfortable or not. I don't want to be married to somebody like that. "

My response to Paul was, "I'm not going to make this a political issue, but Newt Gingrich, a man I don't particularly admire, said something recently that made me realize he's quite a bright human being. I think it totally applies, so I'd like you to hear it. He said, 'I want to address the issue of health care: One, there are millions of people in this country who have no health care, who are dying needlessly. Two, these same people are bankrupting our whole medical system, because they're using the hospitals and the emergency rooms for their GPs (general practitioners) and causing the hospitals to run at a deficit. Many of these hospitals are having to close their doors. Three, medical insurance is being abused by people who are malingering and receiving needless treatment. Four, doctors are ordering more and more needless tests. They feel they have to in order to cover their bottoms because they're practicing in a very litigious society. Five, health insurance companies are making obscene profits. Most people are saying these issues are the problems. My answer,' Newt said, 'is they are not the problems, they're the facts. It is a fact the system is breaking down and going bankrupt. It is a fact that people are suffering and without insurance. It is a fact that doctors and patients misuse, violate, and abuse the systems we have. It is also factual that the insurance companies are making excessive profits. But none of those are the problem. The problem is, how do I, as a politician, deal with them?' "

Based on Newt's words, Paul ideally has to stop, think, and say, "The facts are that my wife is scared of having strangers in the house. Her fear caused her to forget the new policy. My wife is egocentrically involved because she is so insecure that she can't see anything outside of her own self-survival. Those are the facts. How I choose to deal with her is the problem."

And that's what I'm saying to you. How you deal with your "facts" is your problem. If you concentrate on all of the shortcomings in yourself, your wife, kids, parents, friends, and jobs, you never get to deal with the problem. You only get to criticize and find fault with the facts. That guarantees failure, because you can't change the facts. What you can change is the way you deal with them, which may eventually cause others to alter their behaviors or "facts."

So, in the future, when you look at your problems, I'd have you say, "The fact is, I'm in a relationship, or employed by a company, that isn't as considerate, empathetic, understanding, or supportive as I'd like. I have the right to end the relationship or quit the company. I also have a right to approach these facts in a different way, a way that is best for me." But, before you make the choice regarding how and what you should do, you must recognize that the decision needs to come from what you want, not the facts.

This orientation clearly reflects that you are the problem. But you can also change your behavior. Moreover, by doing so, you take responsibility for your failures and your successes. As a result, you don't "quit" because of the way you were treated or because the company sucks; you leave because you choose to do so. There is a significant difference between the two. In one instance, it suggests you had no choice. In the other, you control your own destiny. Because of that, you grow proud of how you behave, and you like the person you are.

CHAPTER FIFTEEN

LEARN TO LIVE WITH YOURSELF

Up until now, I've suggested that, no matter the nature of the conflicts, indecision, and difficulties you face, the problem is always you. You see, the people, situations, and stress you experience are only the facts. In the end, the problem always consists of how you react, cope, or deal with them.

That being the case, the first step you need to take toward altering the way you go about living your life has to be learning to live with yourself. Consequently, I'd have you ask yourself: Do you feel trapped or controlled by others? Are you emotionally dissatisfied with the way your life is going? Would you describe yourself as depressed, having a potential for excess anger, feeling emotionally needy, lonely, unfulfilled, insufficient, or immature? Have you experienced repeated problems in close relationships or in your marriages? If you can say yes to more than two of these questions, I would bet that you have never experienced unconditional care and nurturing from an emotionally healthy, loving mother. Nor did you learn to be a positive parent to yourself. Instead, you are probably still holding on, figuratively speaking, to an old neurotic, critical, manipulative, controlling, or unloving parent model—a parent you are still trying to please or change. But it is time to recognize that neither of these events is very likely to occur. It is you who must change, and you whom you must please, or else you will continue to live your life feeling discontent, spinning your emotional wheels, and going nowhere.

The only viable alternative you have is to learn to live effectively with yourself by becoming the positive, healthy parent to yourself that you wish your actual parents could have been. With each step you take in that direction, you will come to recognize that you are able to stand independently on your own two feet. It isn't that you will no longer experience anxiety, fear, or stress. Those feelings are normal emotions that accompany all new challenges and emotional growth. It's just that those feelings won't have the power they previously had. They won't paralyze you, emotionally or physically, or cause you to feel helpless. Believe it or not, you'll come to welcome them, because they indicate you're growing. Nor will you desperately need someone to share your life with. You may want someone, but you won't require a friend, parent, spouse, or employer to serve as your surrogate parent or caretaker. You will curtail your need to neurotically lean on others. You will stop prostituting yourself emotionally in order to hold on to someone whose love isn't there or isn't obtainable. All of this will come about when you begin to take control of your own life and learn to live with yourself and your inner child.

From that moment on, casual words, criticisms, and even biting comments, accurate or not, will no longer serve to push your buttons to the point that you're devastated or totally paralyzed emotionally. If they do, your reactions will not be excessive. As a result, you will cease having to hide behind flamboyant exaggerations of your accomplishments, passive-aggressive behavior, vitriolic or hostile retaliation, hysterical tirades, prolonged periods of pouting and resentment, days of silent withdrawal, self-pity, or excessive attempts to purchase acceptance.

I know that these words sound like an advertisement for a magic elixir that will cure all that ails you. Therefore, let me modify them by saying that it isn't that you will no longer hurt or feel the sting of real, implied, or perceived rebukes or rejections. Instead, it is a case of being far less emotionally dependent on others. Thus, your reactions, when they occur, will stem only from the hurt attributable to the remarks themselves. They will not include the overwhelming emotional fear associated with your dread of disapproval or rejection—feelings typically experienced by emotionally dependent children. At the same time, when you are finally able to become a positive parent to yourself, your internal conflicts and anxieties will also improve. Specifically, your super-sensitivity will be mitigated and the intensity of your dread of rejection, imperfection, or failure will radically diminish. Consequently, your fear of expressing yourself openly and sharing your true feelings and opinions will be equally lessened. In the process of learning to live positively with yourself, you will become more open, less emotionally brittle, and have less need to control others. All because you have a new parent—one you can trust and lean on and with whom you can honestly share your emotional upsets. The development of this new state of emotional peace within you mitigates your fears of the opinions and reactions of others and, therefore, lessens your need to control, criticize, or defend yourself from rejection or disapproval.

It stands to reason that, at that point, your relations with others should also improve dramatically. With the absence of your former need to impress, your hostile exterior, your need to control, or your blatant displays of emotional neediness and dependence, others will no longer want to avoid you or feel they have to protect themselves from you—some of which may stem from their own feelings of inadequacy and dependence. You see, everyone else, just like you, also harbors a wounded little child inside. Because of that, they are prone to avoid any interaction or situation you may create that might cause them to look into an emotional mirror. In a strange manner of speaking, it explains why, when you can't stand to look at someone, it's usually because you are really looking at yourself.

Now for the bad news. It isn't easy to become a parent to yourself. But it is necessary if you ever want to feel okay. Generally speaking, it is the main step required in the process of living effectively with you. Most of you are apt to say "That's no problem, I live with me every day." And I would say, "Quite the contrary. That's the whole problem."

When I first started out as a therapist, many of my patients would say, during their first or second visit, "I'm here to find myself." At that time, I had difficulty comprehending what they meant. Of course you know yourself; we all know ourselves. You are who you are. Unfortunately, back then I didn't know about icebergs and how little of their entity floats on the surface. I wasn't emotionally aware or fully able to accept the notion that so very much of our behavior is truly unconscious. Nor did I recognize how absolutely powerful, controlling, and designing the unconscious can be. Now I know differently. I know that every one of us has to find himself or herself. That every one of us is at least two people: the person above the surface—your intellectual adult, the person that you generally know—and the sensitive, hurting, emotional little kid who resides below the surface. He may be hidden from sight, but he is omnipresent, ready at a moment's notice to spring to the surface, to protect you from perceived hurt, criticism, or rejection. Even more, he will be there throughout your life. During that time, he will continue to need acceptance and understanding, the emotions he very likely never received during his youth, or experienced too little of, too late. Unfortunately, he will not always be responsive to people who reach out and try to love him. Instead, to the exact same degree as he was hurt or disappointed early in his life, he will doubt their actions, questions their motives, and find it difficult to trust loving relationships. It is only when he feels someone really knows him for who he is and still loves him that he may be willing to lower his guard and to cautiously accept their affections. That, however, can only occur after he is able to honestly see himself for who he is and then has the courage to risk being sufficiently vulnerable to share that person with someone whose love he desires.

There is one major stumbling block. Few emotionally wounded individuals ever honestly look beneath their surface, and they certainly don't invite others to do so. Almost every individual who has ever seen me in therapy has come in blaming "my mother," "my father," "my husband," "my wife," or "my boss." Rarely do they ever come in and say, "The problem is me, myself, and I." Yet I fully believe that only after you learn to see and accept yourself as you are will you be able to deal effectively with yourself, your world, your friends, and your lovers.

Remember: healthy relationships can only come about as a result of the interactions of healthy people. Unfortunately, most individuals, no matter how successful they are outwardly, are lacking in inner emotional health. This statement can best be understood by describing to you three patients I've seen in therapy.

Andrea is a physician. She is a skilled professional with a wonderful reputation. In addition to that, she is an attractive single mother who was involved in a four-and-a-half-year relationship with the same man. During that time, he traveled with her and periodically stayed in her home with her children for days at a time. To the casual observer, their relationship could have been described as "loving and close." There was one problem. She had four or five major grievances against him—none of which she verbalized. She kept them alive in her mind and her thoughts, but she never conveyed them to him. Even more, she set no overt limits or boundaries for herself or for him. Consequently, she was inwardly angry with him for trespassing beyond boundaries he knew nothing about and was furious with herself for lacking the backbone to tell him. It is no wonder that he was always caught off guard when, for no apparent reason, she would become hysterical and lash out with rage and fury. Nor was it surprising that, even when she asked about marriage, he would reply, "There are far too many things that we need to work out. Let's wait a little longer."

Ironically, if you were to observe Andrea in her office, this pattern of behavior would never occur. There, she was the quintessential professional. If there was a mistake on the part of any of her employees, she provided immediate feedback. She told others what she thought, what she wanted, and what she needed. Rules and limits were defined specifically and strictly enforced. Emotional outbursts were absent and resentments were few and far between. Now, I ask you, what was going on? Don't bother to answer. It's a rhetorical question. Andrea is two people: a very successful adult at the office and an emotional child at home.

Paul is a forty-four-year-old entrepreneur who is extremely successful, financially. At the same time, he is a workaholic. If you met him, you would find him to be one of the sweetest men you have ever had the pleasure to meet. All of his friends say that to know him is to love him. But let me relate an incident that took place between Paul and his wife. To set the stage, I should add that they recently had a baby. This is the second marriage for both. Paul has already raised his children, but his present wife had no children by her first marriage. When they married, Paul thought they would live their lives happily ever after, traveling and enjoying the fruits of his labor. However, that wasn't to be the case. A year after they married, "her biological clock began ticking," and she said, "I want a child." After considerable discussion, he agreed, albeit reluctantly. That child was born approximately six weeks prior to this incident.

"Mr. Nice Guy" came home an hour late. He walked into the kitchen, got a plate of food that was being kept warm on the stove for him, and, as he did, he heard his wife say, "Would you please take the garbage out? It's full." He proceeded to go to the garbage can. Then, without warning, he started tossing things onto the floor. Garbage landed over the entire room. A gallon-sized milk container flew through the air. Fortunately, it was empty. Boxes, orange peels, and several dirty diapers littered the floor. When he was finished, he proceeded to verbally chastise her. "If you're going to fill a garbage can, for crying out loud, don't fill it up so high I can't close it. Can't you do anything right?" Then "Mr. Nice Guy" went into a ten-minute tirade, adding one criticism after another. But it didn't end there. Several days later, he came home to find her on the telephone, engaged in a conversation with a friend about the baby. After (he said) fifteen minutes (she said five), he screamed "Get off the goddamn phone and see if you can do a little something in the kitchen so we can eat tonight." My second rhetorical question: Why? His behavior was totally inconsistent with the outward image he portrayed to the world. However, if she had communicated with his previous wife, she would have known that it was not entirely new.

The third example deals with Mark, a patient who in his youth was an All-American college football player. He is now a fifty-eight-year-old successful businessman who owns a large national company. On this particular occasion, he and his wife were going to a homecoming game at his alma mater. Several days earlier, he informed her that a very important client of his had called and asked them to go out to his new home on a ranch close to the town where the game was being played. Driving to the game, he once again said, "Remember, after the game, we're going out to visit with my client." Prior to the game, they went to visit their son, who attended the same university. Later, they all went to brunch. It was still early for the game, and his wife decided to spend some of the free time working with their son on his new apartment. In the meantime, Mark took his son's car out, had it washed and detailed, filled it with gas, and returned to the apartment to find his wife and son still actively involved with their project. Seeing that he wasn't particularly needed, he went to his car, took one of his briefcases from the trunk, and sat outside doing some of the work he regularly carries with him. This was not unusual for him. It was totally characteristic of the way he had lived his life for the thirty-two years since their marriage. He always carried several briefcases in his trunk. It served as a way of keeping him occupied, added to his feeling of accomplishment, and kept his mind off things he chose not to handle.

At about 1:30, they all went to the game. Afterward, his wife said there were "just a few things" that need finishing up in the apartment, and did he mind if she completed them? He shook his head no, took out another briefcase, and went to work while she went to complete the project. Two hours or more later, she came out. By that time, he felt it was far too late to go out to his client's home. It was past dinnertime, and it would be too dark to see the property. As a result, without uttering a word, he headed back home. However, during the next two-and-a-half hours, his wife heard plenty: how inconsiderate she was, what a poor wife she was, how he didn't matter to her, and how her son was more important to her than he was.

In truth, there was probably considerable credence to his statements. At the same time, it was an old argument, one that had persisted over the years and had been repeated on many occasions. If you were to examine their marriage, you would see that she had spent thirty-two years primarily involved with their children. He had spent thirty-two years involved with his business and his briefcases. On that particular day, he spent two to three hours in the car, doing his work, and building up his anger. When she was finally able to get a word in, she said, "Why didn't you come in and remind me?" That unleashed a volcanic explosion. He screamed, "That's the point. If I have to come in and remind you, I'd be begging you to come. Why should I do that?" His statement said it all. "I'm not a priority. I don't count. I really don't matter to you. You don't love me. What you love is the kids. All I am is a checkbook to all of you." There it was. He had set up the test, and she had failed. Now, do you think he would have behaved that way with any one of the almost one hundred employees who worked for him? The answer is absolutely not. At the same time, it is equally important to ask, would her memory have been quite as faulty if one of her children had made a similar request? I strongly doubt it. At this time, however, neither of these assumptions is the real issue.

The relevant question is, why was there such a great incongruity between the behavior demonstrated by these three patients in their most meaningful relationships, as opposed to the behavior they would have undoubtedly demonstrated professionally, or with their children and friends? Before answering that question, I think it is important to say that these three patients aren't alone. They are only a small representation of a problem that exists in almost every human being. I suspect that most of you can readily think of things that you may have done or said that, in retrospect, caused you to look at yourself and say, "I can't believe I said that. What in the world made me act that way? I must have been crazy to behave in that fashion." As embarrassing as it may be, I must admit that, on too many occasions, I have also acted in ways that, if a patient had acted similarly, I would have climbed all over his or her case. You might ask, "How can that be? You know better." I most certainly do, but so do Andrea, Paul, Mark, and you. Yet I feel safe saying that everyone is capable of this same type of incongruent behavior. You, Andrea, Paul, and Mark are equally likely to act in ways that are totally inconsistent with what any one of you wants to be and what you know. Therefore, the question you need to ask yourself is, "Why?" Or perhaps, more specifically on those occasions, "Which one of me is responsible for my action, my emotional kid or my intellectual adult?"

The answer is immediately apparent. There is no doubt that whenever you overreact in what might be viewed as a "crazy" manner, you do so because of your emotions, not your intellect. That doesn't excuse your actions or take you off the hook. It only helps you to begin to understand that each of us is basically two people, both of whom reside in one body, ours. One exists from the tip of our chin to the top of our head. He or she is an intellectually bright person who, from approximately age four up, constantly grows by virtue of every experience and relationship, whether it result in failure or success. He/she learns from every book or magazine we read, every movie and TV program we watch, and every interaction we experience. At the same time, there is another person in us. He or she resides somewhere between the tip of our chin and the end of our toes. That person is a totally emotional human being. He or she is the sum total of all the emotions and feelings we experienced from conception to the time we reached approximately four or five years old. By six, he/she is as mature as he/she will be for the rest of his/her life.

I know that it's hard to believe, but please try to remember my earlier statements and give consideration to the possibility that everything you ever emotionally learned about loving, about your sense of self-worth, about how to get love and how to give love, you learned before you had the ability, neurologically, to verbalize, integrate, synthesize, or conceptualize intellectually. It is a form of learning I call emotional or kinesthetic learning. Remember my examples about sticking your chubby little fingers in the light socket or touching the hot stove? In both instances, it was a case of one-shot learning. In a similar fashion, as a very young infant, you hypothetically learned that: 1) "before I utter a peep, Mother will be by my side"; 2) another infant learned, "Mom doesn't even come when I cry"; 3) still another learned, "If I goo and coo and I'm a good little boy or girl, Mom will be there"; And 4) yet another learned, "She doesn't come unless I'm sick."

Others of you discovered that the way to get love, i.e., garner attention, was to break something, have an accident, or be a problem. Years later, as teenagers, young adults, and even after marriage, these same infants became: 1) people of entitlement; 2) emotionally needy, inadequate-feeling adults; 3) "good guys"; 4) hypochondriacal kids, students, husbands, or wives; or 5) constant screw-ups.

This is, of course, a simplistic explanation, but, I promise you, it's fundamentally accurate.

None of the above occurred by accident. These individuals learned to play their roles long before their verbal or cognitive development could neurologically account for it. Some infants learned that, if it took, figuratively speaking, "two pounds" of energy to get Mother's love, years later, they unconsciously feel they have to expend a similar amount to get love from a spouse. Conversely, some individuals were showered with affection without having to put out any effort at all. The messages these two infants gleaned from their parental experiences were as dissimilar as the adults that resulted from them. One group of infants grew up to be individuals who constantly put out energy, trying desperately to obtain the love that they were deprived of in childhood. The other group grew up to be individuals who expect to receive everything and are angry when others don't come at their beck and call. At the same time, they feel little or no obligation to give anything in return.

There are a myriad of additional examples I could provide but, suffice it to say, it is evident that each of you are two persons: one emotional, the other intellectual. One person reacts and feels in accordance with the early emotional programming you experienced. The other is an individual who is totally intellectually driven. The end result is a constant power struggle between the two. Each one competes with the other in order to determine who will be in control of you at any given time. It is the source of the conflicts that most people engage in throughout their lives. It is also one of the major reasons that many smart people do dumb things. Try to look at it this way: if I asked a series of questions, such as "Should you have affairs? Should you get mad and physically hit someone? Should you use abusive language? Is stealing acceptable? Is lying justifiable?" every one of you knows the appropriate answer to these questions. You would all say the same thing: "Of course not." You're aware of what is socially and politically proper, but you all too frequently fail to behave that way. More specifically, what if I asked the following: "Should you speak up if you're dissatisfied with the way you're being treated by someone? Is it healthy to hold on to anger, to pout, bear a grudge, and build up resentment? Is it appropriate to toss garbage on the floor and embarrass your wife while she's on the phone?" it's a no-brainer. My patients, the doctor, the businessman, and the ex-football player, intellectually know better. But if you're two people, your behavior can't help but stem, at least on occasion, from the emotional reaction of a four- to six-year-old who has taken charge of you.

It's no wonder, then, that in retrospect some of your decisions and knee-jerk reactions seem childish and ill-conceived, as opposed to the actions you might have displayed had you behaved as an intellectual adult who was in control of his inner child's emotions. In that instance, you would recognize and forgive the child for his knee-jerk reaction, understand and accept his emotions, but not allow him to behave in accordance with them. The interaction might consist of saying, "I know you're frightened of being rejected or abandoned emotionally, but you need to speak out. Don't fight or take flight. Your position may be incorrect, but your feelings are there, nonetheless. You need to share them and let your boss, parent, spouse, or friend know where you're coming from. Whatever their reaction is, positive or negative, know that I'll be there for you and we'll make it together."

Let me state that I fully believe that everyone is two people. I know for certain that I am. All I have to do is go through a breakfast buffet line to reconfirm that notion. I can picture it now. There are the waffles, pancakes, pastries, and cinnamon buns, and my adult is saying, "No, you don't need any of that. You have to stay on your diet. You have to cut the carbohydrates." My kid says, "Come on. You can cut down at lunch, or eat a smaller portion. Then again, you don't have to eat all of it; you can just enjoy a couple of bites." In the space of thirty seconds, a half-hour debate takes place inside me over a cinnamon bun. This is only one example of countless other battles that can occur between my child, who behaves solely on the basis of emotions he learned early in life, and my adult, who intellectually knows right from wrong, good from bad, and appropriate from inappropriate. It seems that the two are always at odds and engaged in a constant struggle to see who will control me. Unfortunately, that little kid wins on far too many occasions. I suspect not only in me, but in many of you.

The only solution is for the two to come to peace with one another—to respect, value, and love each other, and to learn to work together, in order to give you the permission to be who you are and steer you in a direction that will help you to more easily be the person you intellectually want to be. However, before these two individuals can reconcile their differences and integrate their efforts, you must first come to accept that there really are two of you.

In therapy, you learn that, no matter how well you get, the little kid never changes; you just learn to see him and recognize his needs more clearly. But seeing enables you to forgive his shortcomings and still deal with him in a loving manner. When this comes about, there is an integration of the child and the adult inside you that, figuratively speaking, makes you a whole person. Sadly, few people achieve that state. Instead, you exist from one power struggle to another, all the while blaming the world and the people around you for your problems, rather than facing the conflict within you.

I could go on at length regarding the two people inside you, but the primary message I dearly would like to convey is that I view the concept of the inner child as an invaluable tool that can help you to cope better with the emotional problems within you, as well as in your relationships. This concept isn't new, but I feel it has never been taken seriously enough. Years ago, Robert Louis Stevenson had the keen insight to communicate the same thoughts, long before psychologists proposed them. Accordingly, I'd like to quote his poem "My Shadow," which you may recall from your childhood.

My Shadow
By Robert Louis Stevenson

I have a little shadow that goes in and out with me,
And what can be the use of him is more than I can see.
He is very, very like me from the heels up to the head;
And I see him jump before me, when I jump into my bed.
The funniest thing about him is the way he likes to grow
Not at all like proper children, which is always very slow;
For he sometimes shoots up taller like an India-rubber ball,
And he sometimes gets so little that there's none of him at all.
He hasn't got a notion of how children ought to play,
And can only make a fool of me in every sort of way.
He stays so close behind me, he's a coward you can see;
I'd think shame to stick to nursie as that shadow sticks to me!
One morning, very early, before the sun was up,
I rose and found the shining dew on every buttercup;
But my lazy little shadow, like an errant sleepy-head,
Had stayed at home behind me and was fast asleep in bed.

It's not necessarily a great piece of literature, but for me it's profound and makes tremendous sense. If you think of that shadow as your little child, Stevenson could have been saying, "He's very much like me, in every sort of way. Sometimes, he's bigger than life, controls me, governs me, and causes me to smoke, drink, eat, to do all kinds of things that I might not otherwise do at all. But when he's absent and your head controls your actions, most of you experience little trouble or internal conflict. It's only when the shadow emerges that the child makes a fool of you, in many sorts of ways." He really is a coward, because he can't face himself. He blames others, rationalizes, excuses, and accepts behavior and thoughts that are intellectually unacceptable. However, in the mornings before the sun is up, you are able to see with joy the dew shining on every buttercup. It makes me think that what each of you has to do is accept your errant little child, keep him peacefully in bed, and put him in his proper perspective so he doesn't control your head. In the chapters to come, I will give you the tools to do so.

In my mind, the poem is proof positive that you needn't be a psychiatrist, psychologist, or social worker to recognize what's going on inside you. You just have to be a human being who is willing to see your shadow, appreciate your childish behavior, attitude, and thoughts, and accept them.

Let me leave you with this thought. The contradictions, conflicts, and tug of war between your impulses and what you know is best for you aren't unique. They're present in every one of us. Consequently, you needn't think ill of yourself because of them. What you must do, instead, is grow up before you grow old, by taking control of you and allowing your adult to interact with your kid. Together, they can control what you do, say, think, and feel.

CHAPTER SIXTEEN

YOUR INNER CRITIC
VERSUS YOUR INNER CHILD

I thought I had said just about everything I had to say about the inner child, the adult, and the need to integrate the two. At least until Bart came for his last appointment.

Bart is an individual I have seen for quite some time, more recently on a monthly basis, and I view him as a post-doctoral therapy patient. He's very bright, introspectively aware, honest with himself, and willing to consider new concepts that might better enable him to cope in the world. Thus, the session proved to be somewhat of a surprise to me. Let me explain. We were talking about his concern over the birth of his first child, the fact that his wife would shortly have to return to her job as her maternity leave was about to end, and that he was happy because the amount of money that they had heretofore been able to sock away for investments and retirement had been depleted since the arrival of their child. Additionally, he expressed concern over his job, what the future involved in terms of his career, and whether, up to this point in his life—the ripe old age of forty-two—he had accomplished anything of significance.

I noted that his concerns seemed unrealistic in a sense, manufactured, and that, from my perspective, they were issues he needed to cope with. He had just bought a new home. They hadn't lost any money during her maternity leave since her company had continued paying her salary. He had just received a large bonus from his employer, along with a note stating how satisfied the company was with him. Their baby was a healthy, wonderful child, who was progressing quite well medically, physically, and emotionally. If anything, there were many facts for him to be happy about. At the same time, I granted that his feelings were real and suggested there might be another reason for his concerns, other than the problems he verbalized. I also suggested that he try to view his situation through the eyes of his inner child—that, since reality played no part in his worries, his emotions had to be the source of his stress and anxiety. It was then that he explained.

"Dr. Ed, I've bought into almost everything that therapy has suggested. But your concept of the inner child is something I could never accept. I understand intellectually what you're saying. But I don't believe that I'm walking through life with a little insecure, frightened, wounded child inside. If there is another person in there, it's someone I prefer to call 'my inner critic.' He pretty much sets me straight, tells me when I'm off the beaten track, doing wrong, having crazy thoughts, not achieving, falling short of my goals, or not putting out enough energy and effort. He's what spurs me on. And I must admit that, to my mind's eye, he also causes me to work harder, to strive for higher goals, and is the basis for much of the success that you're claiming I've achieved. But lately I haven't felt good about me and, in my opinion, having a crippled, wounded little kid inside me would only make me feel worse."

My response was, "You're probably right. If you were to accept my notion that there is a little child inside who is weak, lacking, insecure, fearful, or predisposed to demonstrate impulsive, non-constructive behavior reflective of a five- or six-year-old, you would feel badly, but only for a little while."

The reason you need to recognize this little kid who, I believe, exists inside all of us is to enable you to attribute your childish actions, behaviors, thoughts, concerns, and fears to that kid instead of your entire person. Your adult knows right from wrong, good from bad, appropriate from inappropriate, and excessive from insufficient. Those are concepts your adult learned, but not your little kid. As a result, you occasionally demonstrate actions that are solely motivated by the five- or six-year-old inside you. It's also the reason you sometimes ask yourself, "Why in the world did I say or do that? Where was my head? I can't believe that came from me. I'd never say something like that if I were consciously aware of what I was doing." My response is, of course not. But you weren't aware. It was your little kid who slipped out and impulsively, without any thought of the consequences, hurts, or effects of your actions, reacted inappropriately and demonstrated another side of you. The beauty of this paradigm is that, when you can accept and own that little kid, your adult is better able to take the necessary steps to cope with his or her behavior. The coping process involves recognizing this, intro-spectively looking at yourself, and owning your behavior. No excuses, no justifications, no pointing the finger at someone else, just saying, "Wow, did I show my bottom," then accept-ing your kid with all his warts, bumps, scars, wounds, short-comings, excesses, fears, and threats. Once you accept him or her, you're in a position to forgive his or her actions. This isn't a cheap emotional escape. Quite the contrary, it's a very expensive process emotionally, because it doesn't make you proud, cause you to feel free of responsibility, or eliminate guilt. Instead, it helps you to own your actions, then accept and forgive them. That's the reason I so frequently say that the better you get, the worse you feel. But it's a different kind of worse. It's the feelings that go along with accepting your-self and honestly saying to others, "This is me. I'm sorry if I hurt or offended you or anyone else. I take responsibility for my actions. I only ask you to understand that it resulted from the emotions of my five- or six-year-old and that it's apparent I wasn't on top of myself today." It's a grown-up reaction. It's also behavior that you can be proud of and others can accept.

Once you're able to take those steps, you come to a point where you can laugh at your little kid; you can look at him from a distance with humor and love him for who he is. If you have children, you've seen them figuratively put their feet in their mouths, say things, do things, and suddenly go "oops," and you have to laugh at them. Well, it's the same in dealing with yourself. Your laughter is a reflection of your forgiveness and acceptance of the little kid inside. All of which leads to the final step, being able to share your adult and child, the good, the bad, and, sometimes, even the ugly, with those who are meaningful to you.

Conversely, if who you carry around is a constant critic, he or she may point you in the right directions, but a critic does what a critic is—he criticizes and finds fault. Even if the purpose is to help elevate you, his or her voice is, in varying degrees, always critical, demeaning, punitive, or depreciatory. I should note that, on occasion, I've heard that voice in me. It's the one that causes me to look at myself and say, "You're a loser. I can't stand you," or, "You'll never be good enough." But that isn't the way I want to live life. I want to be able to say to my little kid, "You're only five years old and I love you, but, for now, I'm going to put you in time out." When my adult is able to do that, I'm able to live peacefully with myself. The surprising result is that the better I live with me, the less difficulty I have living with others.

It's my belief that no one needs an inner critic. Your little kid can be hard enough on you. **What your kid needs is a parent who will love, nurture, and accept him. One who can say, "You're not perfect. In fact, you're imperfect, but you're okay and you're worth loving. If or when you don't believe it, come to me. I'll be there to hold your hand and comfort you."** Each of you has a little kid who is desperately in need of hearing those words, having boundaries and limits set for him, and knowing that he is accepted and loved. Your goal should be to become a nurturing parent to that child.

CHAPTER SEVENTEEN

DISCOVER YOUR LUCAP

There truly is a way to learn to live with, accept, and love yourself. **The first step** is to recognize that you have a little kid inside you who has no patience, acts impulsively, and wants immediate gratification and pleasure. Some of the time, his/her voice tells you, "Have fun and enjoy, because life is too short to worry. Forget the consequences." Other times, the kid is afraid, feels lonely, unloved, and inadequate, and prevents you from recognizing you worth, appreciating your capabilities, taking risks, or speaking out. You cannot change that voice, or the message it delivers. You will have to live with him or her for the rest of your life. In most cases, your kid is a wounded child whose actions and thoughts stem from the emotional input he or she received during the first five years of your life. He isn't crazy, but the early input he received may have been. His reactions and feelings are understandable and predictable, based on his early childhood. But they are often erroneous, ill conceived, and impulsive. Thus, they contribute to you making poor decisions, reacting inappropriately, or behaving in self-destructive manners. To understand why, all you need do is recall the old computer saying, "Garbage in, garbage out."

The second step requires that you be able to determine which "you" is in control at any one time. For example, if I had been in the car with my patient Mark and had asked, "Do you believe that sitting here building up resentment over your wife's involvement with your son's dorm room is going to help your marriage? Do you believe your behavior is going to improve the way you feel toward your wife?" He would have known the appropriate answer, as would every one of you. At the same time, there probably isn't one of you that hasn't acted in a similar manner. Think about it. Your partner wants to go to a party that you're both invited to. You don't want to go, but you finally agree. Then, you say or think, "Okay, I'll go. Just get off my back." Inside, however, a little voice says, "But I'll get my pound of flesh." Which "I" wants to get the flesh, the kid or the adult? Without a doubt, the kid is the guilty party. That's how easy it is for you to begin to differentiate between the two of you.

Third, you might assume that as you grow older and wiser, or more mature, your child grows as well. But that isn't the case. As you grow older, your behavior may be tempered, but that's probably because you've either learned to govern yourself emotionally or have resigned yourself to stop fighting and accept life the way it is. But, no matter how much age or success you achieve or accomplish, it makes no impression on your little kid. I can give you a *curriculum vitae* that lists five or six pages of speeches I have given and tell you about the national TV programs I've been on over the years. I can say that I've had my own radio talk show, appeared as a regular for eight years on a morning talk show on the Houston, Texas, NBC station, written several books, and had a successful private practice that spans almost fifty years. I can even tell that to myself. But the emotional little kid inside me can, on occasion, still feel as inadequate and insufficient as he did seventy years ago. He hasn't changed and never will. Nor will your little kid. What you were emotionally exposed to the first four or five years of your life will stick with you the rest of your life. All the therapy in the world won't change that, even if you are seeing the best therapist in the world.

The fourth step requires you to recognize what your little kid needed to help him cope better today was an emotionally healthy parent who could have understood, cared, and accepted him better when he was a small child. Therein lies the problem. Most of you had flawed parents. You may not like that thought, but I'm a parent, and I sadly admit I was a flawed one, no different from most of you. Over the years, I have come to the conclusion that the definition of "parent" should be "failure," and that the degree of success your children achieve is not determined by how successful you were, but how few mistakes you made.

The fifth step is to recognize that all of that was yesterday and you can't change your past. So, if you are going to assume responsibility and take care of your life from here on out, you need to recognize that your little kid will always feel flawed, insufficient, inadequate, unloved, or whatever non-constructive feelings he absorbed in childhood. The problem is that most of you do you develop extremely successful coping techniques that help you avoid looking at your kid's feelings. These techniques, such as rationalization, projection, intellectualization, anger, depression, etc., are effective short term. Long term, they become problems themselves. But if you're willing to face the music, and to look inside yourself, you will be able to get in touch with your little kid, who desperately needs someone to recognize him for who he is and to love, support, and understand him in spite of his fears and feelings of insufficiency.

Then you will have to give thought to flicking your original parent off your shoulder. The parent who, from birth, has been whispering in your ear messages, such as "Do more if you want more love," "Brush your teeth if you want to be accepted," "Be a good boy/girl if you want approval," "Don't speak up or show anger if you want to be liked," "Do your studies," "Don't show emotions," "Be polite," "Don't be selfish," etc., etc., etc. That parent needs to be replaced by a new, healthier parent who can give your kid the emotional support and love he needs. In the process of growing up, your actual parent tends to disappear as a person, and in his or her place is a myriad of dos and don'ts that some of you are charitable enough to view as constructive forms of criticism. But what your little kid really needed from birth to age five was a parent who was insightful and strong enough to say, when the occasion warranted, "For crying out loud, you don't have to throw garbage on the floor. It isn't something you'd do normally, so I know something's hurting and troubling you. Please let me help, but know that your behavior is not acceptable, so it has to stop. But if you will take the time to look inside and tell me what's troubling you, I will try to listen very hard." A parent capable of that is one who loves, sets limits, and supports the child or children she's brought into the world. Unfortunately, there are very few of them.

Do I need to tell you that the patient who threw the garbage on the floor, "Mr. Nice Guy," was unconsciously jealous of the baby that came into his life? That he never felt loved as a child? He never felt that anyone cared just for him, except when he married his present wife. It was then that he finally found the person whose love he needed. But, for him, it was short lived. Their baby came into the world, and he felt as though he lost her. He didn't realize it, because he didn't have a healthy parent on his shoulder who could whisper, "It's all right to be jealous. It's a normal emotion. It doesn't make you weak or bad, and you won't be punished for feeling that way. Instead, tell your wife how you feel and what you need. Explain that you're hurting. You may be pleasantly surprised that she can understand. You see, she may have enough love in her to satisfy both the baby and you."

Few of you have a parent like that on your shoulder, but all of you need one. Therefore, what I would encourage every one of you to do is create a new parent—one who is loving, understanding, caring, and accepting. I know I've said it before, but I can't stress the fact enough that you can't change what you feel. Your little kid is all he or she will ever be. He's there, like a scar or tattoo. You can't alter that. But you can change the parent that you carry on your shoulder.

You can give yourself a new, healthy parent. At this juncture, you might say, "I don't know how to go about doing that." My answer is that you do, but you don't know that you do. Try to look at it this way: Let's say that I get a brand new car and I drive it for about two weeks. One day, as I'm backing into a tight spot in the garage, I wind up scraping the whole side on the garage door frame. I become furious at myself. A voice inside me says, "How in the devil could you do that? Why weren't you more careful? You're so damn clumsy! What's wrong with you, anyway?" At the same time, if my wife, a friend, or a patient had done the same thing, I would have said, "Don't sweat it. You can fix it. No one need ever know. Think about it this way—you got the first scratch, it's over, it's done with, you don't have to worry about it anymore." But, once again, my duplicitous thoughts raise their ugly head because I'm not that benevolent with myself. The parent on my shoulder, the voice I've heard since childhood, comes from a very critical person who felt so poorly about herself that she could ill afford to fail or make a mistake. One who couldn't help me because she had her own problems. She wasn't aware that people can and do make mistakes or fail and are still worthy of love. But, no matter the reason, the fact remains that her voice is still there in me. It doesn't go away because it was unconsciously imprinted in my hard drive by age four or five. In effect, I have, figuratively speaking, become my own mother.

The sixth step is to emotionally rid yourself of that parent and find a new one. You need to find a LUCAP: a loving, understanding, caring, accepting parent. Where can you find him or her? It's simple. She or he is the same one that's there inside you for your family and friends when they scratch their cars or behave in ways you would drastically chastise yourself for. Until now, your LUCAP was only available to others. You now have to make him or her available to you.

One telltale example, with regard to the capacity all of us possess to be that nurturing parent, can be seen in the behavior of Rick, a patient whose wife was told, completely unexpectedly, that her routine mammogram strongly indicated there was a problem. During the week between the time she received the news and the time she could get a second opinion, my patient discovered that he could be a better husband, a more sensitive individual, a less reactive person, and a human being who behaved consciously with concern, care, and compassion. It wasn't that these emotions were absent or unavailable prior to the abnormal mammogram. Rather, they were obscured by his early feelings of emotional insecurity, fears of rejection, and knee-jerk reaction to defend himself from criticism, whether real or falsely perceived. His reactive nature was, for the most part, in no way rational or intellectually motivated. It was, instead, evidence of his little child inside, who didn't feel okay, was quick to feel hurt or criticized, and caused him to constantly search for validation of his own worth. As a result, his behavior was typically defensive, occasionally offensive, and always reactive in nature. Although he intellectually recognized that there was little factual basis to his reactions, his emotions tended to override and suppress his good common sense. From a psychological point of view, it is understandable that he may go through his entire life searching for the emotional security he needs and desires. The sad reality is, however, that others will not always be there to agree with, support, or care for him. Thus, he needed to find a way to fill the emotional hole inside him, particularly when others fail to meet his emotional needs, are insensitive, or are unaware they need meeting. Once again, to do so necessitates that he become a loving, understanding, caring, accepting parent (a LUCAP) to himself.

Developing a LUCAP is an essential step toward your future emotional growth and will benefit you throughout the rest of your life. Similar to Rick, you have one in you, but too often it takes a bad mammogram, a tragedy, a death, or a loss of some type to throw the switch and allow your LUCAP to come to the surface. How many times, in raising children, have you seen a disparity in the attitude, level of frustration, and nature of the response you display depending on whose child it is that you are reacting to? When it is your own child and it's the second glass of milk or juice that has been tipped over in a week, the second glass broken, or the second meal interrupted, you probably act out of frustration and anger. You ridicule, find fault, criticize, and demean. If, however, the glass is tipped over by a neighbor's child having dinner with you, your response is radically different. You are quick to say, "Did you get cut? Are you okay? Don't worry about the glass, it doesn't matter. It's only milk. We'll fill up a new glass. Don't cry, don't be scared. I'm not going to yell at you." In essence, your LUCAP surfaces and takes control of your behavior. Then again, this child has little connection to you. You don't personalize his behavior; you don't see it as carelessness, a mistake which your child shouldn't make, or, perhaps, passive-aggressive behavior directed toward you. With the neighbor's child, you are understanding, caring, and accepting, usually even more so than his own parent. With those closest to you, your little kid inside totally obscures any trace of the LUCAP inside you.

Nevertheless, I believe there is, without any doubt, a LUCAP in each of you. That means that every one of you truly knows, intellectually, how to love in a giving, concerned, sensitive manner. That is, when you operate from your head instead of from your insecurities and fears, i.e., your emotions. It is a strange paradox. The more you feel, the more you fear. As a result, the more you care, or the more someone means to you, the more you anticipate or feel they can hurt you. Consequently, the less understanding you are apt to be of them, with them, and toward them. Exactly the same can be said with regard to the relationship between your inner parent and your emotional child. Try to imagine the difference between how you react, what you say, and the degree of condemnation and guilt you might impose on a friend who lost her wedding ring, failed the state boards, accidentally dropped a crystal vase, spilled a glass of red wine on the carpet, or wrecked a new car, as opposed to what you would be prone to say or do to yourself if those things happened to you. Not to mention how critical you can be toward yourself for gaining weight or saying something inappropriate at a party, versus how forgiving and conciliatory you might be toward a friend for the same behavior. If you can recognize this, you can readily see that your wounded child is in desperate need of a LUCAP and that you can be that loving, understanding, caring, accepting parent he needs. Ironically, in the process of learning to deal with yourself more compassionately by accepting, forgiving, understanding, and consoling your own little child, you will also become more considerate and loving of others in your world.

To begin this process requires that you take the **seventh and last step**. You must learn to literally talk to your inner child as though you were two separate people: one, an intellectual adult, the beneficiary of everything you have learned during your lifetime, who will continue to change and grow throughout the future; the other, a small, emotional child of four or five years of age, who acts and reacts out of his early hurts and the emotional input he has experienced since his birth. At the age of five, your emotional child was as mature as he will ever be. Whether you are five, fifteen, thirty-five, fifty-five, or seventy-five, the feelings that motivate your child are the same. As you grow older, they may manifest themselves in more socially acceptable manners, but, underneath, the need to defend, the feelings of inadequacy, the fears of rejection or abandonment, and the sense of insufficiency prevail, whether real or not. Because of that, you will always need a LUCAP to figuratively and literally hold your hand, hug you, and reassure you that, no matter how many glasses of milk you spill, or how wrong you may be, your LUCAP (you) will be there to support you. Not necessarily to agree with you, or to take your side, but to love and be there for you emotionally, because your LUCAP knows you're okay and sees you as worthy of the love you need, desire, and deserve.

This concept, at least intellectually, makes sense. But the question I am sure you are asking is, "How do you apply it?

What does it entail, pragmatically? Is it just a case of putting yourself in the proper frame of mind?" The answer is that it is more than an abstract notion. It can definitely be used pragmatically, and its application is simple, but may possibly be slightly embarrassing. It was to me initially. But I don't hesitate to demonstrate it to my patients now. Most of them have reported that it is an extremely valuable tool that they continue to use long after leaving therapy.

Essentially, it consists of three steps. The first step is remembering that you are, indeed, two people. One person, as I said previously, is your emotional child—the one who behaves in terms of the inputs he or she received during the first four or five years of life. He is the impulsive and reactive or restricted, defensive kid within you. He is, at the same time, a sensitive being whose actions are the result of one driving force: the need to protect, to defend, and to survive, no matter the long-term cost to self or others. The world, for him, is a fearful place, filled with potential dangers and threats. Thus, he rebels, hides, or capitulates. In the end, he resorts to whatever it takes to survive, emotionally, for the moment, the hour, or the day. Unfortunately, he is blind to long-term consequences. Still further, the choice of his mode of defense was unconsciously determined early in childhood, as a result of his DNA and the influence of his parents, siblings, family, and community. He is omnipresent throughout your life and, in varying degrees, influences all of your behavior all your life. At times, he can be playful, entertaining, and dynamic. But, more often, he is a frightened, wounded child who desperately needs emotional reassurance, support, love, guidance, and, most of all, limits and boundaries. Without them, he will take over your entire being. He will govern your behaviors to the nth degree and cause you to react to events and people in your life as though you were still four or five years old, no matter your chronological age. Thus, it is imperative that you honestly see him or her for who he or she is. Otherwise, you will be unable to help him, because you can't come to the aid of someone who is in control of you. Similarly, when you truly know your little kid, his reactions don't surprise you. Thus, you're able to accept his feelings but not give them credence. Therefore, you don't have to react to him by drowning him in alcohol, hiding from him, denying, aggrandizing, or bludgeoning him. Instead, you may possibly even find yourself able to see him or her as amusing, devilish, or childishly misguided, all of which will permit you to feel positively toward him.

The second stage requires you to commit to being that kid's parent and to take responsibility for him. You do so not only by recognizing him for what he is, but by owning him, without excuses, explanations, or disclaimers. You learn to accept and forgive his shortcomings and to laugh kindly at his immaturity and impulsiveness. In sum total, you need to love him and expose him honestly to yourself and others in your world, so that they can love him as you do, for who he genuinely is.

The third and final stage necessitates that you engage in a continuous form of self-talk between the two of you. For me, looking in a mirror and giving myself affirmations doesn't quite do it. Telling myself how wonderful I am, or that every day, in every way, I'm getting better and better, only causes me to feel as if I'm lying to myself, and the scam doesn't work. However, some time ago, I became aware of how often people in pain, or those who experience anguish, curl up and wrap their arms around themselves, as if to protect themselves and hold everything together inside. It seems to be an almost automatic, unconscious reflex. The individual regresses to a fetal position, which seems to provide some relief or solace from their pain. Following that example, what I did was take my right hand (probably because I'm right handed), which I arbitrarily designated the hand of the intellectual adult in me, and had it grasp my left hand, which I perceived as the hand of the hurting child in me, in a firm but gentle manner. As I did, I literally talked to my child. I reassured him that 1) *No matter how grievous your thoughts and actions, I will be here for you;* 2) *I won't always approve of your behavior or agree with you, but I will love you, and accept you;* 3) *I will be there because I know there is goodness in you;* 4) *I will always try to understand where you're coming from;* 5) *I will applaud your successes, share your sorrows, lament your failures, and attempt to comfort you;* 6) *I will try to guide you and set limits for you, in an accepting manner;* 7) *I will do this without depreciating or punishing you, because I love you.* As strange as it may sound, after just a few moments, my left hand relaxed and I felt an inner sense of peace. At the same time, my right hand felt stronger. So much so, that it contributed to a feeling of pride in what I was doing for the child in me. Today, years later, this same interaction continues to enable me to comfort the frightened child inside, and to strengthen the adult in me. It works almost every time. I strongly recommend you try it. I recognize that it may sound hokey or embarrassing. Thus, I suggest that you take yourself off to somewhere you can be alone—if need be, even to your closet. There, all alone in the dark, you can gently take one hand in the other, affirm your seven-step commitment to yourself, and reassure that little kid that you will be there. I promise you it will prove to be a supportive, consoling, and positive emotional experience.

The one problem you are most likely to encounter when attempting to follow this process is that, in the heat of the moment, when you're really stressed and most in need of the comfort it can provide, you will all too frequently forget that there are two of you. During those times, you will consolidate the two of you into one entity, "*Me*," an insecure person who is only as good or bad as his last magic trick. Consequently, when you are confronted with disappointment, rejection, or failure, none of which can be avoided in the course of living life, please recognize that you will often regress back to being a person who can't afford mistakes or failures. On those occasions, your whole sense of worth will be derived by how well you perform, or what people think of you. Your identity, your worth, and your sense of lovability will all stem from external sources. Consequently, you will have no internal support (LUCAP) to fall back on. The fact is, you can't and needn't be perfect. The saving grace is that sometime later, after you've behaved or said something you regret, your adult will make an appearance and, over time, that period will become shorter.

In sharp contrast, when you are acutely aware of the two of you, your frightened, wounded, fearful, or insufficient-feeling kid always has someone to fall back on. Someone who recognizes him for who he is, accepts and forgives him for his shortcomings, and still loves him. Someone who believes in him and loves him during the good times as well as the bad times. That someone will be you. In effect, you will have become a wonderful parent to yourself, a true LUCAP—a loving, understanding, caring, accepting parent who, figuratively and literally, is there to take your inner child's hand in yours in order to comfort and reassure him when he needs it the most.

CHAPTER EIGHTEEN

BELIEVE YOU HAVE AN UNCONSCIOUS

I'm now telling everyone that when they see me, the first thing they need to say is, "Golly, Ed, you've gotten new glasses. They make you look younger and chic." (You'll understand this after you read the rest of this chapter.)

Hopefully, you'll also come to see that there truly is an unconscious in every one of us—one that controls our behaviors far more than we imagined and contributes to actions that clearly illustrate how the emotional child in us attempts to protect us from immediate pain but, in the process, winds up causing long-term hurts. No one is without an emotional child, but too few of us are able to recognize him or her. It's not easy, because our emotional child is hidden to the eye. Nevertheless, we must become aware of the influence our emotional child or unconscious exerts on us and learn to take control when he or she becomes too impulsive or demonstrates excessively faulty judgment.

You would think that, after forty-nine years in the therapist's chair, listening to myself, I would be in control of my little kid's actions and remain insightful regarding the immature, childish, and manipulative behaviors he's capable of manifesting. Unfortunately, that's not always the case, because our emotional six- or, at best, seven-year-old is apt to sneak out when we least expect it. Figuratively speaking, whenever we open our emotional doors or turn our backs, he or she is liable to run out into the front yard or the middle of the street.

Well, that's exactly what my little kid did when, after weeks of waiting, my prescription glasses finally arrived. Essentially, I picked up the glasses on my way to our beach house, where my wife had been for several days, relaxing and entertaining girlfriends. She greeted me in such a warm, loving manner that it was evident she had missed me as much as I had missed her. But she failed to notice my new glasses. That was Thursday afternoon. Two days later, on Saturday, Harriet still hadn't mentioned my glasses, and I was becoming angry, resentful, and convinced that she didn't care.

At the same time, let me say, I've lived with Harriet for over fifty-five years. During that time, I have learned, on innumerable occasions, that she could walk by the living room and if a chair was missing, it would be a week before she'd notice it. Conversely, I could walk in, and if there was a nail hole in the wall, it would jump out at me and cause me to become fixated on the fact that I had to repair it. This isn't to say that one style is better than the other. It's just that she walks through life not seeing things, and therefore nothing is broken or in need of repair, whereas I become obsessive about having to fix or rearrange things that aren't in place. That being the case, I intellectually knew that she wasn't likely to notice my glasses. Nevertheless, I set up a test which I knew she'd fail. I also created a situation where I would feel rejected, angry, and depressed. Now, I ask you, why in the world would anyone in his right mind have done that? I'll leave you with that question while I return to that Saturday.

Harriet and I were watching TV when a commercial came on about glasses. She looked at me and said, "Ed, have you heard anything about your glasses?" I pointed to the bridge of my nose and said, "Now that you mention it, all Thursday afternoon, Friday, and today, you've been staring at them, but you never saw them, or me."

Her reply was not to take the bait, but to say, "Ed, you're crazy. If I had gotten new glasses, I would have come in saying, 'Look at my new glasses. Don't they look great?' " I can picture it now. That's exactly what she would have done. But if I had done that, it wouldn't have afforded me the opportunity to feel angry, depressed, and unloved. Once again, let me rhetorically ask, why would a sane person want to feel that way? My answer is because even the sanest of us has a little kid inside whose job it is to protect us. As I noted earlier, he or she knows nothing about long-term consequences. Instead, his or her job is to help us survive in the moment, with as little pain as possible. Unfortunately, the result of his actions is short-term comfort and long-term pain.

Well, that's exactly what it amounted to in the end. But, after introspectively thinking about it, I realized the real reason for my inner child's reaction: it was the fact that I had brought my new book with me. It was only six chapters short of being finished, which was wonderful. But, unfortunately, once it's done, I'll have to face the possibility that no publisher will deem it worthy. That would indicate that the "baby" I created was lacking, which would mean I was lacking as well. Not finishing and staying preoccupied with "my wife's uncaring behavior" protected me from that eventuality.

Believe it or not and think about it before you disbelieve it—my little kid set up the whole scenario, none of which was consciously motivated. But, at that time, if you had suggested that I created the situation, I would have been extremely defensive, or even hostile. Yet, I did wear the glasses without saying a thing about them to my wife, even though I was almost positive they'd go unnoticed. I also proceeded to generate feelings inside me of resentment and unworthiness. Why? Because it was far better to feel angry or hurt by someone I could perceive as not caring than to face the fact that it was me who felt undeserving of being cared for. It's a feeling and a coping technique that, I'm sad to say, I've carried with me ever since childhood. One I constantly fight.

The sad part is, I'm not alone. There are all too many other emotionally damaged individuals in the world. Let me share several examples of behavior similar to my own that were demonstrated by two women I've seen in therapy.

The first, Audrey, is an extremely bright, articulate, and, I believe, competitive, controlling, assertive woman, who would disagree entirely with my description of her. She sees herself as a victim, subject to the mercurial behaviors of a husband she described as "angry every other week. During those weeks, he directs all his anger at me, personally. He runs me down, criticizes my parenting, belittles my opinions, and generally attempts to undermine my sense of adequacy and worth. The next week, he's nice. He never apologizes, but he does little things to suggest that he's sorry for whatever took place the previous seven days. I can't live in this seesaw world of his. I've had it. I'm totally emotionally strung out. I don't know if I can make it. We can argue any issue for hours. For example, he thinks he's more important and more valued because he has more stress than me. He worries about the family, supporting us, making payments on the new house and the cars, and performing up to snuff on his job so he'll one day make partner, while, in his eyes, I just sit at home, caring for the kids. Well, I think that's an important job, too. I'm concerned about their future, about their education, about their health, about having good meals on the table, scheduling their activities, and watching out for their safety. So, I'm just as stressed as he is. But, when I say that, he becomes angry and asks, 'Why is it like this? Why do our conversations always result in competition, where you have to be equal with me?' " She then burst into tears. She said, "I'm the victim. I don't want a divorce, but I can't stand feeling helpless." Then she shouted, "And don't you dare disagree with me. I need somebody who can see my side of it and who will understand what I'm going through, because he certainly doesn't."

In many ways, I do understand her feelings, but I also believe that she uses his behavior to help her avoid looking at herself. Without a doubt, his verbalizations are unacceptable, inappropriate, and insensitive. Despite his education and extremely successful practice, his immature actions and high level of emotionality indicate that he has problems. But he isn't her problem. He's a fact. Her problem is how she reacts to him and interprets his mercurial emotional swings.

What Audrey does is reminiscent of a story I once heard of someone shooting an arrow into the air, at a target two hundred feet away. Another individual ran onto the field, jumped in front of the target, and then complained, "You shot and wounded me." The truth, however, is that he didn't have to run out on the field in front of the target any more than my patient had to see herself as a victim of her husband's behavior. Instead, she might have recognized that his behavior was not an indication of his lack of care or value of her. It's very possible that he puts her down, doesn't talk to her, and criticizes her because it's the only way he knows how to ask for the nurturing, care, affection, and attention he desperately needs all because of his feelings of inadequacy. Granted, it's a poor way to ask for love, but it's the same as a little child throwing a temper tantrum when he desperately wants to be held by a parent. Obviously, he needs to alter his behavior if he ever wants to be emotionally healthy, but there's nothing wrong with his need for support. What's wrong is the way he asks for it. At the same time, her feelings of inadequacy are the cause of her discomfort. They disallow her to see him for who he really is, to accept his weaknesses, and, most of all, to provide him with the emotional support he desperately needs. They also diminish her wherewithal to look at herself and see her extreme sensitivity, as well as her inability to express to him in a nonconfrontational manner how needy she is, how important he is to her, and how hurtful his disparaging remarks and attitude are to her.

The second example is that of an exceptionally beautiful, very intelligent, sensitive woman who is married to an abusive, unloving, angry, but financially successful husband. He figuratively and physically demeans and controls her and their children. Her friends, family, and associates at work all view this hostile, threatening individual as someone she should have divorced years ago. If you were to ask her why she stayed, her answer would be, "Because I'm fearful that, if I divorce him, when he has possession of the children, he will hurt them as a means of punishing me. So, I stay for the kids. Second, I don't believe in divorce. Third, I'm waiting until the kids are old enough to leave home before I leave him." Behind her back, most individuals would state that she stays for other reasons, i.e., her expensive lifestyle, and the financial benefits and perks his success in business affords her. However, I strongly disagree with all of those reasons. Instead, I believe that, despite this woman's interpersonal acumen, her emotional warmth, intelligence, and beauty, she, too, is a damaged soul. Her sense of inner worth was severely crippled early in life, long before she met her husband. Moreover, the abusive relationship she presently stays in is one that is highly similar to the one she grew up knowing. Even more, the problems, upsets, and emotional stress she experiences in her marriage blind her to the fact that she is paralyzed by her fear that she can't make it on her own. In effect, her inner child unconsciously keeps her in a situation that is painful, but it's pain she can deal with, because it's familiar. The benefit is that she doesn't have to look at herself.

It's ironic that a majority of human beings prefer to see their difficulties as stemming from problems between themselves and someone else, when, in fact, the problems they experience are almost always between the two individuals, the child and the adult, residing in them.

The primary reason I shared these stories is to help you see that if you ever want to be healthy, it isn't a matter of changing you. It's a matter of first seeing you and then learning to live with, accept, forgive, and love the person you are, shortcomings, fears, and all. Shifting the blame to others never works long term. It only serves to eventually push them away. Attempting to improve or change who you are on the inside is futile because it's impossible. But trying to do so only validates that you are unworthy because you aren't perfect, strong enough, or without fears or anxiety. Of even more importance, however, is the fact that if you believe the scenarios you create, you will never see the need to alter your behavior, which is something you can change. As a result, you will never grow emotionally. Some people are willing to settle for that because emotional growth is almost always painful, oftentimes noxious, and, certainly, extremely anxiety producing. After all, seeing yourself for who you really are can be overwhelming, distressful, and terribly upsetting. It's no wonder, then, that people in therapy who begin to change often feel worse and believe that therapy isn't working. It's difficult for them to see that the better you get, the worse you feel. However, once you get over feeling worse, you realize that it's only after you can grab hold of your problem that you can get rid of it. It's similar to having a hot potato in your lap. The pain is excruciating, but you do nothing, because it's hot and you're reluctant to get your hands burned as well. Whereas if, despite the heat, you grab hold of the potato, you're able to toss it aside. It's simple. You cannot get rid of something that you don't first possess.

One last thought. Remember, the next time you see me, mention how wonderful my glasses make me look. I'll love hearing it but, because of my little kid's feelings, I probably won't believe what you say. I'll think, "You're only saying it because I asked." Fifteen years ago, that would have been the absolute truth. Today, I'm better able to look at me and affectionately say, "Ed, you're an idiot. Don't believe your own BS." That statement says far more than the words imply. It is my way of remembering that whenever you react to excess, you need to look at yourself and ask, "Who is causing me to act this way, my adult self or my unconscious kid?" The answer is always the same. Excessive verbalizations and behaviors only come about because of your emotional child. Ask, "Where is he coming from?"

---

1. Determine what you want.
2. Decide if your words or actions will get you what you desire.
3. Determine if there is a more positive, proactive way you can behave.

NOTE: Just asking these questions is a means of putting your adult into play, thereby enabling you to behave in accordance with your intellect, as opposed to your emotions.

If you can relate, you can approach yourself with the same honesty and affectionate introspection that I'm finally able to demonstrate. I believe it will help you to discover that you truly are okay, even if your kid doesn't feel it.

CHAPTER NINETEEN

SEVER YOUR UMBILICAL CORD

When I look back at the adult patients I've seen over the years, I would say that 90 percent of them had little trouble in high school, weren't continuously spaced out on drugs, and didn't cause their parents tremendous problems. Quite the contrary. They were the good kids, the ones who went by the rules and made few ripples, except for typical teenage rebellious behavior. Their parents would have described them as "darned good kids." For the most part, they were bright, excelled in school, and, later in life, proved to be rather successful. Yet they were also the ones who often experienced more difficulties in their relationships with themselves than others. It seems odd that this would be the case. You would think they would have been the ones who had perfect marriages, perfect children, and perfect lives. Indeed, that often appeared to be the case on the surface. But, inside, they and their children are the ones who most often wound up in my office.

Perhaps the puzzle could be better explained if you thought about it this way. Many of the individuals who experienced difficulties in high school, or stretched the limits during their teenage rebellious years, learned they could make mistakes and deviate from the norm and still be loved and accepted. They were able to cut their emotional umbilical cords and survive, whereas so many of the "perfect" individuals were too frightened to even stretch theirs. What they needed to recognize is that none of us is perfect. People have faults, shortcomings, fears, and confusion. They can be frightened, anxious, insecure, needy, and lacking in confidence—none of which needs be considered sick, weak, broken, inadequate, or representative of emotional problems. It might be less upsetting if you call these states of mind or feelings normal emotional human characteristics inherent in every individual. The result might be that there would be less psychopathology in the world and far fewer people thinking they need a pill every time they experience sadness, stress, or feelings of insufficiency.

The problem is that no one ever said that to you. Instead, you were supposed to be good, better, and best. You were supposed to achieve, to cause few problems, and to adhere to what was politically and parentally correct. And, if you could be perfect, all the better. You were supposed to be confident, assured, independent, self-sufficient, and personable. If you weren't, you were taken to a therapist, provided a tutor, or sent to another school, because your parents loved you, wanted the best for you, and were willing to sacrifice financially for you. The least you could do in return was behave in accordance with their expectations. Thus, if you had problems, you knew that it was because something was lacking in you. It wasn't that your parents necessarily verbalized these thoughts. In fact, they overtly said the opposite. Their words were usually something similar to, "I can't understand how someone as bright or good as you can bring home a report card like this, or act that way."

Once again, it isn't that they were consciously trying to find fault or criticize. It was their means of motivating you to work harder, perform better, and fit in with their expectations. It's no different than their saying, "You don't have to get all A's; you just have to do your best." Please explain to me how any child or even adult can determine when he/she is doing their best. Or, what about this one: "You're the most wonderful child in the world. You're my whole life. If it weren't for you, I wouldn't want to live." How much pressure does that create? What I'm faulting isn't their motivation, intention, or whether their behavior was conscious or unconscious, or even if they were only doing what they themselves learned or experienced as children. It's the message parents overtly or subtly deliver and the effect it has on you throughout your life.

These messages don't come from parents alone. Society, religion, and even literature are all equally influential or responsible. Parents are often portrayed as being good, wonderful, loving, caring, and nurturing. The conclusion is obvious. If they're perfect, every conflictual interaction is your fault, because your behavior contributed to and caused them to act the way they did. Even when you intellectually know better, unconsciously, you feel, "I must have done something wrong." Those thoughts and feelings aren't always conscious, but they're there, and they control you to the point that, throughout your life, you attempt to do your utmost to live up to what you might describe as your parents' expectations, but which, over time, you have adopted.

For example, I recently heard this story from a forty-year-old executive who quit the company he had worked for since college and joined with several colleagues to form a start-up company. His salary was doubled, his move was reported in the *Wall Street Journal,* and his mother e-mailed distant family, acquaintances and all her friends about his accomplishments. Two years later, the company disbanded because of the economic condition of the country, and he was emotionally devastated. He was extremely concerned about finances and whether he could keep his home and how his wife and children would react to the changes that might come about. All of which made good sense. Two weeks later, he sheepishly confessed that the only person he hadn't informed about his loss was his mother. He said, "I'm afraid to tell her. I hate to disappoint her."

In many more cases than you might expect, that is the very reason many of you wind up anxious, stressed, conflicted, angry, feeling inadequate, and frequently unable to experience joy. The reason is that you're still carrying with you the notion that you're not okay, that something is lacking inside you. This feeling, in most instances, isn't a conscious one, it's kinesthetic—it's your emotional little kid, not your adult. Therefore, it might be said that you don't know it, but you feel you're not okay.

Let me give you two illustrations that might help you to better understand this concept. Rhonda was beautiful, bright, curious, and verbally articulate at a very young age. She showed tremendous future promise. Her mother never ceased from complimenting and encouraging her and informing her how lucky she was to have those qualities and how much she had to do to live up to them. In many ways, Rhonda was going to make her mother's life worthwhile. She was going to be a success story whose accomplishments stemmed from her mother's rearing, which would, therefore, imply that mother was "okay."

Rhonda not only lived up to her mother's desires, she went a step farther. Sadly, however, despite her accomplishments, Rhonda's self-image trailed drastically behind. She felt her sense of worth was dependent on what she produced and accomplished. Love wasn't something she received for who she was; it was something she earned on a daily basis, twenty-four/seven, fifty-two weeks a year. When it wasn't forthcoming, when it seemed as though she had failed to live up to her mother's (and later her husband's) expectations, she felt guilty and tried harder. But, deep inside, she also felt anger and resentment. Nowhere in her life did Rhonda feel emotionally secure. There was no one whose love she trusted would be there, no matter how she performed or whether she succeeded or failed. As a result, her life was a series of mountains that she climbed on a daily basis. After climbing one, she always felt the need to find another, still higher, in order to obtain the nurturing and accolades she so strongly desired. But, all the while, she experienced constant stress and fear over her next challenge and the possibility that she might not succeed. As you might suspect, her relationship with both her mother and her husband deteriorated over the years due to her unfounded belief that she hadn't ever been loved just for who she was.

Eventually, the bubble burst and Rhonda came to therapy depressed, resentful, and paralyzed by the possibility that she could never again achieve the success she had known previously in her life.

Brandon was a good boy, a sweet boy, a loving boy, a caring boy, and, in his mother's eyes, a darling boy. He was smart and performed well at school, but he had difficulties relating to his peers. He was either totally shy and retiring, or excessively talkative and animated. Either extreme contributed to his being viewed as peculiar, odd, or different.

At home, Brandon was chided constantly by an older brother, who saw him as an embarrassment and whose friends teased him regarding the possibility that Brandon was gay. Understandably, Brandon's brother constantly pushed him to "be a man," to be tough, strong, and aggressive, all traits that were absent or lacking in his makeup. As a result, he felt himself inadequate and insufficient in the eyes of his brother and his peers. His mother made excuses for him, but his father and brother, both of whom were athletic outdoorsmen, constantly pushed him to live up to what they needed him to be. To avoid facing his feelings of insufficiency, he developed phobias related to the weather, driving in traffic, and having to speak out in a crowd. He was especially self-conscious when it came to relating to women, except as "a friend." He also eventually found his way to my office.

Both of these individuals wound up in therapy. The things they had in common were that neither of them had ever severed the umbilical cord that tied them to their parents, their families, and society. Neither of them fully experienced teenage rebellion. As a result, they went into adulthood without a sense of emotional self-sufficiency, independence, or adequacy. More importantly, there was nothing wrong with either of them. They were both okay, but they didn't know it. What they needed to do was recognize that who they were and what they had accomplished came about as a result of the combined influences of their DNA and their parental rearing. But it couldn't have taken place without their individual efforts, capabilities, and energy. Those things came from within them. They alone gave them the right to feel adequate about themselves and to know that they were entitled to whatever rewards they had already achieved, or would experience in the future. Most of all, they needed to be aware that any love or approval they received should have been given unconditionally, for who they were. Moreover, that love in no way obligated them to live up to their parents' expectations for the rest of their lives, and, further, any debt they felt, or had been led to believe, that they owed was invalid.

I should add that there is another group of equally adequate individuals on the other end of the spectrum who received messages they interpreted—sometimes rightly, other times wrongly—as indicating that they were basically inadequate, personally lacking, and in need of improvement.

Their reactions, however, were to behave in completely opposite ways. They unconsciously chose to reinforce that notion by angrily or passive-aggressively sabotaging positive achievements and seeking negative attention. All because they either doubted their wherewithal to achieve or rebelled against what they viewed as controlling behavior. In either case, they were also "okay," but they didn't know it, either. Unfortunately, some of them whose behavior excessively exceeded what society deems normal or acceptable wound up hospitalized and medicated in order to "help them fit in." Mind you, I'm not saying that fitting in is wrong, but when it becomes the only road available to you, you lose the capacity to be you, to be creative, and to think outside the box. It is too great a price to pay for a coping mechanism that, long term, fails to produce genuine contentment or emotional peace. All of these individuals needed to cut their umbilical cords, figuratively and emotionally.

But, then again, it's an essential step every one of you needs to take in the course of becoming an adult. At a certain point in your life, you must assume total responsibility for you. After all, you are the only one who determines what you do and why you do it. It is you who must take responsibility for where you are in life. Intellectually, it readily makes sense. Emotionally, it's extremely frightening. But, when you finally reach that point, you will feel a sense of peace within you that you have never experienced before. Your fears of others' reactions and opinions will be diminished, and your confidence will increase—all because the primary factor that really counts is how you feel about you.

Therein lies the real seat of the problem. In most instances, when you attempt to meet the expectations of parents and society, your efforts are directed toward external accomplishments which will primarily be judged by someone else. Conversely, in order to genuinely feel good about yourself, the focus is reversed. The judge and jury are primarily you. The axiom is that when you do things that you judge to be good, it winds up being good for others. Although it sounds simple, it isn't. Your focus needs to be totally inverted. Instead of attempting to please others to feel good about you, you have to look toward pleasing yourself to feel good about you. Somehow that seems to make more sense. The problem is that, for the most part, it doesn't work that way in your everyday interactions, and, when you initially attempt to please yourself, others tend to react negatively. You're told you're selfish, self-centered, and uncaring for not meeting their needs. It's ironic, but your parents do the same thing. They say they want you to be happy with you, but they reward you for pleasing them.

Therefore, it's important that, whether you're an individual who is attempting to sever your umbilical cord or a parent who feels surprised and hurt by a child's newly expressed dissatisfaction with your parenting, no matter how hurt or angry you may be, you need to recognize that the conflict wouldn't exist if each of you wasn't important to the other, didn't matter, or didn't love the other. Please, try to remember this when you attempt to cut your umbilical cord. It's much easier to sever a codependent relationship with scalpel and anesthesia than it is with a dull knife while biting on a leather belt.

Having said that, I'd like to share a story about a couple's sad experience with their son, which caused them to view him quite differently from how they originally saw him and to realize that what's on the inside is of far more importance that what's on the outside.

Jack Jr. was the son of a fairly affluent couple whom I briefly saw in therapy. His father, Jack Sr., was a successful insurance company executive whose mother, after her husband's death, worked two jobs to support Jack and his two brothers. Life wasn't easy, but Jack Sr. worked his way through college and started at the bottom of the insurance company he now heads.

Jack Jr.'s mother, a litigator in a law firm, was born into more comfortable surroundings. She was the only child of a high-powered attorney and a socially conscious mother who expended more time toward her charity interests than she did to her daughter. As a result, she became her father's "successful surrogate son." It's no surprise that she is a respected professional, but severely lacking as a nurturing parent.

In light of their own accomplishments, you can imagine their feelings when they finally conceded that Jack Jr. wasn't going to be the scholar, the high achiever, the son they'd always dreamed of. Instead, he struggled through high school with the aid of tutors and later flunked out of junior college. He then worked at a multitude of odd jobs until he found employment as an electrician's helper, a position he excelled at and thoroughly enjoyed. Sadly, his enjoyment wasn't long lived. Jack Jr. died of a heart attack at the age of twenty-seven.

His parents grieved over Jack Jr.'s death. They lamented what he could have been. They spoke of his innate intelligence, his never living up to his potential, and what he could have been if only he had applied himself.

However, from the time Jack Jr. was put in intensive care, a strange entourage of young men and women appeared at the hospital and remained there until he died. They were a clean-cut group of warm, caring young people. There probably wasn't one college graduate or Phi Beta Kappa in the group, but they were people who showed loving concern, and whose hearts appeared broken over what was happening to their friend. They joked, they cried, and they kept the vigil. They hoped for the best and were there for the worst. They were there for "plain, inadequate Jack." They never spoke of any disappointment over who he was, or his lack of achievement. They spoke of their love for him and the many ways he reciprocated their feelings.

It was only after viewing this that Jack Jr.'s parents realized they never knew or fully appreciated their son. Because he wasn't what they needed him to be on the outside, they never looked to see who he genuinely was on the inside.

There is a powerful lesson to be learned here. *When you are consumed by what's on the outside, you're blind to the things most worth seeing, because those things are primarily on the inside.* Your quest, then, has to be to learn to look at others and yourself for who they and you are on the inside. To start, you need to cut your emotional umbilical cord in order to be able to see yourself through your own eyes, instead of the eyes of others.

Remember that there is so much to love about our little kid, but we simply don't give enough attention to his positive traits. Instead, we often try to totally change him. But without him, life would be mechanical, or boil down to an intellectual exercise. He is the spice that adds zest to our lives, and for that reason alone he deserves to be valued.

CHAPTER TWENTY

LOOK OUT FOR YOURSELF

S ome time ago, I went to a lecture on introspection. The speaker began with the statement, "Half of you in the audience need to do a better job of looking out for the individuals you interact with. The other half has to do a better job of looking out for yourselves."

With one exception, I couldn't agree more. If he was talking about the population in general, he's 150 percent correct. But I doubt that he was accurate with regard to his audience. The reason is that individuals who need to do a better job of looking out for others don't generally go to lectures of that type. Nor do they generally go to therapy. At least, not for more than one or two sessions. What they do, instead, is complain about the people with whom they interact. They rarely see themselves as having a problem and almost always attribute their difficulties to others. They leave therapy the moment their therapist suggests, "You might benefit more if you were to look at yourself, because you can't change someone else. But if you're successful at changing you, it might have a positive effect on those around you."

Having said that, let me speak to those of you who have to do a better job of looking out for yourselves. I cannot stress this thought enough. As I have stated over and over again, *you need to dare to be selfish.* For most of you, that's almost an impossible task, because your whole sense of worthwhileness is dependent on an image you developed early in life, still strongly cling to, and project to the world. It's that you are a good, emotional, caring, helpful, generous human being. It's even possible that you occasionally hear a little voice inside you saying, "You're a better person than other people who are selfish, egocentric, and insensitive." All the while that voice is speaking, there's a bit of a grin on your face that implies, "What a good person I am." That's your identity. It's one you learned early in life. In many ways, it permeates every interaction you engage in and, in many more instances than you might suspect, it is far more destructive to your relationships with others, particularly those you love, than the selfish, egocentric characteristics demonstrated by people who need to do a better job of looking out for others with whom they interact.

Initially, it may appear that what I'm saying is totally inconsistent with basic beliefs. After all, what's wrong with being a good guy? Nothing, but when that behavior is excessive or applied to your long-term relationships, it's hurtful. An identity that stems from being a "better" person, turning the other cheek, and waiting for bad people to "get theirs" in life, or after death, never helps you. I know you've heard the expression thousands of times, "What goes around comes around." But, I ask you, is that really true? I haven't found that to be the case. I have known a great many people who've behaved in terribly selfish, dishonest, abusive ways. They took advantage of and disregarded the feelings and welfare of others. But, generally speaking, I haven't seen them "get theirs." Conversely, I've seen a multitude of good people who tempered their feelings of anger and resentment, avoided negatively judging others, and even felt guilty for thinking selfish thoughts who wound up living lives filled with pain and disappointments. They mean well, but, too often, their self-righteous, overly considerate, or generous behavioral orientation serves as the seed for hidden resentment, self-pity, passive-aggressive behavior, and emotional disappointment.

If you constantly do more for others than yourself, see yourself as a victim who is always taken advantage of, and think the world is unfair because good things don't happen to you, you may be one of those people. What may be a more accurate description of you is that you've hidden behind "goodness" and made yourself a martyr. In effect, you became a highly judgmental, moralistic, self-righteous victim, who is quick to, at least unconsciously, criticize anyone who doesn't share your values or sense of right or wrong. I can say this because I feel I am a converted "good person" who got tired of living in an "unfair" world and thinking good things should happen to me because, in truth, I didn't have the backbone to stand up for myself and make those things happen to me.

To better understand this, let me give you an example.

It was a very special therapy session. Gus was there with Mickie, his possible future fiancée. She was attractive, tall, intelligent, and personable. But, then again, so were his three previous fiancées, all of which is a testimony to Gus's good taste. This time, however, Gus was more intent on developing a permanent relationship, getting married, establishing a home, and creating a family. It was apparent because, for the first time in all the years I had known him, he was able to say the word "marriage" without whispering or stuttering. During the session, Mickie noted how absolutely thrilled she was with a conversation that had taken place between them the night before. In the past, it could have developed into an argument that would have lasted for days. But, with pride, she said, "This time I said what I really felt. I had the courage to tell him what I wanted. Next Wednesday, he's scheduled to leave on a ski trip to Colorado with four of his best friends and return Sunday night. That's perfectly all right. I understand that his friend Jay is getting married and this is the last time the four single guys can make a long weekend of it. There's only one problem. Thursday is the one-year anniversary of the day we first met. It's a very special time for me, and, though I don't resent him going, I really wanted to be with him on Thursday to celebrate that occasion. Well, I had the courage to ask him if he would consider the possibility of not leaving for the ski trip until Friday morning so we could celebrate together on Thursday night."

I looked at Gus quizzically to see what his response or reaction was to her statement. He said, "It was no problem. I mean, I thought maybe we could celebrate Tuesday and then I could leave on Wednesday night. I even suggested the possi-

bility of us celebrating it the next weekend. But once I understood how absolutely important it was to her, it made me
happy to think I could please her and be with her. It was difficult for a moment, though, because I felt that I was caught
between them. If I did what Jay wanted, she'd be unhappy. If
I did what she wanted, Jay would be unhappy. I had to decide
which one I was going to please. Hands down, I love her so
much that the answer was obvious." It may have been to him,
but I doubt it was as honest a statement as Mickie's.

Before I continue to describe the therapy session, I'll ask
you to stop for a moment and think what you would have done
in the same situation. Who would you have pleased? Should
Gus have agreed so readily? Did he owe something more to his
friend who was getting married? Or was he negligent in not
remembering that the following Thursday was the anniversary
of meeting Mickie one year earlier? What was the right thing
for him to do? Think about it. You may want to compare your
thoughts and your answer to what occurred in the second half
of their therapy session.

In therapy, I frequently find myself saying there is no
right or wrong. Your feelings have to be taken into consideration. Stop trying to be perfect, or to do "the right thing".
Do what you feel is best for you, even if it may hurt someone
else, as long as it isn't your covert motive or conscious intention. In this instance, however, there was a right thing to do,
and that was for Gus to recognize, first and foremost, that
his thought process was flawed. Truly, he could not win for
losing, because his problem had little or nothing to do with
whether he satisfied his soon-to-be fiancée or his soon-to-be-
married friend. Gus saw himself as having to decide between

the two of them. What he failed to recognize was that there was a third party he had to deal with—he had to ask himself not "What do Mickie or Jay want," but "*What do I want? What do I really prefer?*" You see, for him it didn't matter what he did. It mattered whom he chose to please.

When I said that to Gus, he looked dumbfounded. His mouth gaped open. He stared out almost blindly at the two of us, and you could literally see the wheels turning in his head. Then he said, "I know, in ways, we've talked about this before, but I have never had it so vividly displayed to me. I can see it perfectly clearly. I never even think to ask the question, 'What do I want?' Now, as I'm sitting here, I realize that I haven't really asked that question of myself throughout most of my life. At least not when I interact with people I love. Instead, I concentrate on doing whatever pleases someone else. It is the most overwhelming realization I've had in years. On one hand, it's mind boggling. I'm filled with the endless possibilities it presents for me. On the other hand, it scares me to death. I'm afraid if I really ask that question, I'll be selfish, just thinking of myself. Years ago, my father told me, 'Before you do anything, you have to think about the other person and where he or she is coming from.' Then he told me the saying 'To really understand another person's situation, you have to walk a mile in his moccasins.' I always thought that was such a good thought, and that it was the way I should behave throughout my life. Now, after hearing what you've said, I'm beginning to think that he forgot to tell me that, before you can walk in someone else's moccasins, you have to be able to walk upright in your own. As crazy as it sounds, I'm afraid what other people will think. I don't want Mickie or Jay to think that I don't care, or that I'm not a good person. Yet I can't wait for another opportunity to do what's best for me. It is emotionally terrifying. It's like doing something totally new that I've never done in my whole life. I'm excited and overwhelmed at the same time."

In many ways, Gus had discovered the key that would open up his understanding of what I mean when I say to every one of my patients, "I want you to come to therapy and learn to be selfish. To look out for yourself. To adopt a *rational self-interest*, which will influence how you act and behave and the kind of decisions you make." It is the biggest step most of you will ever take in your lives. It doesn't mean that you will become inconsiderate of others, that others don't matter, or that you are no longer going to share. Nor does it mean that you will always make sure that you get the biggest piece for yourself. It just means that you are going to make yourself a part of the equation you use in making your choices, determining how you behave, and influencing the decisions you make.

Far too many people go through life negating themselves. As a result, their identity is nullified and their perception, accurate or not, of the expectations of others serves to influence who and what they think, say, and do. These individuals do not, however, always appear the same on the surface. Similar to Gus, some are compliant and chameleonlike. Others are totally selfish and do not seem to care for anyone. Those individuals may act that way, but their behavior is primarily a form of compensation. Their authoritative, unbending, rigid attitude is designed to obscure their inner feelings of weakness and desire for love. Unbeknownst to others, they, too, censor many of their actions in accordance with what they believe will please others. At the same time, they abhor the weakness they perceive in themselves because of it. Thus, they attempt to appear strong in the only way they know how. Ironically, it does little to impress others; it only serves to estrange them further. Note, however, that their actions in no way reflect the selfish attitude I am speaking of. Behavior that is genuinely derived as a result of a rational self-interest takes into account the thoughts and desires of others, and though it may ultimately differ from popular opinion, it is expressed with understanding and awareness of what other people may feel.

For example, I said to Gus, "After asking yourself, 'What do I really want,' you could have appropriately decided that you wanted to go for the extended weekend with your friends. After all, it had been planned months before. Your response to Mickie might have been, 'I love you to death. I recognize how important celebrating on Thursday is to you, and I'm sorry to say that I never even thought about or knew when the one-year anniversary of our first meeting was. It doesn't mean I don't love you, and it doesn't mean that your desires and feelings aren't important to me. In fact, part of me wants to please you and stay. But if I do, I'm going to feel guilty about not going on this extended weekend with all the guys. I may even be resentful toward you, because I'll feel controlled and forced to stay because of my love for you and my reluctance to hurt you. I see myself going for a hurried evening out to celebrate our anniversary and the next day scrambling like mad to pack, catch a flight, and get out to Colorado to spend two days with the guys. I will have cheated you, I will have cheated them, and

I will have cheated me. I don't want to do that. I want to go with the guys this weekend and make next weekend very special for both of us. I'm sure there will be other times when we won't be able to make things work perfectly, or will choose to celebrate events on an alternate day. But we will be able to make the time we spend together very special and make each other aware of how much we love one another. I hope you understand.' "

Mickie was quick to say, "If he had said that, it's all I would have had to hear. After listening to you, I now realize it really wasn't the day that was so important; it was probably my way of asking him to prove that he loved me. I needed reassurance of his love more than I needed him to demonstrate it by doing what I wanted."

Unfortunately, Gus behaved in accordance with the way he'd learned early in life. He clammed up, kept his feelings inside, and agreed to stay with her. His behavior, however, only served to create an escalation in Mickie's fears and doubts concerning his love. How would she be able to trust his behavior in the future? How would she know when his agreement was real or capitulatory?

The story doesn't end there. Later on the day of our session, they arrived home to spend an evening together. She made dinner and he went and got his mail. As he looked through the letters, he saw a card, obviously written by a woman, and an invitation that said "Mr. Gus Jones and guest." Without consciously thinking it through, he placed both behind a picture frame on the shelf by his chair. When I questioned his behavior, he said, "I didn't want her to get upset because some girl from the past had sent me a card.

After all, I haven't been out with anyone else in a year. Also, why should I let her see an invitation to 'Mr. Jones and guest'? I did once before, and she was hurt and angry at the sender for not inviting her as an individual."

As you might suspect, Mickie noticed his attempt to hide the letters and she questioned his motivation. Once again, an argument ensued. He apologized and explained that he had totally forgotten the lesson he'd learned earlier that day. He went on to say that his behavior was designed to protect her, to keep her happy, to avoid upsetting her. He went so far as to say, "I should have just said, 'Hey, there's a card here from so-and-so. It's about a month late and it says 'Happy Birthday.' And look, so-and-so is having a party, so put it down on your calendar." His good intentions only reinforced his self-perception of being the "good guy." They certainly did not evoke appreciation in her. Instead, they proved to be only one more indication to her that he could not be trusted, that he was a liar. As you might imagine, her inability to trust him created even more doubt in her. Before he could realize any of that, she put her shoes on and stalked out of the house. He stood there, watching her go, almost glad she was leaving and, at the same time, confused with regard to how he might have acted differently. He forgot to ask, "What do I want?" Once again, he saw himself caught between the devil and the deep blue sea. He spent most of that night going over the situation in a myriad of different ways. He finally recognized, "I am tired of playing this game. I don't want to go through the rest of my life this way. From now on, I'm going to ask, 'What do I want?' "

He never bothered to call Mickie to apologize any further, or to plead with her to forgive him. He called for another therapy appointment the next morning and, after relating the story, said, "You know, I really love this lady. I'm not mad at her. I'm really angry at myself. For the first time in my life, I feel liberated. I know it sounds crazy, but I'm free to love her and she's free to do what she wants to do, to make her own decisions. I also recognize something else. From now on, I'm going to make myself a part of the equation. I have the right to do that and to go to Colorado as planned. You know what else I have a right to? To be human. To make mistakes and to still be loved because I'm worthy of being loved. And, you know, I recognize that I lied to her. It's no wonder she can't trust me. But I was living a lie. I rarely considered me. I only gave people what I thought they wanted. Now they can know me, they can take me or leave me, and I can be who I am."

Gus had listened well and learned fast. But there was one problem. He had experienced what I call the "pendulum clock syndrome." It is a common occurrence to which no one is immune. It is usually the first perceptible step in the process of growing. Invariably, when an individual commits to an act of change, he alters his behavior 180 degrees. There is an equally intense act of change in the opposite direction. For example, when an aggressive individual determines that he needs to alter his behavior, he generally becomes as passive as he initially was aggressive. Similarly, when an individual who has, throughout his life, given little consideration to self realizes that a change of attitude is in order, he becomes full of himself, just as Gus did. Have no fear, however. This is only a temporary reaction. Try to imagine the pendulum on a clock that has stopped. After setting the right time, you pull the pendulum as far as you can to one side and release it. What does it do? It swings to the extreme in the opposite direction. In a short period of time, the pendulum will find a happy medium. The same process took take place in Gus. After a period of time, he discovered a happy medium and struck a balance between a healthy interest in self and an appropriate consideration for others. By the way, he and Mickie wound up reconciling, marrying, and, based on the last time I saw him, seem to be doing very well.

It can be the same for every one of you. Once you recognize that you have a right to be in the equation, that what you want counts, you are liberated. You are free to love. You don't have to control others because you are no longer fearful of being controlled. Other people can have their reactions, and you don't have to resent them. Nor will you feel the martyr, plagued with thoughts such as, "Look at all I've done for you. Look at all I've sacrificed to please you and make you happy, and now you won't do 'X' for me." That won't apply, because, in effect, almost everything you do will be done for you and by you. You will no longer have a need to hold any resentment. It will make you free to love without fear that you're controlled or manipulated. It isn't easy to do. In fact, it is a hard step to take. Generally speaking, few of us ever achieve a state where we fully recognize that there is a world out there that we belong in, one in which we serve a purpose and where our feelings are worthy of being accepted by ourselves and by others. It is, nevertheless, a goal you can strive toward. You have a choice. You can be a victim for the rest of your life, or you can decide to open the door to freedom. The first option is too emotionally costly. Therefore, there really isn't much of a choice. It is a difficult step, because it's unfamiliar, places responsibility on you, and forces you to be honest with yourself. But it also allows you to behave in the world with a rational self-interest. All it takes is to ask yourself "What do I really want, and do I dare to take that step?"

Your reaction to all this may be, "He wants me to be selfish." You're absolutely right, if selfish means having a rational self-interest. Note that I say, "Dare to be selfish," because if you are a "good person," you have to work at it. When you initially put yourself first, you'll feel guilty. To help you deal with these feelings, remember that "God only helps those who help themselves." I interpret that to mean that, long term, when you do for you, you wind up doing more and better for others. You've also heard that good people are supposed do good things for others without expecting anything in return. But I know you've also heard the expression "Cast your bread on the water and it will be returned tenfold." I believe that as well. When you do good things, people often return the favor. But where do you get your first "bread"? I think, by doing something for you! In effect, I am trying to say that it's all right to have a rational self-interest.

I learned early on, as a child, that whenever I had a friend come over, my mother told me, probably because we never had very much in the house, "Here's a cookie. Break it in half and give your friend the biggest piece." Even then, it didn't sound right. Now, I'm aware that my mother spent most of her life doing just that. She lived her life as an angry, resentful person, constantly complaining that she always got the smaller piece. As a result of her instruction, I became the world's best divider of any portion of food. Give it to me and I promise you, it will be cut so close to fifty-fifty that I at least ensure that I get my equal half.

Let me assure you, however, that if you're one of those good people, similar to me, you'll never be a totally selfish individual. You'll always feel more comfortable giving more than you get, but you won't resent it, because when you have the wherewithal to say "no," it's easier to say "yes." Even so, the first few times you look out for yourself, you may fear that others won't love you or will reject you. But I've learned they're more likely to look up to you and respect you for not being a self-sacrificing, self-righteous person who makes your life and theirs hell on earth. What do I mean by that? Essentially, that when you're excessively helpful, put yourself last, and only consider what others want, you almost always elicit guilt in others. They feel indebted to, controlled by, and beholden to you. Without realizing it, you rob them of their freedom, because of their guilt. Long term, they'll strive to create distance between you and them. That is, unless they're users, who will take from you without compunction and without feeling any obligation to reciprocate.

CHAPTER TWENTY- ONE

LIVE LIFE FROM THE INSIDE OUT

I believe, without a doubt, that when you are consumed by what others say, what they think, what they want, or what you assume they'll approve of, you're blind to what is essential, because what is essential or most worth seeing is those things that are primarily on the inside. They're what you believe, feel, value, and desire. Consequently, it seems essential that you learn to live life from the inside out, as opposed to from the outside in. Let me explain what I mean by that.

Harry was devastated when, after less than six months of marriage, his third wife left him a note saying she loved him, but wasn't in love with him. That was fairly obvious, in light of the fact that she left for New York with one of his coworkers. In therapy, he spoke about the futility of living life, the fact that no one could be trusted emotionally, and that he had decided that three was the magic number. He would never marry again. "God obviously doesn't want me to do that, but I can't understand why."

Another of my patients, Millie, was equally despondent, but it manifested itself by rage, retaliatory behavior, and threats of suicide. She constantly poisoned her children's minds against their father, instructed them to call the girl-friend he was living with "a whore," and periodically called his parents and siblings to recount his marital infidelity and his numerous transgressions. In the process, she drove everyone away from her. Even her closest girlfriends found it difficult to spend a prolonged period of time with her. One of them told her directly that she could no longer tolerate her piti-ful hysterics, her self-consuming martyrdom, and the intense emotions she showered on everyone. Millie heard her words but gave them little credence. During her therapy session the following week, Millie said, "If it ever happened to her, she'd know how it feels and would regret her advice to get over it." It was apparent that what her girlfriend said wasn't what Millie wanted to hear, and that she had plans to suffer considerably longer than anyone thought was appropriate.

Each of these examples is somewhat similar, in that each of the individuals involved was reacting to an emotional loss. But they were radically different people. Harry was the fatal-ist. The situation was, in his mind's eye, what God chose to deal him. He would accept it, but it was difficult for him to see why life hadn't been kinder to him. Perhaps he'd never heard that God helps those that help themselves.

Millie was the quintessential victim. She totally lacked introspection, took no responsibility for her lot in life, and had only one goal: to get even, no matter who or how many others it might hurt. It was an effective means of avoiding looking at herself, but in the process, she not only hurt many others, but hurt herself even more.

To a great extent, the same observation also applies to Harry, Millie, and a host of other individuals. I believe that, when upsetting or disappointing events or losses occur in one's life, it is not only appropriate, but even necessary to be able to experience your emotions and express your feelings in a healthy manner. In each example, it's apparent that neither was the case. A balanced combination of experiencing, accepting, and expressing their emotions might have served all of them a lot better.

At the same time, there are several very important lessons that can be learned from each of their reactions. First and foremost, ***most people in the face of loss of any kind, be it financial, physical, or emotional, tend to behave on the basis of an outside-in, as opposed to an inside-out, orientation.*** To understand why, let me facetiously say, you need to totally blame your parents for being imperfect and making mistakes while rearing you. As a result of their imperfections or humanness, they, their parents before them, and many of you today fail to instill in your children an inner sense of worthwhileness and adequacy that is essential for the development of an emotionally healthy, inside-out-oriented person. Lacking these core feelings, most people become outside-in persons, whose habituated knee-jerk reaction is to let the world and others determine how they feel, think, and respond. They feel totally subject to the whims of their environment and blame their problems on others. Therefore, disappointments of any kind cause them to lose any sense of well-being or self-esteem that they may possess. Since they see themselves as and act as victims, they are often overwhelmed by their problems, feel victimized by life, fall into depression, and question the value of living. They then react out of grief, either angrily or passively, but always out of a sense of insufficiency. Outside-in people rarely appreciate their own worth because they're blind to the disparity between what they feel and what is real. For them, what they feel *is* real. Thus, when life deals them a bad hand, they say, "If it weren't for that, them, or this, I wouldn't have my problems." Conversely, an inside-out person says, "What can *I* do about this bad hand?"

Let me share an example that will help you to better understand this behavior. Jason was one of the most boring, uninteresting, mildly offensive individuals you could ever meet. His father was an abusive individual who constantly beat him. Even when there was good reason, the beatings were radically excessive in comparison to the crime. The abuse only reflected his father's emotional state that day. But it totally eroded Jason's sense of worthwhileness. As a result, he was deprived of any feelings of confidence or lovability he might have gained had he been reared in a healthy home.

His mother was his only salvation. She dearly loved him, but only showed it when father was gone. During his volatile and abusive episodes, she just stood by, too frightened to stand up for her son or herself.

Jason's defense was to hide, emotionally and physically. In his own words, "A good day was one during which I avoided my father's attention." He went through school in a similar fashion, trying to be invisible and hoping not to be noticed. Again, "A good day there was one when I wasn't picked on or singled out by the bullies."

Although Jason was a bright, sensitive young man, he had no awareness of his capabilities. Instead, he viewed himself as undesirable, unlovable, and unwanted. Years later, at work, he performed well and even excelled, but his work record included frequent job changes due to difficulties in relating with coworkers. He spoke only when necessary and exhibited little warmth, all of which served to estrange him from others and perpetuate his negative self-image.

In therapy, he learned that *what you feel isn't necessarily real.* Further, that when you act on erroneous perceptions, your behavior is often inappropriate and incomprehensible to others. That's exactly the way it was in his marriage. Periodic arguments, misperceptions, and conflicts kept Jason and his wife apart. He perceived himself as unloved, uncared for, and unappreciated, and if you viewed his wife's behavior, you would have had to agree. What you wouldn't have seen was that she spent years living with a man who spoke and explained little. Her unloving, rejecting reaction to him was just her defense against his behavior, which said to her, "You don't matter. Leave me alone. Just let me get through the day without any conflict or pain."

During his initial therapy sessions, Jason complained about his financially successful son-in-law, who never talked to him. Jason thought his son-in-law saw himself as better than Jason, who was unworthy of his attention. After a period of time, Jason's eyes opened to the fact that people only know you in terms of the way you present yourself, and if you're silent or unresponsive, they keep their distance. I'd like to think that as a result of this awareness, Jason did something that he had never before attempted. While walking his dog, he saw someone standing on the sidewalk, directing moving men who were loading furniture into a van. He said his usual behavior would have been to lower his eyes, avoid contact, and pass him by.

This time, he looked the man in the eye and said, "Hi. I'm Jason. It looks like you're moving. I'm sorry."

The man said, "Yes, we're downsizing. The kids are gone and we're moving to a condo in a new development. Where do you live?"

"Just down the street", Jason said, pointing to his car four houses down.

"Did you just move in?" the man asked.

"No, I've been there for eighteen years."

"That's strange", the man said, "I've been here for fifteen and I've never seen you before. I'm sorry. I wish I had met you earlier."

"Well, I'm sorry you're moving," Jason said, then proceeded on with his dog. But his footsteps were far more brisk, his heart warmer, and his feelings lighter.

He returned to therapy the following week with an extremely positive attitude. He said, "I would never have done that before. I would never have spoken up, because I didn't want to bother people. I guess what you said was right. I must have a huge sign hanging around my neck that says,

'No entrance, no trespassing, stay away,' because I also interacted with my son-in-law. I was at one of my grandchildren's birthday party and it was unbelievable. He spoke with me. We had a long conversation and he took time to listen to what I expressed. It was amazing.

"Now I'm having a devil of time at home with my wife. It's obvious she doesn't care because she's angry all the time. For example, I was leaving for my meeting with you and she said, 'Where are you going?' I said 'Therapy. You know I go on Thursday afternoons.' She said, 'No, I don't. You told me a month ago that you weren't going to go for a while, so I had no idea where you were going the last two weeks. You never talk to me, so I have to assume things.' " When she finished, he turned and walked out. It was a decidedly pre-therapy behavior.

I said, "It sounds to me as though she was jealous and suspicious regarding your absences. It suggests to me that your notion she doesn't care is more indicative of where you're coming from than what she's feeling. People who don't care have no interest in where you're going. They're just glad you're going to be gone."

He paused, thought for a moment, and said, "I understand. I'll go home today and try to correct that." He did. But, more importantly, there is something that every one of you can learn from this example. Although what you feel is real, it isn't necessarily reality. Therefore, when you have a strong feeling, check it out by opening up. For example, if you're Jason's wife, risk saying, "I'm not accusing you, but you've been gone two weeks in a row and it scares me. Are you meeting someone or having an affair? I'm asking because I care, and I need you to reassure me that you care as well." It's significantly better than getting angry, waiting to communicate on the day someone is moving out, or, even worse, after they've left. You also need to be aware that people often feel what they fear, so when you perceive your feelings as truths, you frequently wind up increasing your fears and protecting yourself by either pushing others away or shutting them out. In either case, you estrange yourself from persons who might potentially be there for you. It's typical of behavior exhibited by outside-in people.

As you can see, outside-in people let what they feel control what they think about themselves. Even when they have an inkling of positive self-worth, their feelings of fear override it. They tend to overanalyze. Consequently, right and wrong, acceptance and criticism, compassion and harshness, desires and obligations all become intertwined and confusing. The result is that they either react emotionally and impulsively or have extreme difficulty making decisions. As a result, the process is slow and, more often than not, their conclusions are determined by what others will think, rather than by what they themselves want. You might say they are controlled by emotional logic. For example, if they perceive themselves as rejected, criticized, or demeaned, they feel "I'm not worthwhile" or "I'm a victim. No one cares for me." If the world deals them a low blow, they feel "I don't deserve any better" or "What's new? This is my life."

In contrast, inside-out people start out with a positive sense of worth. They know that bad things can and do happen to all people, but they view them as natural occurrences, or the breaks of life. They recognize that it's how you deal with the bad breaks and whether or not you take advantage of the good ones that determine how you come out in the end. That being the case, they take their lumps in stride and learn from their mistakes or disappointments. They don't blame others, because they take responsibility for their own behaviors. At the same time, they are neither destructively self-critical nor overly pompous. They recognize their humanness, accept the fact that they have shortcomings, and tolerate their fears and indecision. But, in the end, they behave out of a rational self-image, rather than from a sense of insecurity and inadequacy.

The second lesson that needs to be learned from these examples is that **emotional loss or disappointment includes hurt and pain, which you have a right to feel and react to without shame or embarrassment.** Inside-out people know that loss is tragic and that they have the right to express their hurts, to feel them, and to share them with others, but not to wallow in them. Despite their anguish, they're able to walk upright through difficult times, as opposed to running or hiding from them. They don't keep problems tucked away inside, or let them ferment and grow and then covertly react to them for the rest of their lives.

The third lesson is that **the best revenge is not getting even, hurting others, or wasting your time trying to make these people feel as badly as you do; it's to do well.** Unfortunately, some people never learn that lesson. Thus, they devote all their energies toward getting even rather than doing well, which implies to me that they want to pull the other person down to their low level. I can't help but think that's a poor way to squander your energy and your life. Think how much better off you would be if your efforts were directed toward activities that would positively enhance your feelings of well-being.

You should note that no one is 100 percent an outside-in or inside-out person. The likelihood is that you can find traits of each of them in you. I know I can. But you need to strive to ensure that 65-80 percent of the time, you behave from an inside-out orientation. The question that follows is: how do you go about that? Your first thought might be, "I need to fix me, so I'll never have those feelings again." If that's your thought, you're in trouble, because that's not the way it works. Think about it: if you approach the problem believing you have to be cured, it clearly means you haven't accepted the child within you as he is. Nor have you learned how to live with him or her, because you're still trying to fix him or her, which suggests that you're broken. That approach won't improve your inner sense of self-esteem, but it will support my notion that the majority of you "are okay, but you don't know it."

Another alternative would be to resolve to think positively and improve your basic self-perception, thereby causing you to become an inside-out person. That's a thought in the right direction. Feeling more positively about yourself can, indeed, help you to cope more effectively in many areas of your life. However, it won't fill the hole that has existed inside ever since childhood, or alter the fact that you are basically an outside-in person. Nonetheless, in some facets of your life, you may have already augmented your self-perception. For example: the surgeon who, once he or she dons scrubs, becomes an inside-out person. Any problems that arise during an operation are considered par for the course, a glitch that needs to be overcome. In this setting, his/her feelings of adequacy resulting from having completed medical school and a prestigious internship provide the inner confidence required for him to act as an inside-out physician. However, the same human being may go home and behave in quite an opposite manner when dealing with his spouse or children. You see, even medical school couldn't change the basic outside-in personality he developed early in childhood and still demonstrates in intimate relationships. It's a part of his hard drive that's there to stay.

That fact is also true for you. You are who you are. No amount of therapy with the best therapist in the world can alter your hard drive. But what you can change is how you cope, deal with others, react, and behave. Pragmatically speaking, however, it's extremely difficult to change your habituated reactions. You can attribute a portion of the blame to habit alone, but your DNA, parental role models, upbringing, environment, and the amount of stress you experience accounts for the rest. In order to help you develop new behavioral patterns, you need to develop manual override. In the vocabulary of RET (Rational Emotional Therapy), you would call it reframing. In computer terminology, it would be called reconfiguring. For example, if, in the middle of a document, your computer suddenly stops responding, you turn the computer off, wait two or three minutes, and turn it back on. That delay provides sufficient time for the computer to readjust or reconfigure. It almost makes you wonder how much your mother knew when she said, "Before you react, count to ten."

Analogously speaking, that means that when you catch yourself overreacting emotionally or physically, whether expressed by hostility toward others, drinking, taking drugs, etc., or by punishing and demeaning yourself or others, you don't drown yourself in self-pity or depression. Instead, you recognize that you are basically an outside-in person by virtue of your early programming. It's no different from having blue eyes versus brown eyes, blond versus black hair, or being five feet eight inches or six feet two inches. You may wish you were five feet seven inches, with long, straight black hair, a 36-24-36 figure and an inside-out orientation, but you have to come to understand and accept yourself for who you are. Further, if what you are isn't to your liking, you must learn to forgive yourself for what you can't change.

For example, a mother gets a scathing letter from her child at college, chastising her, berating her for the way she raised him, and furious because she won't give him more allowance. Her knee-jerk reaction might be to write a check to gain his favor, get angry, and be resentful toward her offspring for being an unappreciative human being, or to feel depressed over having been a poor parent. The latter is often reinforced by old tapes from childhood, which elicit thoughts such as, "Mom or Dad always said I'd never amount to anything. I always screw up the things that matter." When you adopt a pattern of manual override, your reactions differ. You may well have the same thoughts, but you accept them. They're okay because they're just your automatic response to stress of that type. At the same time, you recognize that you are acting from your typical outside-in direction. Recognition, however, doesn't come about immediately. It may require an interval of time ranging anywhere from several minutes to several days or weeks. But the longer you practice manual override, the shorter the time it takes. Once you're aware, your adult takes over. You turn the automatic switch off and click into manual override. You look at the situation objectively instead of responding emotionally. You should stop, take a breath (or several), and realize, "My inner child must be hurting a great deal for me to be acting this way. I know better than this. I'm not going to be provoked by guilt or react out of anger. Nor am I going to push him away. Maybe it's his way of not telling me that something is really bothering him, i.e., his girlfriend may have broken up with him and he's feeling unworthy of love and screaming for help. Possibly, he's having problems at school and would rather I get angry with him for "unacceptable behavior" than for being a failure, emotionally weak, or exercising poor judgment. All of which says to him that he's undeserving of the love and support he needs." Those are only several of the considerations she might make after reconfiguring. You see, after you reboot, you can address the problem from a new direction, one which will serve as a corrective device for habituated reactions learned earlier in your life.

Rebooting consists of taking a step back and looking at the stressed, frightened, or angry child inside you, then taking his or her hand and soothing, comforting, and supporting him or her. After he or she calms down, ask yourself, 1) What do you want to achieve? 2) What's your goal? 3) Can you reach that goal by behaving from the outside in? 4) How can you deal with this issue as an adult instead of a child?

Perhaps the best example I can give you is that of a patient of mine whose use of manual override brought tears to my eyes. I feel confident that his story is one many of you can relate to. I also believe that it will instill in you hope with regard to your ability to positively readjust your own reactions.

If you ever wanted to see an outside-in person, Paul would take the prize. Everyone liked him and truly, they should have. His prime objective in life was to garner love by pleasing others. Your slightest wish was his command. To that end, he was extremely sensitive to others. He always knew if something was bothering you and he'd be there with genuine concern and support. But he had one major problem. He was only able to focus outward. He was blind to himself. Therefore, no one really knew him, because he was unable to share what he didn't know about himself. At work, he was diligent, responsible, and conscientious, yet others, many of whom he trained, were promoted over him. At home, he shared the load. He was amenable to any request or suggestion his spouse made, but he rarely demonstrated spontaneity or initiative. Consequently, his wife, Joyce, ran the show. All the while, she complained that she resented having to be in control. Their marriage eventually ended in a divorce that she sought.

Several years and two or three failed relationships later, Paul decided to come to therapy. He, by that time, truly desired to alter his behavior and discover how he ticked. Those were essentially his words.

It might interest you to know that, about eighteen months later, his ex-wife was in the midst of ending her third marriage, while Paul was involved in what he described as the healthiest relationship he had ever experienced in his life. This time, he assured me, "it's different." I believed him. His sense of self-worth had grown to the point that he no longer looked for women whose love he had to earn. Instead, he saw himself as deserving of someone who would care and want to be involved with him.

You might ask how this came about and why it took so long for Paul to grow. My answer is that therapy is a process. During the actual sessions, you gain recognition. Insight and acceptance can take much longer to occur.

However, his ex-wife must also have perceived the difference. He was no longer responsive to her demands for additional support, or intimidated by her threats. The better his new relationship became, the worse Joyce behaved. She even used their children as a means of getting him to return to his old compliant self. It was evident she saw the new woman in his life as more of a threat than any of the women he had dated previously. It was also apparent that he was a different person—more decisive and confident in both his interpersonal relationships and at work, where he was more successful than ever before. This basically outside-in person had finally learned to behave from the inside out.

All of which leads to the incident that I want to relate to you. Paul called his daughter on a Tuesday evening in order to confirm his Wednesday night visitation. He said "Hi. Just want to talk to you for a minute and let you know that I'll be by tomorrow night to pick you up for dinner." She hesitated, started breathing heavily, and said, "I can't come." He asked, "Why not?" He heard a voice in the background say, "I've got to feed the horse," whereupon his daughter responded, "I've got to feed the horse."

"Perhaps someone else can do that," he suggested. "It's Wednesday night, it's our time together, and I'm more important than the horse."

The voice in the background said, "I spent all day Father's Day with you," and his daughter repeated, "I spent all day Father's Day with you."

"That's right," he said, "and I expected that. Just as I fully expect you to spend all day Mother's Day with your mother. But Wednesday night is our time, and we have a date."

The voice then said, "I wish you'd stop putting this kind of pressure on me." The words were awkwardly repeated to him. By that time, he was beginning to lose his cool. He was exasperated by the three-way conversation and resented Joyce's interference. He hated feeling controlled by her and saw himself helplessly trapped between this manipulative woman and his victimized daughter. Finally, he lost it and screamed, "If you don't want to go, forget it, stay with your mother," and he hung up the phone.

Twenty minutes later, he discussed the problem with a divorced friend, who advised him to "show up tomorrow and if you have to, kick the door in. She's your daughter. You've got visitation rights." Paul didn't have to think very long about the advice. It just didn't fit his style.

He called me and we discussed whether he wanted to respond from the outside in, i.e., to react to the situation, Joyce's manipulation, and his fear that his daughter wouldn't love him; or whether he wished to behave from the inside out. That meant questioning himself regarding what he desired, what he wanted to achieve, and how to best accomplish his goals. Ten minutes later, he called his daughter again. She answered the phone and he said, "Honey, I apologize for hanging up. I was hurt. But I've collected my thoughts and I still want to go to dinner with you. I'll be there tomorrow night at six. I love you."

The next evening, when he picked her up, she seemed a bit uneasy, but after a period of time, they fell into a comfortable conversation and everything appeared normal. In the restaurant, he leaned over to her and said, "Honey, there's something I want to talk to you about."

"Is it about me and my mom?" she asked.

"Well, kind of. It's really more about you and your mother and me."

"Well, I don't want to talk about that" was her immediate response.

He nodded, and ten or fifteen minutes later, he said "Sweetheart, there's something I've got to say to you."

"What is it?" she said, defensively.

"It's that I'm sorry."

For a moment, there was a marked silence. Then she looked at him quizzically and asked, "Sorry about what, Dad?"

"I'm sorry that I let you get trapped in the middle between me and your mother yesterday evening. I swear I'll never let that happen again. I don't want you ever to be part of our disagreements or fights. It was a terrible situation for you and a horrible experience for everyone. I promise you the next time that occurs, if it does, I will say to you, 'Honey, I know this isn't a good time for us to talk and I don't want to argue with you. I'm going to say good-bye and call you back later when you can talk more freely. I'm going to hang up now, but I want you to know that I'm not angry with you or rejecting you. I'll be loving you and trying to help you out of the middle of a bad situation.'"

He watched as a tear rolled down her cheek. Then she got up, rushed over to him, kissed and hugged him, and whispered, "Thank you for understanding".

Paul is still a basically outside-in person. He learned that role extremely well in childhood and behaved that way a good deal of his life. In therapy, he learned to practice manual override. Remember the steps he took. He was able to see the inappropriateness of his reaction to his daughter the night before. He sought out advice, curtailed any further kneejerk reactions, collected his thoughts, and decided the end he wanted to reach and how best to achieve it. Every one of you is capable of following his example. Believe it or not, even older individuals can learn new tricks. It is never too late for an old outside-in person to learn to behave like an inside-out individual. All you have to do is practice manual override. It is a backup system which helps you to better cope with difficult times, loss, and disappointment. It aids you to recognize and sometimes circumvent your knee-jerk reactions. Because of manual override, you are better able to accept unacceptable behavior, whether you recognize it before or after it manifests itself, and then to forestall, mitigate, or make the necessary alterations for the actions you wish to change. Even more, it can alter your orientation from that of a resentful, angry victim who is self-centered, egocentric, and holier-than-thou to a sensitive, understanding human being, one who is sufficiently accepting of self to be able to open up and be vulnerable to others, as opposed to constantly needing to aggrandize or protect yourself.

To summarize, no matter how bad a hand you may feel life has dealt you, you cannot alter the world. *You can only change your world by learning to behave as an inside-out person,* one who uses his or her strengths to face the world and to deal with it directly. You must also recognize that **you have a right to feel bad when the world disappoints you**, and that you have an obligation to yourself to express those feelings openly and honestly and to look for support from others. But you cannot use your sadness to justify living a depressive lifestyle or hurting others. Lastly, you should never forget that *the best revenge is living well.* You need to make that a primary goal in your life and direct your energies and efforts toward that end. The way to do that is to install a manual override system in your life—a behavioral pattern you can use as a backup system if and when problems befall you and you begin to overreact emotionally. It will enable you to cope with your world from the inside out instead of the outside in.

There are several hints I'd like to share with you to help you with this endeavor.

1. Periodically remind yourself that someone else's feelings, moods, and opinions don't have to affect how you feel.
2. You can be happy even if someone else—friend, parent, spouse, or your children—is upset. It's not your job to "fix" them or solve their problems. Recall that it's better to teach someone to fish than to give them fish.
3. Even if you're blamed by others for their problems, you needn't feel guilty or at fault unless you caused their upset with malice aforethought. Otherwise, their problems are theirs.
4. Remember that, generally, how others feel has little to do with you or what you do and more to do with their own issues.

To think otherwise is to be totally egocentric, i.e., to believe that you are the sole source and cause of everyone's feelings, both good and bad. You need to let go of that form of thought, because there is no way it's real, no matter how you feel.

CHAPTER TWENTY-TWO

RUN TOWARD YOUR PAIN

O ver the past three years, Laurie's life has consisted of one doctor's visit after another. After tearing all the ligaments in her left ankle at age fifty-two, the rest of her body seemed to cave in. She had run cross country in junior high school and throughout her life continued to be an avid jogger and a regular at the health club. She loved Pilates, ate healthily, and rarely, if ever, consumed carbonated drinks, alcohol, or carbohydrates. Then, all of a sudden, she found it difficult to wake in the morning. She lacked energy and, on occasion, experienced muscle pain which was totally incapacitating.

Initially, Laurie tried seeing a chiropractor. Later, she consulted an acupuncturist and finally wound up in a neurologist's office. But he could find nothing wrong. Nor did he see her as a malingerer. She abhorred her pain and often tried, in spite of her discomfort, to return to the gym and exercise. She described her life as consisting of pain pills, limited sleep, and constant searching for a new doctor who could cure her illness.

Finally, an internist had the courage to say, "You might consider psychotherapy." His statement offended her. She said, "I'm not crazy! My pain is as real as childbirth." However, in spite of her disbelief, she sought therapy.

During our first session, she was adamant. "I am not imagining this, doctor. Never in my life have I felt this way. I have always been an outdoors person. I've hiked, I've trekked, I've gone on mountain-climbing trips. I'm not someone who pampers herself, but I'm in real pain, and if there's nothing else you can do, maybe you can help me to live with it."

Laurie wasn't the first patient I'd seen under these circumstances. Most individuals, when faced with excessive fears, stress-provoking situations, or hurtful insights that are too difficult to swallow, feel forced to create a smokescreen to avoid the pain of coming in touch with their reality. In fact, many of you probably do the same. For example, one solution is alcohol. If you drink enough, you don't have to worry about what's really bothering you; you're anesthetized. Drugs are another. If you swallow, sniff, or shoot up enough, you don't have to face you. Similarly, if you're sufficiently depressed, physically sick, hurting, or create a problem with parents, spouse, children, or coworkers, you don't have to look at you. For others, weight or an eating disorder can also serve as a way of avoiding reality—i.e., if you lose or gain enough weight, you don't have to look at you, because your problem isn't you, your problem is weight. So you diet over and over again, but never lose weight, because you need the fat to hide behind. Of course, the opposite is also true. Either way, you jeopardize your health. It is almost a case of flirting with death. But the supreme act of avoiding self is suicide.

Note: I am not saying that every angry, depressed, physically sick, overweight, addicted, or suicidal individual is hiding from himself. But I am saying that many people do use these behavioral patterns as a defense for avoiding coming to grips with themselves. At the same time, I must admit that when you see someone wracked with pain, someone whose discomfort is so great that he is willing to endure repeated medical tests and procedures, medications of all sorts, and incapacitation due to the pain he is experiencing, it's hard to believe that he would do that to himself. The truth is, he wouldn't, if he did it consciously. But, for the most part, doesn't decide, "I'll get drunk so I don't have to look at me. I'll get fat, angry, create sufficient mental stress, i.e., have a panic attack, get fired from my job, stay angry, play the victim, blame others, or cause my children to have problems, so I can become preoccupied with them, rather than myself" (Munchausen syndrome by proxy). Instead, it's an unconscious process. Many of you might find this hard to believe, but before you reject this notion, let me say that your unconscious is often far, far stronger and more persistent than your conscious.

After hearing the same statements that you've just read, Laurie looked at me and said, "Doctor, you don't expect me to believe that I would do something like this to myself. No one would do that."

My answer was, "People do, and it's possible that you may be doing it as well. This isn't an accusation or a criticism of you. Instead, it's an attempt to offer you a new way to look at the pain you're experiencing."

"I appreciate your being kind enough to say that," she said, "but why in the world would I do this to myself? Wouldn't it be just as easy to face whatever it is that's bothering me?"

It was a logical, intuitive question. What I'd like to do is answer it for Laurie and any of you who can relate to her, i.e., anyone whose coping techniques are devastating to their life, damaging to their relationships, or destructive to their daily adjustment. Let me give you a personal example. Several years ago, while I was walking through the bedroom, my wife looked at me and said, "What have you been up to?"

I said, "What are you talking about?"

"I'm talking about that contusion on your leg." I looked down and there was a horrible, red and black bruise, fully eight inches wide. It looked as though I had blood poisoning.

She said, "How could that happen without you knowing? It had to be very painful." Her words seemed perfectly logical, but the truth was, I had no idea what had caused it. Her next statement, I'd like to think in jest, was, "Maybe you were in bed with some wild woman, having wild sex."

My thought was, "No, I'd remember that!" But, short of having Alzheimer's, it made no sense to me. Several days later, while sitting in my office, the answer shot through my head. I knew how that bruise got there. Two or three days earlier, I had gone to the dentist with an abscessed tooth. In order to anesthetize me, the dentist gave me what seemed to be a dozen shots. Now, I'm kind of a wuss when it comes to dentists and needles and pain, so, while she was giving me the shots, I grabbed hold of my inner thigh with my right hand and squeezed for dear life, in order to avoid the pain resulting from the injections. To do so, I had to create an even greater pain to obscure the discomfort associated with the needles. You've probably heard of it before. How do you cure a headache? Stomp on your toe. How hard should you stomp? Harder than your head hurts.

If that's true, Laurie must have been experiencing an awful lot of inner pain. Think about what I've said so far with regard to her running since junior high school. Could it be that her running was both emotional and physical? That something occurred at that early age to cause her to run? Now, let me add that, despite being an attractive, professional woman, Laurie had never married. There were men who sought her out, but, to say the least, they were never encouraged and were frequently replaced. She wasn't a lesbian, but her sex drive was severely compromised.

Lastly, let me add that her mother had abruptly divorced her father when Laurie was in the second half of seventh grade. Laurie had no idea why. I'm sure that, by now, every one of you has already drawn a conclusion with regard to the source of her pain. The surprising fact is that Laurie never did. Now, I ask you, how much hurt did Laurie have or experience? The answer is, probably very little until she was no longer able to run, literally, or to figuratively escape her past. When it came time to do so, she created a new, very effective way of not facing herself.

Let's go back to what Laurie initially asked: "Why in the world would somebody do that?" I've already answered the question: to override the pain of a lesser nature from a different source. Initially, that makes little sense. What is the difference between the pain of the needle and the pain I inflicted on myself? Why would I prefer a greater self-inflicted hurt to the pain created by the needle? The answer: *I was in control of the pain in my thigh.* Even though it hurt more, I knew that I caused it and I could stop it. I was in charge of that pain. The pain from the injections was something I had no control over.

Please understand that what I've given you is an intellectual explanation that makes complete sense to me for an almost knee-jerk reaction that isn't the result of conscious thinking. It is my strong belief that on occasion, and in varying degrees, all of us practice the same behavior in order to avoid looking at what's really bothering us. The curious paradox is that we create discomfort far worse than the upset we're trying to avoid. Think about it. How many times have you anguished over a decision, an appointment, a confrontation? Or stressed out over having to be honest and tell someone the truth about what you really feel, or that you don't want to go somewhere with them? The reason is that you didn't want to disappoint them, or you were frightened they might not like you or would reject you. The stress you felt probably disallowed you from being an effective, functioning person and even caused you to be unable to think about anything else clearly. However, after you finally faced the issue, your thoughts were, "Why didn't I do that to begin with? It was so much easier than the upset I caused myself." But, over time, you forget, and later, given a similar situation, you repeat the same behavior.

That being the case, let me suggest that, whenever you find yourself responding, behaving, or reacting in a self-destructive or excessive manner, it is important that you:

1. Do a reality check. Make sure that what you're feeling, saying, or doing and responding to is really the issue. Be careful, however, because oftentimes we lie to ourselves, so you may have to ask yourself the same question two or three times, i.e., "What am I really upset about?"

2. Look for what else may be bothering you. Consider what else is going on in your life that may be causing your upset. It may be something at work, at home, or at school. Whatever it is, it's causing you to feel, think, or hurt because of something that, in your eyes, is too painful to look at.

3. Run toward what you discover to be the real source of your problem. Fretting about it, suffering over it, obsessing over other issues to avoid it, or trying to destroy yourself won't help. The only solution is facing it.

The adage is, you cannot drink enough, drug enough, eat enough, sleep enough, be angry enough, suffer enough, deny enough, or screw enough to make you mentally healthy. I should add that, over time, Laurie discerned the source of her pain and learned that by facing and accepting it and her feelings and fear, she could take control of and diminish the majority of the stress, depression, and pain she'd previously experienced. This discovery was the first step in the process that enabled her to better understand how she got to be who she was, accept herself as she was, and efficiently cope with her life in spite of her early emotional trauma. It worked for her, and it can do the same for you.

CHAPTER TWENTY-THREE

BE OPEN TO CHANGE

L earn to be flexible and to bend with the times, whether favorable or not. The alternative is to eventually realize that you can't control everything in your life, which will result in you breaking down or falling apart.

Nothing is more beautiful than a large oak tree whose branches stretch from its trunk in a multitude of directions and in countless geometric forms. For a child, it provides a place to climb; for loving adults, a shady spot under which to picnic; and for homeowners, an added attraction for their residence.

There is a problem, however. In the face of strong winds that accompany a hurricane, tornado, or cyclone, the mighty oaks are the first to be uprooted. Unlike willow trees, they're inflexible and unable to bend in the presence of a storm.

In many instances, it's the same for human beings. Rigid, inflexible individuals who need to control can't cope with change. They do well when they're in control and others lean on or look up to them. But, in the face of excessively strong ill winds, or even unexpected good fortune, their unbending strength winds up being their undoing. I can't begin to tell you how often I've seen rigid, strong men and equally stubborn, inflexible women refuse to bend or consider alternate positions. For the most part, they are the individuals who refuse to go to therapy with their spouses. They're also the people who will stand by their so-called principles, or adhere to old beliefs, while their relationships and marriages crumble and wind up, often unnecessarily, in divorce. You know them and may even be related or married to one. They're the ones who say, "If it was good enough for my parents, it's good enough for me." Though they may appear very strong in form, they're actually weak in substance. They hide their fears of the unknown, their dread of anything new, and their reluctance to learn or enter into anything they perceive to be different or difficult tasks, behind a stubborn reluctance to change. Well, they're in deep trouble, because the world, role models, styles of life, technology, and values are presently changing at an almost unbelievable rate of speed.

To better illustrate this problem, I'd like to share the conflict that Lori and Irv brought to therapy. Hopefully, it will help you to see the need to be receptive and open to change.

"I've had it." Lori said. "I can no longer live with him. I finally realize I don't have to. I can make it on my own. I don't have to have my heart broken and my emotions acting as though they're on an elevator that's bouncing from the basement to the penthouse. With him, I never know how I'm going to feel from one moment to the other."

"I can understand why you wouldn't want to live that way," I told her. "But I don't understand why you've had to."

"Simply because of my husband. I can't depend on anything he says. It's always a case of building up my hopes, looking forward to something, and having the rug pulled out from under me. He's a mystery to me and I don't want to live with it anymore."

"You don't have to," I said. "However, it sounds to me as though you're living your life from the outside in. You're letting all his actions, promises, and moods control you. In addition, you're using him as an excuse for how you act and feel. There is another alternative. I can't help but feel that you might be able to stay in your marriage and deal with his behavior in a far less disturbing manner to yourself. Tell me, what was the straw that broke the camel's back? What brought you to therapy and caused you to think you had no other alternative but to leave a twenty-eight-year-old marriage?"

"You'll laugh. It seems crazy to me, particularly when I think of standing in front of a judge, saying, 'The reason I want a divorce is because of the way he acts before every vacation,' but that's the basic truth. We'll be at a dinner party and people will say, 'Why don't we all get together and go on a trip? The evening has been so much fun; it seems a crime for us not to spend more time together.' Guess who is one of the most enthusiastic members of the group? Guess who stirs everyone up, initiates plans, and acts the tour leader for the forthcoming event? It's always Irv. And what an idiot I am. I get excited, my friends and I make plans, and the week before we're ready to leave, you can't imagine the hell I go through. Let me tell you, Doctor, I'm not exaggerating. These are his words: 'I don't know why we're going on this trip. I didn't want to go in the first place. It's going to cost a fortune. I can't be away from work that long. I haven't been feeling that good and, you know, all this preparation, getting ready, is too much. If it hadn't been for you, I wouldn't even have considered it. I'm constantly doing things to make you happy and then I regret it. And do you care? No. You're out there buying all kinds of clothes for the trip. It doesn't cost enough and already you're making the cost double? I don't think I can possibly live with this pressure. Isn't there a way we can just cancel?' From then on, anything I say that pertains to the trip gets blown up into an explosive situation. It just isn't worth it anymore. His behavior is driving me crazy. Do you think it ends there? It gets worse. The day before the trip, he starts in. I'm packing too many things. I'm taking my whole wardrobe with me. Who do I think is going to wind up carrying all those bags? Then, before we leave, he says, 'Get ready, we're going to be late. You're taking too long. You know how long it takes to go through security at the airport.' I tell you, I'd rather stay home than go through this every time we plan a trip. And you think it's just the big trips? It could be a weekend, or off to visit our kids. He's a crazy man, and the older he gets, the crazier he gets."

"Let me try to explain", I said. "Right or wrong, men have, for centuries, been brought up to feel that it was their job to protect, to take care of, and to assume responsibility for their families, but, most importantly, their wives. As a result, when you go on a trip, unconsciously he begins to feel, 'I have to take care of this. I have to make sure things are okay. I have to be in charge of organizing, planning, carrying out, and expediting this trip that, in theory, initially sounded wonderful, but, in actuality, causes me to have an intense feeling of responsibility and obligation that I fear I can't meet.' For the most part, these thoughts are unconscious. They're cognitively unavailable to your husband, and other men as well. They are, nevertheless, controlled by the fear that if anything should go wrong, if any problem should arise, they have to be able to cope with and resolve it in a manner that reflects their adequacy, self-sufficiency, and masculinity. It's understandable that, as a man grows older, his fears are exaggerated, often to the point that couples stop traveling altogether. The husband refuses to go, but has no conscious awareness of the emotions driving his behavior. At the same time, the wives say, 'He doesn't have to do everything. I'll take care of making the arrangements, setting things up, and causing them to happen. After all, he works. I don't mind taking on that responsibility.' You would think that would alleviate the problem. It doesn't. It creates another one, which causes the husband to feel even more inadequate and insufficient. For one thing, it takes away many of his excuses. For another, he begins to feel, 'I'm not handling everything. My wife is taking over. I feel more inadequate than I can possibly allow her, or anyone else, to realize.' As a result, he becomes more stubborn, more controlling, and more determined that they not travel, justifying it on the basis of health and financial problems, lack of energy, or even by creating conflicts that mitigate his wife's desire to go anywhere with him."

Lori can't solve Irv's problem. Nor can any of her girl-friends fix that problem in their husbands. But they can come to understand the emotional dynamics underlying their husbands' behavior by learning to read between the lines. At the same time, if anyone needs to be introspective and honest, it's men who desperately need to look inside themselves. They have to accept their limitations and learn to forgive them. They need to recognize that times and people change over the years and that the man they were at seventeen to twenty isn't the man they're going to be at seventy. Let me use Lori's words to illustrate a problem that's far more wide-spread than you might imagine. In the course of sharing a lifetime together, traditional roles and positions change. It often becomes more difficult to live up to the expectations that were there when you first married. When it comes to the notion of masculinity, men are particularly sensitive and threatened by the changes that occur physically due to their age, the technological advances they can't fully understand or handle, and the cultural changes contributing to significant changes in the roles played by women and children in today's world. I can't count how many times I've heard women say, "I don't cook anymore. When I make dinner, it means I make reservations. I have the maid come in several times a week to clean and do the laundry. The kids are gone and I don't feel my old sense of obligation." Or, conversely, "You know, I work, too, I have a career. I put out as much energy as you do during the day and I don't want to take full responsibility for the family. We have to share those duties." In many instances, they seem to say it with little compunction, guilt, or feelings of obligation. In fact, it's quite the opposite. It's almost a declaration of independence. I'm in no way criticizing these changes. In fact, I feel it's about time they've come about, because the world of the "Stepford" woman is long past. But if men can't bend, then, like oak trees, they'll splinter and crack.

There is little doubt that today's women feel more empowered than in previous years. In general, they have a new sense of entitlement and a feeling of adequacy that doesn't depend on or stem from their spouse or their marriage. Unfortunately, that doesn't seem to be the case for Lori. Her boundaries stem from an earlier generation. In addition, she has little insight regarding where her husband is coming from. Thus, she blames him for what she feels and how she reacts and then wants to run from him. Perhaps she needs to feel sufficiently entitled and empowered to not only have her own feelings, but also to comprehend why he acts the way he does so that she doesn't have to leave. That way, even if he's griping, she can be happy about the trip. She can roll her eyes and say, "He's scared. I understand. But, no matter his behavior, I don't have to react or be angry." In this scenario, his behavior doesn't serve as an excuse for her actions. Note: I am in no way telling her she has to stay with him. I am, however, suggesting that there are many men who share his problem and that, with some insight, she could possibly stay and have a loving but newly defined relationship with the man she already has. Of course, that would require that she be able to change. The alternative is that their marriage will also go the way of the oak tree.

There is another possibility: both Irv and Lori learn to bend sufficiently to create a new relationship between them, one in which she can be more independent and self-sufficient and have the right to her own emotions, opinions, and positions, which would allow her to voice her feeling about his behavior with understanding and compassion. For that to take place, it would require Irv to admit that, at times, he feels frightened, inadequate, and insufficient. To do so, he would have to emotionally accept the notion that a man doesn't have to be Rambo in order to be a worthwhile male deserving of love.

You see, it's a new age, one in which you have to accept that gender is only an indication of physical genitalia. It has nothing to do with the stereotypical roles that you previously had to live up to. To live life in an emotionally healthy manner, both men and women must learn to bend with the changes that are taking place in the world. They need to realize that they're okay, whether or not they fit old role models, and that they deserve to be loved for who they are, as opposed to the image they project, the way they look, the money they earn, or the possessions they've acquired. Because, in the long run, the true test of a human being isn't determined by external factors. It's based on what's in his or her heart and whether or not he or she can share those feelings and emotions with you.

CHAPTER TWENTY-FOUR

LET GO TO GROW

Y ou've read the books and you've heard the term, probably too many times, and you've said, "Now I know who I am. I know what I am. I've found myself. I am a co-dependent person! I'm an adult child of an alcoholic parent. I'm the 'chosen child,' the neglected middle child, or the indulged baby. But, most of all, I am the product of a dysfunctional family."

As I noted earlier, a dysfunctional family is one in which people compulsively protect their inner emotions. Only certain feelings are permissible, and performance is more important than the person. It is a group which harbors many secrets and includes a myriad of surreptitious interactions, hidden agendas, and taboo subjects. It's a unit where everyone must conform to the strongest person's ideas and values. There is a profusion of control and criticism, punishment and shaming, and long lists of shoulds and should-nots, along with a superabundance of guilt. Discipline is either absent, inconsistent, rigid, or excessive. Parents are manipulative and insensitive (or too sensitive), and the atmosphere is tense. Thus, members of the family are forever hiding behind their emotional defenses to avoid stress. They constantly feel tired, sick, angry, fearful, hurt, or disappointed. Emotional growth, if not openly discouraged, is certainly not encouraged. As a result, most family members have low self-esteem which carries over from generation to generation.

It's difficult to imagine any family devoid of all these characteristics. Consequently, most of you share some of them. Therefore, despite the fact that you may have learned all the psychology terms and can repeat a good deal of the psychobabble, you very likely still have unresolved issues that interfere with your enjoyment of life. It's because you're from a dysfunctional family. That's the cause of all your problems, right? Wrong! Absolutely not! All the therapy in the world isn't intended to provide you with excuses to hide behind. Its purpose is to provide you with an explanation—an understanding of how you came to feel as you do and to view yourself for the person you believe you are. It is not intended as an out, an excuse, or a justification for your feelings or actions.

You see, I too, read the books and said to myself, "That's you, Ed. You're an adult child of a depressed, narcissistic mother. You're the first born, the Type A overachiever who has to please, and your mother's chosen child. You are destined to be on a treadmill for the rest of your life, trying to live up to the expectations of your birth order and prove you deserve the "love" your mother professed for you. You are the classic "good kid" who feels obligated to please and, at the same time, resents that he can't say "no." It was clear to me that my family was dysfunctional. My parents were far less than perfect, and, looking back, I can see that they had numerous shortcomings. Most of all, they failed to be the people I would have liked them to be. As I mentioned previously, after all these years as a therapist, when I look back on my family, my parents, and my own behavior as a father, I realize that the definition of "parent" should be "failure," because there are no perfect parents, perfect children, or perfect families. In fact, it may well be that every family can, to some extent, be described as "dysfunctional" in nature. I now believe that a dysfunctional family is one which has more than one person in it. Perhaps it's more accurate to say that a dysfunctional family is the norm, rather than the exception, especially if "the norm" means common to all of us, traditional in our society, or typical of family units throughout the world. It is the healthy family that is "abnormal." Without a doubt, the exception is the family that teaches individuals that they are worth something despite their failings and insufficiencies, the one that gives unconditional love, acceptance, and care, as well as appropriate discipline, and a healthy dose of reality. It is, indeed, unfortunate that this kind of family is the exception, but, in my opinion, it is the truth.

As a result of this truth, each of you must find some means of breaking that chain of tradition. You need to create new "abnormal" family structures which can help you to realize that, although you may be created equal, none of you are perfect, and that striving for perfection is striving to fail, striving for the impossible. Why not use the energy you waste in that endeavor for something that is within your grasp? Why not attempt to give yourself, your spouse, and your children the opportunity to see you for who you are, the permission to forgive you for your shortcomings, and the wherewithal to accept your humanity? It is the only path that will "cure" what you feel is wrong with you. Thus, you need to look at yourself and discover that you come from a dysfunctional family, and that you have wounds of varying degrees or intensities which were collected in the course of growing up. Those wounds left you scarred, and the scars make it impossible for any of you to ever be perfect. This is a fact with which you must learn to live. Accept that you are imperfect and have shortcomings, that you have been hurt, and that your life will always include stress, emotional conflict, and problems. The solution is that you must learn to live in spite of, rather than because of, all of these factors. If you can accept these thoughts, you will also become aware that you wasted too much of your life trying to hide, or to be someone different than who you are. Someone you thought would be better than the real you, more acceptable to others, and, consequently, someone you could view with greater pride. But it doesn't work. Because of that, I would have you commit the following thought to memory, so that you can refer to it whenever the need occurs:

Accepting what you find unacceptable about yourself is the only healthy way to self-actualization.

What does it mean? Just giving up on yourself? Saying, "This is all I am, and if no one likes it, that's tough"? Looking at yourself and saying, "I can't accept what I've been. There's no way I will ever be remotely acceptable to me. I'm doomed to live with unhappy, inferior me for the rest of my life"? Should you pick up one of those books on positive thinking and say, "I know I'm supposed to like what I am, but I don't. But if I keep saying I do, one day I will"? The answer to all these questions is, "Of course not!" Absolutely no to all of them. What that statement says is: Be you! Who you really are is better than anyone you pretend to be! So stop trying to change or fix you. Realize that your parents and family tried in their own dysfunctional ways, to give you the best they had to give. If they didn't love you, it was because they didn't know how to love. If they didn't care, it was because they didn't know how to care. If they didn't provide support, it was because they didn't have the support to provide. It wasn't because you were worthless, or lacking, or because something was inherently bad in you. It was because they, too, were human beings bereft of the benefit of having parents any better than they themselves were. As a consequence, they lived their lives neurotically, blindly, sometimes even cruelly. But it says nothing about you, only about them. To be sure, each of you was, in varying degrees, wounded by your childhood, but how long do you hide behind that excuse? When do you finally come to the realization that, at some point in your life, you have to take responsibility for yourself, go about healing old wounds, and live the rest of your life in a manner that is truly acceptable to you?

It is only after you can accept who you are that you can begin to go about the chore of truly living your own life. At that point in time, you can also begin to accept your parents, spouse, partner, and others for who they are. It's then that you can give them the opportunity to love you. You can ask for it without feeling weak or dependent. You may even have to draw pictures to describe what you want or teach them how to give you what you feel you need. If it isn't forthcoming after you have expended positive, conscious, loving effort toward them, you will be able to say, "I tried. It isn't there. I needn't bang my head on a brick wall any longer. I must go into the world and look for the love I deserve from someone who is capable of providing it. Not just because of the image I painted for him or her, or the accomplishments I worked so hard to achieve, but also because of the limitations, the inadequate feelings, the ineptitude, and the insufficiencies in me that I have come to accept as part of me and now perceive as human traits in spite of which I deserve to be loved."

Once you reach that point in your individual growth, you no longer need to look over your shoulder, lament the past, or be consumed by your anger and resentment toward people who could not give you what they didn't have within themselves to give. Think about it. You don't get mad at your cat because it can't bark. How can you get mad at parents for not loving you when they don't know how? Let me answer that question. You can get mad at parents for not loving you because it's a great hiding place for you, a great way to play the victim, to forgive yourself for not having the courage to dedicate yourself to a new way of life, including learning new rules to govern your thoughts and improve on past behaviors. *The path I would have you follow in the future is to make this commitment: for the rest of my life, I will attempt to run toward and through the things I fear, instead of away from them. I needn't be perfect. I won't always succeed, but if I achieve this goal 75% to 80% of the time, I'll feel proud of myself."*

The commitment isn't easy. No commitment is, and those involving growth and change are the most difficult and the most frightening. There is a technique that may help you in this endeavor. Again, I will use the example of a trapeze artist. Try to visualize yourself as this trapeze artist, high in the air, hanging onto a trapeze and swinging back and forth, building up the momentum to let go and fly through the air. Your purpose is to grab onto another trapeze that was sent from another platform, where all the things you're searching for are available. Some of you will let go and fall to a net far below. Some of you will successfully grab hold of the other bar and take advantage of what life has to offer. All too many of you will merely swing back and forth over and over again, too fearful of letting go. Years later, you'll find yourself still hanging from the original bar, looking over at the same goals you set eons ago, but were too frightened to attempt reaching. You were reluctant to risk the chance of failing or being imperfect. Let me remind you that living life well requires that you grow as an individual, and grow you must. No one can do it for you. Growth takes courage. It takes letting go of the old hurts, wounds, losses, feelings of being the victim, acting codependent, and your dysfunctional family. Your motto should be: *you have to let go to grow.*

There is a problem. You can't let go of anything until you first grab hold of it and accept it. Only then can you release it. When you finally do, it will no longer have power over you. You will be free to be you.

CHAPTER TWENTY-FIVE

TAKE RISKS

t started out as a special day. The Baxters packed a picnic lunch, put the top down on their convertible, and set out on a two-hundred-mile trip to see wildflowers and stop in at some roadside antique stands. Their expectations of closeness and joy were high. Consequently, their disappointment and hurt increased exponentially when their hopes failed to materialize. Initially, Sandy Baxter was feeling emotionally closer to her husband than she had in months. Jake shared her feelings and thought, incorrectly, that it was the perfect time to tell her about the scuba trip he had planned for the following month with his sons from a previous marriage. He assured her, however, that she was also welcome. Her hurt over not being consulted or invited until after the fact was painful, but she attempted to conceal it. Thirty minutes later, however, his cellular phone rang. It was his ex-wife calling to say she would be unable to pick up the boys at a little league game that evening and needed his help. Without hesitation, he agreed to be there. Sandy exploded. She ranted and raved and threatened divorce. She reiterated all of her hurts and grievances from day one. She questioned his manhood, his backbone, and his ability to love based on his relationships in two previous failed marriages and his inability to discipline his children. Having finished her verbal tirade, she lapsed into silence, which continued for the next five days. Sandy had a fifty-dollar reaction to a fifteen-dollar problem.

From my vantage point, many of Sandy's perceptions had merit. Her husband's priorities were skewed, with Sandy seemingly at the bottom of the pecking order. His primary allegiance to his children from his previous marriage, whether out of love, guilt, fear of risking rejection, or a combination of all these feelings, provided little indication that Sandy, their union, or the family they were attempting to create was a priority. At the same time, Sandy's reaction did little to enhance her attractiveness. Even worse, her exaggerated emotions only served to diminish the credibility of her justifiable feelings of rejection and abandonment. It is very possible that she was unable to recognize or articulate hurtful feelings any other way and that the only reaction to hurt she learned as a child was fight or flight, both of which she now demonstrated all too well with Jack. In either case, her behavior defeated her purpose. You can readily see that Sandy vacillated from one extreme to the other. She kept things inside, brooded over them, and let them ferment until she could no longer control her emotions. At that point, she became verbally abusive, after which she sank into a state of depression and withdrawal.

When she came to see me, it was obvious, even to her, that she severely overreacted and that she harbored a great deal of inner hurt and fear. Helping her to become aware of the excessive reaction she demonstrated was not meant to demean, to cause her guilt, or to judge her. Instead, it was intended as a catalytic agent, designed to encourage her to ask herself, "What am I really reacting to? What is it I want?" and, "Will what I am doing get it for me?" Sandy's recognition of her propensity to overreact did not occur immediately. However, over time, she did come to recognize the inappropriate nature of her behavior and to discern the roots of her fears. From then on, she was able to begin establishing control over her explosive emotionality. It was only a matter of time and repeated reinforcements until she was able to risk sharing her fears of abandonment and need for emotional security, as opposed to becoming defensive and vitriolic. You can do the same if you are able to be truly honest with yourself. It's a different step to take, but it is possible. If not, seek some professional help, then go about practicing manual override.

Still another example of excessive behavior can be seen in another patient's brooding. Although Jan's overt behavior was radically different from Sandy's, their dynamics were remarkably similar. Jan never exploded, but she worried about everything. If her mother promised to call around noon, by twelve fifteen Jan began to think that her mom had had an accident. She would contemplate calling the local hospitals or the police department. On several other occasions, she left work when her mother failed to answer the phone, to see if something had occurred that prevented her from coming to the phone. She reacted in a similar fashion to weather reports predicting heavy rainstorms or the possibility of tornadoes. Jan was a consummate worrier who could create a state of anxiety over any issue related to or indicative of the possibility that harm had come to someone she loved. It was not a case of inappropriate concern, but it was always fifty dollars' worth of anxiety over a fifteen-dollar problem. The nature of her behavior wasn't my greatest concern, but the inappropriate degree and the intensity of her reactions were. Worry served as her primary defense. It enabled her to see herself as a caring, sensitive person, without her having to reveal herself as the weak, timid individual she perceived herself to be.

No one can go through life without experiencing difficulties, upsets, or "bumps in the road." But when we make those bumps into deep potholes, we exaggerate the degree of the problem and magnify our upset. Typically, a fifteen-dollar problem deserves a reaction of approximately equal value. It may vary a bit—we may see someone who has a thirteen-dollar reaction or a seventeen-dollar reaction to a fifteen-dollar problem. But when we observe a fifty-dollar reaction to a fifteen-dollar problem, we know immediately that it is totally excessive. Excess, however, not only manifests itself externally and internally, but can also be seen in demonstrative versus restrained emotionality. For example, when an individual only has a three-dollar reaction to an eighteen-dollar problem, his behavior must be viewed as equally inappropriate and worth exploring. It is important to note that the lack of a response is in no way indicative of a lack of emotions. There are just as many over reactors as there are under reactors. The difference is that one individual protects himself with anger, the other with silence or avoidance. In both cases, the individuals experience emotions which they find disturbing, or even threatening to their self-image. One reacts excessively, the other displays restraint, but, in this instance, the lack of response can be considered a response in its own right. For example, consider a conflictual marriage which is emotionally hurtful. On the one hand, the overt expression of excessive anger, caustic accusations, and criticism serves to temper or mitigate intimacy. On the other hand, the covert display of dissatisfaction through silence, lack of emotions, and a loss of sexual desire alleviates closeness. The motive in either case is to prevent anticipated hurt, criticism, or rejection. Behavior of this type is primarily defensive in nature and stems from the fear of exposing one's feelings. It is not the result of a desire to consciously hurt one's partner. None of the individuals described are bad people. They're scared people who don't feel okay or don't believe they will be accepted for who they are.

That being the case, my way of dealing with their reactions is to say, "You've had a fifty-dollar reaction, but it's only a fifteen-dollar problem. If you subtract fifteen dollars from fifty dollars, what's left?" The answer is obvious—thirty-five dollars. In this instance, a fifteen-dollar reaction is justifiable, even expected. It can be accounted for by the degree or intensity of the problem itself. The thirty-five-dollar excess, however, suggests something else. It is a measure of the amount of emotional upset, pain, sorrow, fear, hurt, or any one of a number of other hidden emotions that exist within you. It has little or no connection to the experience you believe you are responding to at the moment. Therefore, the answer lies inside you. It cannot be blamed on or attributed to an external situation or problem or another person. Your inner fears, however, are buried so deep inside that they are obscured from conscious awareness. Because of that, it is easier to yell and scream, or be passively resentful over a minor issue, than to get in touch with what really troubles you. But it solves nothing, because the recognition of your fears is the only key that can unlock the door to your true feelings. It forces you not only to face your problems instead of running from them, but to realize that "excessive" behavior of any kind is a last-ditch effort to redirect your own feelings of insufficiency, neediness, and weakness toward someone else.

The logical question that follows is, if behavior is expressed in a pathological manner—i.e., excessively—is the individual expressing that behavior also pathological? The answer is, not always. For a moment, let us assume that each of us is at least two different people. From the neck up, we are the sum total of all our life experiences, our interactions with others, the classes and teachers we were exposed to, the books we've read, and the movies and television programs we've seen. We are an intellectual machine that constantly collects, sorts, and filters information which can affect our thoughts and, hopefully, our actions. In contrast, from the neck down, we are the sum total of the emotions we experienced from birth to possibly age six or seven. By that time, we are fully emotionally mature. Our emotional patterns, including our fears, threats, sense of self-worth, and notions of love and how to get it, are fully developed. The way we express them may change over time, consistent with our level of learning, but the early messages and their themes persist. They are the same at age six, sixteen, thirty-six, and sixty-six. The child who ran from the dinner table at age five is the teenager who leaves a ball game at age fifteen because he isn't allowed to pitch, and is the adult who gets in his/her car and drives away from a spouse at age thirty-five. In each instance, his behavior is the result of the same feelings of unimportance, rejection, or need for added attention, all controlled by the emotions of a five- or six-year-old.

The existence of these two separate people or motivating forces can be seen in a myriad of everyday situations. If you have ever been on a diet and found yourself facing a luscious piece of strawberry cheesecake, had a problem with drinking and found yourself in front of a beer, or needed to study for an exam and received an invitation to a movie from a special person, you have probably come face to face with both of them. In the space of thirty seconds, you experience a debate between the two. The adult says, "You don't need that." The child says, "Well, I can have a little bite. After all I didn't eat much today." The adult responds with, "You know that's not on your diet." The debate continues until one finally wins. In the cases of Sandy and Jan, their excessive behavior is the result of their emotional little child winning too frequently. At the age of five or six, their reactions may have been seen as somewhat inappropriate. At the ages of thirty-five and thirty-one, respectively, their responses can be viewed as unacceptable and totally out of control, but not necessarily crazy or pathological. The solution is evident. You need to be in control of your emotional little kid, not eliminate him or her. You must integrate the thoughts and behaviors of your intellectual adult and the emotions and feelings of your inner child into a healthy emotional union that allows you to recognize your feelings, but not necessarily to act because of them.

Here are the first four steps toward this objective:

1. Your job is not to rescue, fix, or cure your partner. It is, first and foremost, to save yourself.
2. You need to examine the degree of influence that adverse factors and attitudes and the behavior of others have on you.
3. Albeit subjective, you must then determine, by virtue of the frequency and degree of the excessive behavior you demonstrate, the amount of stress and the number of feelings of inadequacy and anger you carry within you.
4. If you see yourself as having a hair-trigger temper or are easily hurt and defensive, you know the degree to which you may be broken and behaving inappropriately.

These four steps will aid you to honestly determine the amount of control you need to exert over your emotional child. Once you are able and willing to see your own excesses or inappropriate actions and to take responsibility for them, you can then begin to investigate their origin. The goal isn't to find fault or punish you. It's to have your adult accept and forgive your childish, inappropriate thoughts and actions, but, at the same time, to love and guide the emotional child who resides within you. Beware, however, because there is another alternative: you can blame your excesses on others—friends, family, spouse, etc.—thereby justifying your lack of personal growth or maturity. Although blaming others is an extremely poor choice, your fear of change and a reluctance to give up familiar coping behaviors can often supersede sensibility and cause you to choose not to risk exposing your inner self. Consequently, your inappropriate or excessive behavior tends to escalate, enabling you to hide who you are, but eventually severely damaging your interpersonal relationships. After all, why would a "healthy, loving" adult choose to maintain a continuing relationship with an emotional child who is out of control?

On the other side of the fence, if you are involved with an under or over reactor, it is essential that you recognize that his/her reaction is not about you. You may contribute to or even provoke his/her reaction, but you are not the cause of it. The propensity for his/her excessive behavior was there long before he/she met or married you or any of his/her previous spouses. Unfortunately, if you are the type of person who would pick an "emotional child" as a partner, you are very likely a person who also has the propensity to accept responsibility for his/her criticism. You must, therefore, ask yourself, "What's wrong with me? Where did I learn this?" (Look to your own childhood for this answer) and "What can I do to stop it?" Assuming responsibility for the behavior of others only serves to undermine what little self-esteem you may have and will circumvent any possibility of you contributing to your partner's growth. More importantly, if you accept the blame for your partner's actions, he or she doesn't have to. Thus, it is you who needs to change.

In every dysfunctional relationship, you need to remember that:

1. Your job is not to save, fix, or cure your partner. It is, first and foremost, to ave yourself.
2. You may feel sorry for or victimized by him, but your job is only to support and provide him with his own reality. The latter requires that you have the courage to speak your mind.
3. Whenever you or your partner engages in any form of inappropriate behavior, it stems from your fears, not your strengths. During conflictual times, what your partner needs from you is strength, not an uncontrolled reaction of a similar or opposite nature to his own.
4. If you feel the need to stay in an emotionally unhealthy relationship, it is not because you are a nice person; it is because you are frightened of losing what you've known all your life: hurtful feelings, criticism, and abuse, lack of emotional support, fear, and insecurity. Despite the fact that these emotions are painful, they're familiar and preferable to risking having to cope with a new, uncharted relationship.

For you, just as for your partner, to risk exposing who you are, what you feel, and what you fear is your only solution. It will not only enable you to recognize and gain healthy control of your inner child and his emotions, it will enable you to learn to like him better. As a result, you will be liberated from being controlled by the impulses and emotions of a child. You will be free to openly share your honest feelings while responding out of your intellect and knowledge.

Perhaps the following poem dealing with risk will aid you to consider betting on yourself and on life.

Risks

To laugh is to risk appearing the fool
to weep is to risk appearing sentimental
to reach out to another is to risk involvement
to explore feelings is to risk exposing our true self
to place your ideas, your dreams before the crowd is to risk loss
To love is to risk not being loved in return
to live is to risk dying
to hope is to risk despair
to try at all is to risk failure.
But to risk we must,
because the greatest hazard in life is
to risk nothing
The man, the woman,
who risks nothing
does nothing
has nothing
is nothing

—Anonymous

CHAPTER TWENTY-SIX

TRUST YOURSELF

In case you haven't noticed by now, you are the only solution to the stress you feel, the conflictual relationships you're exposed to, and the troubled marriages in which you're involved. Although you might not realize it, you have the power to make your relationships work, to break them up, or to just tolerate them. You also have the inner strength to relate with others honestly and forthrightly, and to stand up for yourself. Moreover, you are capable of making the final decision regarding your actions and reactions. But if you don't, if you blame others for your behaviors and look to them to decide what's right for you, you will never learn to trust yourself.

What does trust mean? In the way I'm using the word, it has nothing to do with others. It assumes you realize that you can't control the world, other people, or the way they act or react; that you also know that, whatever happens, you can trust that you'll be able to take care of it or cope with it. On the occasions that you can't, you'll accept that you're not perfect and that you don't have to be. Also, that you can call in an expert or a professional to take care of any problem you're unable to handle and trust you're still okay.

When you reach that point in your individual growth, the world and its burdens become far lighter than ever before. On the one hand, you no longer have to control what goes on around you or in you. You have the freedom to experience your world as it is. You don't have to make excuses, rationalize, distort, deny, or mitigate it. You can deal with reality because, inside, you know that whatever comes about, you trust you'll handle it.

Consequently, you can live with less fear. You won't have to be troubled by countless worries, problems, or circumstances that may or may not occur, because the feeling that you can trust you will prevail.

As a result, you won't have to control people around you, absolving you of a tremendous burden. It will enable you to recognize that others will be who and what they are. Those who are important to you, you'll deal with; those who aren't, you won't have to. Nor will you lose sleep over the fact that someone may or may not be angry, upset, or about to reject or abandon you, because even if they do, you trust you'll be able to live through it. What a wonderful comfort that could be.

But that's not typically the way it is. In life, the normal inclination is to blame the problems you face, the choices you make, and the stands you take on someone or something else—your early upbringing, your lover, the fact that the world has treated you badly or that your love has died because of your spouse. For the most part, those are all excuses. It may be true that the world has dumped on you that your childhood was lacking, that your partner's behavior needs a major tune-up, that you've grown over time and/or your love seems distant and irretrievable. But your love isn't dead. It doesn't just disappear, die from pneumonia, or atrophy due to some form of cancer. More often than not, it is obscured by old hurts and bitter resentments, blurred by fears, or hidden by a host of negative childhood events and memories. All of these need to be dealt with up front, discarded, and then forgiven in order to enable you to first trust yourself and then get in touch with the loving emotions that are there inside you.

Dan's history exemplified this problem. He was a forty-five-year-old confirmed bachelor, as well as a handsome, successful individual every woman saw as "a good catch." There was one problem: all of his relationships were short lived. His longest involvement only lasted three years. That was because he didn't know how to leave her without hurting her feelings. He followed his usual pattern of behavior with Anna, but she didn't respond in the same manner as the previous women in his life. His typical pattern was to search out a tall, very attractive, caring woman who, despite her outward appearance, lacked inner confidence—one who had severe conflicts with her father, was emotionally responsible for or very dependent on her mother, and desperately wanted to be loved by "a good man." It wasn't a conscious process, but it was a repetitious one that began when he was fifteen years old.

Dan was a good man. It was no wonder that women were attracted to him. He was gentle, solicitous, generous, and sensitive to their needs. He was also slow to trust, easily hurt, and reluctant to express his feelings. As a result, he built up huge amounts of resentment, which eventually caused him to lose interest. When he did, he would retreat emotionally, lose his sexual drive, and spend more time with his male friends and his business. After a while, the woman would get the message and leave him. In that way, he was never responsible for the breakup, although he was always the one who initiated it. In the three-year relationship with Anna, he reached that point on several occasions, but her emotional neediness overrode her sensitivity. Consequently, she was willing to accept his neglect and rejection. Finally, he was forced to take a stand, a very difficult step for him, but, in this case, very likely a fortuitous one. It was the first step in the process of his recognition that he lacked trust in himself and, as a result, could neither trust nor love anyone else. It took every bit of courage he could muster to ask her to leave. When she expressed a desire for them to enter therapy and try once again, he reluctantly agreed. He stayed in therapy, but about six weeks later he repeated his request that she leave.

Dan's emotional growth increased by leaps and bounds after their breakup. Several months later, he met and became seriously involved with Nancy. Although she initially filled the bill—i.e., she was tall, attractive, and had the prerequisite problem with her father and a highly dependent relationship with her mother—Nancy, unlike all the other women in his life, also had a backbone. After a year and a half of serious involvement, she questioned his plans for the future and indicated that she needed some evidence of a commitment. When this was not forthcoming, she called the relationship off, despite his protestations and his vague promises regarding the future. In less than three weeks, Dan actively proclaimed his love. He asked that she reconsider her decision and promised a commitment in the very near future. Unbeknownst to her, he had already bought an engagement ring and given serious thought to how he would present it.

But, before his plans were complete, Dan began to have second thoughts. "After all," he said during a hurriedly scheduled therapy session, "she's no pantywaist woman. She's got a backbone, which I really admire, but I'd hate to think how strong she could become. She certainly didn't back down about the breakup. Maybe I'm rushing into this thing too fast."

"You're obviously scared," I said. "I understand that. But before you attempt to make any major or definite decision, please try to determine what the problem really is."

"I don't understand what you're saying. I'm scared to death she'll try to control me. Isn't that enough?"

"Is that the problem? Or is it that you're really frightened that you can't stand up to her?"

"What's the difference? It sounds the same to me."

"There's a huge difference," I said. "On one hand, the problem is between you and Nancy. On the other hand, the problem is you."

He was silent for what seemed an interminable period, then looked at me wide eyed and said, "You're absolutely right! isn't the problem; it is me. I'll be back for my regular appointment this week, and we'll discuss 'me' issues."

Dan did well in therapy and eventually went on to marry Nancy. But don't think for a moment that his problem is unique to men. Women experience the same blindness with regard to their self-worth, their special qualities, and the feelings of their partners. They are just as likely to search for excuses to justify their actions and vindicate any of their behaviors that they perceive to be unacceptable, weak, or reflective of a lack of trust in themselves and their worth.

For example: Evelyn was the quintessential caretaker. She had a unique way of dealing with her problems. She said it all in five sentences during her first therapy session. "I have an eighteen-year-old son and twin eight-year-old daughters, yet I feel like I have four children. Let's face it, Dr. Ed, John is a good man, but I'm the one who takes care of everything in our house. Sure, he goes to work and brings home a paycheck, but so do I. In fact, I make more money than he. He's like an exchange student we had living with us one summer, except he did more to help at home than John does."

She then went on to explain, in detail, all of the chores and responsibilities that fell on her shoulders. She added that her original decision to marry John was not an easy one. She was on the rebound from a six-year relationship with an older man who desperately wanted to marry her. "And still does," she added. The only problem was that he was a very successful, widowed, entrepreneur who was used to getting his way. He wanted to care for her, but she knew she wouldn't be able to call all the shots with him. John, on the other hand, was an easygoing guy who never questioned her or asked much of her. From the day she met him, she was certain that he would continue to behave the same way after they were married. She was also sure that she could not expect very much from him emotionally or sexually. To be frank, she said, "He never stirred me sexually, but I knew he would always be here. Now I feel sorry he is."

On the surface, it seems pretty obvious that Evelyn took no emotional risk. She settled for "Mr. Steady," and now she regretted it. There was one problem, however. Evelyn did not go into this relationship with her eyes closed: she knew exactly what she was doing. The decision had little to do with the facts. It had everything to do with her emotions. As a child, she learned to be a caretaker. Much of the responsibility for her younger siblings fell on her shoulders. Her mother was, in Evelyn's words, "a child in her own right who should never have had any children. Most of the time, she was in her own world, which was a lot better than when she tuned into yours and lost her cool." As a result, Evelyn grew up totally dependent on herself. Her survival techniques consisted of never needing anyone so she would never be disappointed. "It worked pretty well for the first forty-one years, so why change now?", she said. The answer to that rhetorical question is "Because somewhere inside is a little girl who desperately wants to be taken care of, to lean on someone, and to be able to let her emotional guard down, but she's too frightened to risk it."

The solution, however, isn't necessarily to leave John. Before she can pragmatically consider that alternative, she has an awful lot of rebuilding to do in herself. For starters,

Evelyn is basically a good person. She is intelligent, successful professionally, and a wonderful caretaker. But she isn't the confident, happy, loving person she portrays herself to be. Nor is she the victim of John's lack of a sense of domestic responsibility. No matter who she married, she would have eventually trained him to lean on her and to expect her to care for everything. She neurotically needs the paradoxical feelings of competence and martyrdom to justify her emotional existence. It provides her with a sense of adequacy, albeit a false one. Her actions speak for her. They say, "I am capable, I am needed, therefore I am. That I sometimes resent the role I have created for myself is true. But I know no other role in life, because I do not trust that, ultimately, anyone will be there to care for me, because I do not trust that I am worthy of being loved."

It is plain to see that Dan couldn't trust himself to stand up for himself. Similarly, Evelyn couldn't trust that anyone else would be there for her if she didn't care for everything. In both cases, Dan's and Evelyn's lack of trust in self was the result of their depreciatory self-concept developed early in childhood. This same poor self-concept served, throughout their lives, to actively influence their behavior and thoughts. The erosion of their self-concept started early, but, years later, it still contributed to their behaving in accordance with the rules learned from their relationships with their mothers. This behavior is not likely to ever change on its own. Their one hope is that, through therapy, they can learn to accept their childhood fears of insufficiency and come to recognize that they are of greater worth than they initially felt they were. It is the first step toward becoming the responsible, loving people they are capable of being: i.e., people who can trust that they are worthwhile, who will be able to take the risk of trusting others because they value themselves.

In the course of reading *You're Okay, But You Don't Know It,* I hope you come to learn that "okay" or healthy people are individuals who trust themselves and don't need, use, or hide behind excuses. When you do, you need to understand that excuses are your attempt to justify or defend certain actions or thoughts whose origins or motivation you do not want to confront. However, more often than not, the motivation underlying your overt behaviors is the true indicator of who you are on the inside. Consequently, based on the belief that thoughts and actions do not come about by coincidence, by accident, or as a result of some magical force, you need to see and, hopefully, understand the motivations driving your behaviors.

To be "okay," you alone must become the guiding force in your life. You must make what you do, say, want, and think the direct result of who and what you are on the inside. Your actions must reflect your inner emotional state, your intellectual wherewithal, your values, your constantly updated or modified beliefs, and your newfound sense of confidence. As a result, your behavior will be influenced by their collective input, as well as by the fund of information you have gathered throughout the years and the thoughts of others whose opinions you have learned to trust.

It is only after you learn to live with yourself that you will be able to effectively live with and love someone else. However, in order to love self, you must first become the responsible person described previously. You must develop integrity within you. That means that harmony will prevail between the things you say, do, think, feel, and want. Without that harmony, you will experience a constant sense of inner discord and conflict. You will be pulled and pushed internally in different directions, and you will be eaten up by the guilt you feel over your actions that do not coincide with your beliefs and thoughts. The end result is that you will be pulled apart inside and tormented emotionally. In that state, you cannot love self, and you certainly can't adequately love someone else.

If you truly desire to be a healthy, loving person, you have no choice but to become a responsible person in your own right. Becoming responsible, however, doesn't come easy. It involves:

1. Being able to recognize and own your feelings and opinions, in spite of how unpopular or unacceptable they may be.
2. Trusting enough in yourself and your feelings to openly express them to others.
3. Exercising your right to take stands, set boundaries, and establish limits for yourself in all your relationships.
4. Risking the possibility of being disliked or rejected for the positions that you take.
5. Having sufficient emotional flexibility to bend; i.e., to change your opinions and alter your positions without feeling that you are a loser or weak, and without harboring misdirected resentment toward others who have proven themselves to be right.

6. Expressing your love to someone in spite of your fears and the possibility that it may not be returned.

7. Accepting and believing the love you get, without doubt, suspicion, and/or running from it because of your fear of being disappointed.

8. Believing in yourself sufficiently to show yourself when you're not at your best—during a bad hair day, with a zit on the end of your chin, when you've erred or failed and everyone knows it, or when you feel weak and needy.

9. Refraining from buying the love of others, emotionally or financially, because you believe you're worth loving for who you are.

10. Admitting you love someone who doesn't love you back, all the while knowing that:

   a) You won't die because of it;
   b) It isn't the end of you, even though it feels like it; and
   c) You'll live to love again, to give your love to another person who will return it more or better than you have ever experienced before.

These ten requirements for being a responsible, trustworthy, loving person, i.e., being "okay," are far more than a group of words or psychobabble. The likelihood is that very few of you can live up to all of them. Essentially, they ask that you look inside, without outside influence, and see yourself for who you are. They require that you own your feelings, in spite of popular opinion. To relate to them, all you have to do is ask yourself, "How many times have I had a thought that I immediately rejected because of what I learned as a child, or because I was told it was too evil, immoral, or bizarre and, therefore, unworthy of expression?" You may even recall a flitting voice inside you saying, "You can't think that. Stop it! Get it out of your head, it's bad, wrong." These requirements also involve you thinking about how many times you decided not to speak up, or express an opinion, or take a stand, for fear of it being unacceptable and having others reject you for it. They encourage you to face how many New Year's Eve resolutions you have broken. You know the ones: lose weight, stop drinking, smoking or taking drugs, get out of an affair, or stop being a couch potato who does nothing, accomplishes nothing, and feels nothing. They suggest that, in the past and very likely in the present, you too frequently alter your position and decisions in order to be politically correct and not offend others, or diminish the risk of failure or disappointment. Try to recall the occasions you were cajoled into going out with friends in spite of all the things you wanted or needed to do at home. The piece of birthday cake you ate, even though you promised yourself you wouldn't (but how could you possibly hurt the honoree's feelings by not eating it?) Or the jobs you didn't apply for, because you didn't want to be rejected. Each of these incidences is a small crack in the trust you have in yourself. To be responsible, you need to recognize them and take steps to mend them or, more specifically, mend you.

These requirements remind you that you aren't perfect. You can and do err; thus, you need to be sufficiently strong to admit your mistakes and, when appropriate, change previous stands, apologize for past acts, or alter your behavior. It might be important to add that there are many instances where inflexibility represents a false attempt to convey inner strength and trust in oneself. Therefore, you mustn't confuse being wishy-washy with flexibility, or stubbornness with strength. Overall, they direct you to believe in you enough to take risks, to fall on your face, and to get up and try again, because there is no sin in failing, but there is in not trying.

In themselves, none of these requirements involve issues that are abnormal, atypical, or uncommon to most individuals. Quite the contrary, I doubt that you cannot plead guilty to at least several of these shortcomings. That being the case, you may have to seriously question how trustworthy you really are. Your answer is extremely important, because it directly affects how much others can trust you. It also reflects the degree to which you can trust yourself and love others. Remember, however, that there are few people who can honestly claim to live by these ten requirements 100 percent of the time. To be frank, it really isn't necessary that you do so. What is essential, however, is that you try, because living by these ten simple rules will help to rid you of your excuses. It will enable you to accurately see yourself and to take credit, or blame, whichever is appropriate, for your behaviors. The end result is that it will help you to trust yourself; to know that your actions and your thoughts come primarily from you, and that you have the courage to risk being honest with yourself and those you love. As a result, you will be able to react honestly in your dealings with others and with the problems or weaknesses you discover in you.

There is only one additional thought that I hope you will remember. You need to take chances, trust yourself, and speak out to develop a life that will enable you to experience the loving relationships you desire, but which, in the past, always seemed to elude you. I have heard so many times that this approach isn't worth it. That bucking or trying to stem the tide will only result in an argument or a fight. But I assure you that standing up is a courageous behavior that, in the long run, your partner will admire, because there is such a thing as constructive confrontation. The motto I hope you will hold on to is that it is better to risk getting into a fight than to risk getting into a divorce, or never having a relationship at all. Honesty and/or conflict will not necessarily curtail the possibility of establishing healthy relationships, or carry you to a divorce. However, the lack of openness, truth, and trustworthiness will.

CHAPTER TWENTY-SEVEN

PUTTING IT ALL TOGETHER

By this time, you've learned that there are any number of steps you have to take to know you're okay and to be the person you want to be. I hope you've accepted the notion that these steps don't occur overnight, and that it's not an event, it's a process. It's an ongoing battle between the two individuals in you; one you will experience all the rest of your life. There will be days when you wake up on what, for lack of a better term, people call "the wrong side of the bed." On those days, you'll want to climb back in, pull the covers over your head, and ask, "What's it all for?" The reason this can happen is that, at least for me, sometime during the night, my intellectual processes (the parent in me) go to sleep so deeply that my child sees his opportunity to come out and play. Figuratively speaking, my child looks out and says, "I'm free to be me, but I don't know what I'm doing, why I'm doing it, and if it makes sense long term. I just want to be me, but, in all truth, I haven't yet discovered who I am or what I want."

Inside, emotionally, there are times I still feel I'm not good enough, that I'm too weak, a wuss, and I haven't lived up to my capabilities. Those or feelings of a similar nature can come about in any one of us, on any given day, week, month, or year. And that's okay, too. At those times, your LUCAP has to make itself evident and say, "For crying out loud, Eli (Jim, Helen, etc.). I know you feel that way, but you're okay. After all, you're only four or five or six years old. You're not crazy, dumb, or terrible, and having those feelings is different from acting on them. In fact, sometimes you're even allowed to give in to them and say, 'I've had it. I don't want to see, hear, think, and feel anything. I don't want to hurt or fight any more. I just want to retreat and crawl into bed in a fetal position.'" That's perfectly fine for two or three hours, or even a day. But when it goes on too long, you've got to see that your inner parent is overindulging your child. It's on those occasions that your LUCAP has to step up, grab you by the scruff of your neck, and affectionately say, "You little idiot. You're not going to accomplish anything by this behavior, except to dig yourself deeper into your morose, helpless state. So get up, drag yourself out of bed, take a shower, exercise, walk, call somebody, go to work, do something constructive. It doesn't have to be discovering the theory of relativity. It can be cleaning out the garage and getting rid of stuff you've dragged with you for years. Stuff that you haven't looked at or felt a need for, but couldn't part with for years. It can be cleaning out the attic of the boxes you piled up there that you were going to look at fifteen or twenty years ago when you moved into your house." It's the satisfaction we can get from getting rid of some of the physical baggage that we carry with us, although, more often than not, it's emotional baggage that we need to discard, at least enough to show us that we've moved one step closer to making our lives brighter and proving that we can organize and deal with things that, heretofore, we refused to face. That's what growing up means: taking responsibility for yourself, facing reality, and pushing, pulling, or cajoling yourself enough that you're able to recognize and accept your fears and turn them into challenges. I know that it's worked for me, and I believe that taking these small steps can work equally well for each of you.

In order to help you with this endeavor, I've created a list of seven steps I believe can aid you to integrate both your child's and adult's efforts and facilitate putting your life together. I wish I could guarantee that if you follow these rules, you'll be totally emotionally healthy, but it doesn't work that way. Some days you'll work on step one, and another day you'll wind up on step four and then find yourself way back at step one again, realizing, "I didn't really see it all, or do it fully. Let me go back and do it a little better this time." But it's not a sin to hone your behavior over and over again. Please try to remember that none of us is perfect, but there is an okay person in each and every one of us. Believe me, I'm no different than any of you. I have to perfect the way I act more times in a month than I'd like to think I should. However, these seven steps have helped me to accept my insecure feelings and myself. As I've said throughout this book, you can't change your child, but you can alter his/her reactions and behaviors. The rule I try to live by is the same one that AA repeatedly expounds: "one day at a time." You mess up today, you've still got this evening or tomorrow morning to start over again. Having said that, here are my seven steps.

1. ***Recognize* who you really are**. Introspectively look into yourself. Be honest. Remember, I've said on numerous occasions in this book that we lie to ourselves, but we need to be honest, no matter how painful it may be. Let yourself emotionally feel and touch those things in your past that you don't want to look at, that make you uncomfortable, and that you previously obscured, rationalized, denied, and refused to acknowledge. They're the feelings that you shook your head to rid yourself of because they weren't politically correct or reflected weakness, dependency, helplessness, and futility. All emotions you weren't supposed to own, because strong, adequate, good people would never have those feelings. Well, I don't accept that. I believe that it's our job not to run from, but to face our dark side and go through it so that we can see that there is a light at the end of every one of our tunnels. The first step in that process is for you to recognize it, be honest with yourself, and face the pain from your past.

2. ***Own what it is you've recognized*.** You may say, "That's redundant. It's the same." No, it is not. I cannot begin to count how many people I've seen in my office who have said, "Dr. Ed, you're beating a dead horse. I know I'm insecure. I don't

deny that I'm anxious or feel bad sometimes. But doesn't everybody?" And that's when they reveal where they are emotionally. They've intellectually subscribed to the notion or the awareness that they're anxious or insecure. But they haven't bought or assimilated it. They haven't owned it. They haven't come to the realization that I don't care about "everybody" and, even if "everybody" has it, that doesn't make it any better. If there's an epidemic of smallpox or the black plague, it's going to kill you whether everybody else has it or not. And, to be really honest about it, sometimes the pain associated with my hangnail bothers me more than your appendectomy. It's not that I'm not sympathetic or empathetic; it's not that I don't care about your pain. It's just that, selfishly, the pain that I experience hits me harder than the pain you experience. I believe that's the case with all of us. Even more, I believe it's important that we experience the pain. Doing so will force us to go through our fears. That's essential, because you can't walk around them, jump over them, deny, avoid, or mitigate them. Therefore, you have to experience them. That's also what owning is all about. You have to acknowledge the emotional hurts, wounds, and disappointments in your past and, at the same time, fight for your right to have and to react to them. To use them not as an excuse for the mistakes you've made, but, rather, as an explanation, not a condemnation of how your parents or other people and situations affected you in the past. As a result, I'd have you be able to say, "My parents did the best they knew how and, unfortunately, it wasn't good enough. I'm the result of their child-rearing deficiencies. I vow to remember that, but not to replicate it or use it to justify my actions as an adult; rather, to learn from it." All of which is a part of the process of owning. It's one step beyond recognition.

3. *Accept you.* Once you recognize, own, and accept what your little kid feels, you will no longer need to fix or make him better. You've been doing that all your life and it didn't work. All you did was hide those feelings under the carpet and, over time, the lump only got bigger. More specifically, your underlying anxiety, stress, and distress made itself evident in every walk of your life, even when you weren't consciously aware of what it was that was causing you to be upset. The alternative is for you to accept them. To admit, for example, that you felt like a wuss, didn't feel brave, wished you were Rambo and knew how to defend yourself and to stand up to all the evil forces in the world. But think about it. Sometimes, it's hard enough just to stand up, let alone to battle all the forces in the world. It's not a matter of judging whether your feelings are right or wrong. It's accepting that they're a part of you; a part of the little kid inside you who represents the baggage you carry with you. That little kid is always going to be there. If you

don't accept him, you're likely to do the opposite. You're going to hate him, be embarrassed by him, and constantly try to hide him. It will force you, in the long run, to unconsciously punish him by sabotaging your own successes and achievements. After all, if you hate him or her, you don't deserve success or rewards. So, acceptance becomes an extremely important step for each of us to strive for. It's similar to a chapter in my book *Hungry for Love*, where I talk about the fact that every one of us should have a label, similar to a plant tag that says whether it needs shade or sun, wet or dry soil, or a soup can label that tells that the soup contains a certain amount of sodium, carbohydrates, and fat. These labels help the buyer make wise purchases. Our labels need to list our faults and assets, what we require, and how we behave, as well as the statement "Do not remove under penalty of law." If we can't wear or openly share our labels, it's because we can't expose who we feel we are. It then becomes apparent that we haven't owned who we are. Sadly, that's the case for most of us. At some level of awareness, most of us know who we are and what we are, but, more often than not, it's not who we show to the world or share with others, because, "Oh, if they really knew me, they wouldn't like, respect, or love me." Thus, we create an image of self who, much like a chameleon has the capacity to fit into whatever environment we're in; someone who has no stable identity that others can count on. In some instances, we play so many different roles that we ourselves are unsure of who we really are or what we think or feel. There is no way to bring this behavior to an end until we take step four.

4. *Forgive.* I have heard it said by many people and seen it included in many religious doctrines that forgiveness of self and others is an essential and heroic step toward living a healthy emotional and spiritual life. I strongly believe that if indeed charity begins at home, so does forgiveness. As I stated earlier in this book, until late in my life, I couldn't make a mistake, spill anything, mess up, or fail. If I did, I lied about it to others. I tried my best not to expose the human person in me to anyone. I had to be the great Dr. Reitman, instead of the real Ed Reitman. I couldn't accept "Eli" at all. The reason was because I couldn't forgive him if he spilled his drink, broke something, or scraped the side of his car. Too much of my energy and too many efforts were directed to avoiding mistakes, rather than to living life, taking risks, and recognizing I couldn't be perfect. As a result, my life really wasn't as productive, satisfying, or emotionally comfortable as I wished, all because I couldn't forgive my imperfections. I have finally reached the point that I'm able to say and believe that getting something done is far better than devoting all my attention all my life to doing something perfectly. In part, it's my way of accept-

ing and forgiving my imperfections. Another way I say it is, "I accept the kid I am, but I don't have to let that inadequate-feeling little kid control what I do. I can't change his feelings or emotions, but I can change the way I think about them and the way I react to them. By virtue of that, I'm now in charge of me, far more than ever before. At least I'm forgiving of my past behaviors, but I don't want to display them in the present. As a result, I don't have to criticize or blame myself. Nor do I have to punish myself because of my kid's "unacceptable" feelings. I just have to accept and forgive them.

5. *Laugh at yourself.* After you have genuinely accepted and forgiven yourself, you will no longer need to take yourself quite so seriously. You can be amused by, accepting of, and forgiving of the emotions, thoughts, and actions you previously would have used to punish yourself. For example, if you haven't ever had the experience of looking at a little child who has just eaten a candy bar, try to imagine the chocolate smeared all over his face, from one ear to the other. His hands are covered with chocolate, which he's wiped on his shirt. The picture is a "Kodak moment." That's the way you've got to be able to deal with yourself, because if you can't laugh at yourself, you're going to cry. You're going to be like the uptight mother of the chocolate-covered child, who is furiously wiping chocolate from her child's face, hands, and shirt. You're going to be consumed with cleaning

yourself up and making yourself presentable. All of which indicates that you haven't fully owned, accepted, or forgiven you. Face it, human beings are funny. We do dumb things. We behave in accordance with AA's description of insanity by doing the same thing over and over again and expecting different results. We persist in repeating old, habituated behaviors, and then punish ourselves because of this behavior. Why? Because we don't recognize or own who we are or how we act. Instead, we run and hide from ourselves. But if we stopped long enough to first see ourselves and then forgive ourselves, much as we forgive the child who's stained his clothing, his plate, his high chair, his face, and his hair with chocolate, we could learn to laugh at ourselves. The extent to which we can achieve this is an indication of the degree to which we've accepted and forgiven ourselves. As a result, we'll no longer need to yell, scream, holler, or punish our kid by thinking, "God, I'm going to have to wash your clothes and put you in the bath. I don't have time for all this, or you." Every bit of joy that child may have had, we take away because he acted like a child. How sad. Sad because when you can't laugh at yourself, when you're critical and hostile toward yourself, you're unable to laugh at or accept the child in others. It's a curious paradox. On one hand, similar to our own parents, we rear our children thinking we're doing the right things and saying the right words.

But, on the other hand, we fail to provide our children with the freedom to live with themselves; to mess up, literally and figuratively; to be children and to openly demonstrate emotional zeal, because we weren't given it. Therefore, we don't know how to give it to them.

6. **Love yourself.** By this time, it should be fairly easy to do because, when you can recognize, own, accept, forgive, and laugh at yourself, that's what you're doing: loving yourself.

Think about it: a LUCAP is someone who loves, understands, cares, accepts, and parents, but doesn't punish. There is an added bonus. When you can love yourself, it's amazing how easy it is to genuinely love someone else.

7. **Share yourself.** It's simple to do but, to be honest; it's far simpler when I say it to you than when I say it to myself. Why? Because I still occasionally experience days when everything seems overwhelming and I think, "Who am I fooling? It's just a bunch of psychobabble words and everything sucks." Those are the days when I don't want anyone to see who I am. This reminds me of a very successful man I saw in therapy who grew up on a "dirt farm" in Oklahoma, a fact which embarrassed him most of his life, at least until he came to therapy. At one point in his learning to accept himself, he drove back to the little town he came from and took a picture of the small shack like home he grew up in. He had it framed and hung it in his office. He later

said to me that of all the awards, plaques, and commendations he has on his office walls, the one he's most proud to point out to others is that picture. It represents an acceptance of himself that could never have come about if he hadn't taken steps one to seven. That's when he could finally say, "This is who I am. This is what I am, an imperfect but caring, loving human being from Oklahoma, who went from rags to riches and now feel proud of my roots and feel that I'm worthy of being loved."

So, there you have it. Seven steps. Recognize, own, accept, forgive, laugh, love, and share you with the world. I hope that puts it all together for you and helps you to deal better with all the previous steps and stories in this book. The purpose is to congeal them into a Unified whole that's bigger than the sum of its parts and allows you to feel bigger and better than the sum of yours.

CHAPTER TWENTY-EIGHT

FEEL FREE TO BE YOU

f you've reached this point in *You're Okay, But You Don't Know It*, you've probably come a long way emotionally since you started reading it. Hopefully, you're now more liberated from the weight of your past, have decreased the pressure you used to experience to be perfect, and have accepted your need for recognition, care, and love from others.

There's one problem. Remember the adage "Be careful what you ask for, you might get it"? Well, you've got it. You are free to be you. At first, you may feel peculiar, awkward, or uncomfortable. You may even question whether or not you have the right to do what you want, to not have to totally answer to someone, to laugh, to be joyful, and to feel unencumbered. Those questions stem from a mix of old, childish messages and fear of casting them aside. My advice is to enjoy them, take pride in your growth, and search out new challenges and the feelings of fulfillment you experience when you face them, because you deserve it.

But before you rush off to your new life, let me leave you with several last thoughts. One of the most important is that the fight to find you and to accept you is an ongoing one. It isn't as though you took the bar exam, passed it, became certified as an attorney, and no longer have to worry about your professional status. It's altogether different. It's a lifetime process which requires you to constantly recertify yourself, sometimes on a daily basis, in order to:

1. Ensure that you retain your grasp of the adult identity you have chosen to live by.
2. Help you remember that there are two of you, a child and an adult, both of whom reside in your body and compete to see who will drive you.
3. Remind you that no matter how healthy you get, your child will ever go away. He or she will be there throughout your life. Your job is to accept, forgive, and love him, not chastise, hide, or punish him. To the degree you forget that, you will find it increasingly difficult to live with yourself and almost impossible to sustain a healthy, long-term, intimate relationship with anyone else.

Why? Because the feelings, the coping techniques and the identity that little child inside you had at ages one, two, three, four, five, and possibly six never die. They stay with you. I have repeatedly tried to stress that point throughout this book. On any given day, you can wake up feeling wonderful and on top of the world. It will seem as though the sun is shining extra bright and all is well with you. Then, without warning, several hours later, or the following morning, you may wake up in a funk, feeling depressed, anxious, or confused. Does that mean that you're no longer okay, that you've taken ten steps backward, that your life sucks, and that all the therapy and learning you've derived from this book were useless? My answer is an adamant *no*. Instead, it means that your situation outside probably changed. That should be no surprise, because the world is ever changing. It also means that things aren't so cozy today; that the economy is topsy-turvy; that your health isn't as good as it was; or, possibly, that a friend, family member, or someone meaningful to you isn't as cooperative, loving, or attentive as he/she was heretofore. Most of all, it means that your little kid, who is ever present, saw his opportunity and, to the point that you were stressed, he and his childish fear and feeling of inadequacy came to the forefront and overwhelmed you. On that day, it's likely that your adult stayed in bed, didn't smell the dewdrops, and let your child take control of you.

The last statement comes from the poem "My Shadow," by Robert Louis Stevenson, which I shared with you earlier. It's strange, but sometimes I believe that the real experts in human dynamics aren't necessarily psychologists. They don't have degrees or clinical training. They're playwrights, poets, authors, and composers; especially talented people who are insightful, far beyond any professional training. They can see and feel the emotions inside human beings with surprising clarity. As a result, their creativity consists of bringing those insights to the surface through their words, illustrations, and music

Think about Stevenson's poem. That shadow is more than just the physical shadow all of us know. Shadows don't make fools of us, nor are shadows cowards. But the little kid inside each of us is the quintessential example of those words. He does cause us to behave in foolish ways. He is a coward. He's filled with fears and insecurities and feelings of inadequacy that he doesn't face squarely but, instead, runs from, denies, compensates for, and is reluctant to confront. The coping techniques he displays are his way of dealing with emotions that he's carried with him since childhood. At the same time, his intentions are often noble. He does his best to help you avoid the pain and hurt you might experience if specific experiences or events were to come to the surface and force you to face them. However, in the course of trying to protect you short term, his behavior long term causes you to carry extra emotional baggage throughout most of your life. It's almost analogous to riding in a boat with the motor going full speed and the anchor dragging the bottom. No matter how well the engine functions, you never travel near the level of your potential. The kid's intent is far from that. It's just that he's shortsighted. He helps you to avoid immediate hurts and pain. But, long term, you suffer more.

Just as the poem says, your inner child has a way of "suddenly shooting up taller, like an India-rubber ball, and sometimes he gets so little, there's none of him at all." That being the case, you have to be able to accept the fact that the child within you is, thank goodness, still alive and kicking, or you wouldn't be. Therefore, you need to recognize that he's not wrong, bad, or terrible. He's just a kid, six years old at best, who doesn't want to hurt and is screaming for attention, support, direction, and reassurance that he's okay. Your job, as an adult, is to take care of the child inside you, because when he's screaming, he has probably run amok or screwed up and is in need of help. On those occasions, your adult needs to come to the forefront in order to comfort your little kid and control, support, and direct him. It's what a parent does. Unfortunately, the sad commentary is that most human beings are pitifully poor parents to themselves.

Let me share one last story with you that I believe will help to clearly exemplify what I am trying to say. It has to do with a female family attorney who refers a great number of people to me. She's a wonderful person whom I care for a great deal. Therefore, when she called and asked if my wife and I would go to dinner with her and her husband and another couple. I readily agreed. Several days later, I found myself in the midst of their company at a very nice restaurant. During the evening, she repeatedly touted my abilities to the other couple. It was very complimentary, and I basked in the sunshine of her words. The rest of the evening progressed very comfortably until she turned to me and said, "Ed, I just got your latest article by e-mail. It was the one called 'That's My Nature.' I'm sure you remember it. It talks about how so many people use that line to excuse their behavior and to justify actions they're not necessarily proud of. I not only saw myself in it, but others I know, as well. I thought it was a great article." You would think that would have lifted my spirits even further. I won't go into deep analysis regarding why it happened, because by now, you know I don't believe you should go through life analyzing your navel to see where the lint came from. Let me just state that I heard a voice from deep inside me whisper in my ear, "What does she mean by 'that article was great'? I think a lot of my other articles are much better. Does she mean she doesn't like the other articles? Why? Aren't they all great?"

Years ago, that voice would have been enough to lower me into the pits of despair, cause me to doubt my abilities even more so than usual, and either retire from the conversation or become a motor mouth. But not that night. There were too many lessons to be learned from this story. One is that most of us, including me, hear what we fear. We have creative hearing that reinforces the notions already inside us that we learned as children. Two, there really are two of me, and you never know when that little kid is going to, figuratively, open the door and run out of the house and into the street in front of an oncoming vehicle. Three, and most importantly, I was able on that particular occasion to say to my little kid, "Get the devil out of here. I don't need that kind of chaos. Enough of your insecurities. I know you're there, but I don't have to give credence to you or allow you to control my behavior." Intellectually, I knew full well what she meant. She was, once again, complimenting me. At that moment, however, I wasn't consciously aware of what was taking place. I just experienced a blinding flash of my kid's underlying insecurities, but this time, I didn't let them control me. I just waved them off casually, with little thought or concern. It was only later that I recalled the incident, smiled to myself, and said, "That little kid's still there. But you took care of him. You didn't criticize him, find fault with him, feel a failure, feel weak, justify, or have to overcompensate for him. You accepted him and went on." I wish I could have done that for the first three quarters of my life, but I'm pleased as punch that approximately 75 to 80 percent of the time, I'm able to do it now.

Today I can accept the little kid in me. I can be more forgiving of his behavior and I can recognize that he's a scared, ornery, insecure, sometimes sad little boy, who needs to be laughed at, hugged, and loved by the adult in me. My wish for all of you is that you will one day, at least in part as a result of this book, come to peace with yourself and be able to say, "I'm okay and I know it." That day will come when your wherewithal to integrate the child and the adult inside you reaches the point where you can say, "I no longer feel trapped, victimized, or obligated to agree, act, or commit to anything I choose not to do. Nor am I fearful of being rejected, or of not being loved. I know that I have worth and that there will always be someone who, when they come to know me, will recognize that." As a result of those feelings, your resentments and fears of others will be alleviated, and you will be free to be you.

EPILOGUE

The other day, as I was sifting through my papers, I found an old letter that had been sent to me by a patient. I had saved it because it touched my heart and seemed to say how a person should go about living and accepting his or her life. I'd like to share it with you, in the hope that it will serve to say to each and every one of you that there can be a light at the end of your tunnel, no matter how black your world may appear to you today.

Dear Dr. Ed,

I thought it appropriate at this time that I try to summarize some of my thoughts and feelings, along with some of the things that I've learned from you in therapy. So, I've written them down in hopes that you will have an understanding of how much help you've given me and where I am at the present time.

I realize that a time comes in your life when you finally "get it." When, in the midst of all your fears and insanity, you stop dead in your tracks and somewhere, the voice inside your head cries out "Enough! Enough fighting and crying and struggling to hold on." And, like a child quieting down after a blind tantrum, your sobs begin to subside. You shudder once or twice, blink back your tears, and begin to look at the world through new eyes. This is your awakening. You realize it's time to stop hoping and waiting for someone to change, or for happiness, safety, and security to come galloping over the next horizon. You come to terms with the fact that you are neither Prince Charming nor Cinderella and that in the real world, there aren't always fairy-tale endings (or beginnings, for that matter) and that any guarantee of "happily ever after" must begin with you. In the process, a sense of serenity is born of acceptance.

You awaken to the fact that you are not perfect and that not everyone will always love, appreciate, or approve of who or what you are. But that's okay. They are entitled to their own views and opinions. And you learn the importance of loving and championing yourself. In the process, a sense of newfound confidence is born of your own self-reliance.

You stop complaining and blaming others for the things they did to you (or didn't do for you), and you learn that the only thing you can really count on is the unexpected. You learn that people don't always say what they mean or mean what they say, and that not everyone will always be there for you, and that it's not always about you. So you realize that you have to stand on your own and take care of yourself. And, in the process, a sense of safety and security is born of self reliance.

You stop judging and pointing fingers. You begin to accept yourself and others as they are, and to overlook their shortcomings and human frailties. And in the process, a sense of peace and contentment is born of forgiveness.

You realize that much of the way you view yourself and the world around you is a result of all the messages and opinions that have been ingrained in your psyche. And you begin to sift through all the junk you have been fed about how you should behave, how you should look, how much you should weigh, what you should wear, what you should do for a living, how much money you should make, what kind of vehicle you should drive, how and where you should live, who you should marry, the importance of having and raising children, and what you owe your parents, family, and friends. You learn to open a window to a new world and different points of view. You begin assessing and defining who you really are and what you really stand for. You learn the difference between wanting and needing and you begin to discard or modify the doctrines and values you have outgrown, or should never have bought into to begin with. And, in the process, you learn to go with your instincts. You learn that it is truly in giving that you receive, that there is power and glory in creating and contributing, and you stop maneuvering through life merely as a "consumer" looking for your next fix. You learn that principles such as honesty and integrity, are not the outdated ideals of a bygone era, but the mortar that holds together the foundation upon which you must build a life. You learn that you don't know everything; that it's not your job to save the world; that you can't teach a pig to sing; and that you shouldn't get angry at a cat because it can't bark. You learn to distinguish between guilt and responsibility, and the importance of setting boundaries and learning to say no. You learn that the only cross you have to bear is the one you choose to carry, and that martyrs only get burned at the stake. And, let me add, "and then you begin to live life."

My patient said it so very well that I wished I could be as articulate as she. My consolation is that, to some degree, I played a part in helping her to discover her light. I think her words provide a model for each of us to follow in the future, and I urge you to try it, one step at a time. I truly believe it will help you to recognize the goodness in you and the serenity, acceptance, and zest in life that is there for each of you to discover.

—Edward Reitman, Ph.D.